BY TOM DOYLE

The Glamour Chase: The Maverick Life of Billy MacKenzie
Man on the Run: Paul McCartney in the 1970s

MAN ON THE RUN

TOM DOYLE

BALLANTINE BOOKS NEW YORK

MAN
ON THE
RUN

Paul McCartney

in the 1970s

Published in the United States by Ballantine Books, an imprint
of Random House, a division of Random House LLC,
a Penguin Random House Company, New York.

BALLANTINE and the HOUSE colophon are registered trademarks
of Random House LLC.

Originally published in hardcover in Great Britain in 2013 by Polygon,
an imprint of Birlinn Ltd.

ISBN 978-0-8041-7914-0
eBook ISBN 978-0-8041-7915-7

Printed in the United States of America on acid-free paper

www.ballantinebooks.com

987654321

First U.S. Edition

Title page photograph © Clive Arrowsmith

Grateful acknowledgment is made to Toby Greenberg
for her photographic research.

Book design by Carole Lowenstein

To Thomas Corrigan Doyle,
for fixing the plug onto that first record player
and setting me on my way

CONTENTS

INTRODUCTION

The first time I met and interviewed Paul McCartney, he kept stealing distracted glances at his watch.

It's tough enough to consider the fact that you're interviewing the most famous musician on the planet, someone who was being interrogated by other writers before you were even born, but it's more disconcerting to realize that you're failing to engage a former Beatle and, as the old song goes, stop his mind from wandering.

The date was Monday, May 15, 2006, and the location was a photographer's studio in Kentish Town, North London, where McCartney was having his picture taken by his similarly doe-eyed daughter Mary for one of a series of *Q* covers to mark the magazine's twentieth anniversary. I was there to talk to him about his experiences of the past twenty years, their events and innovations.

During our half-hour-long conversation, I managed to keep him on the subject long enough to discuss everything from his eyewitness account of the immediate aftermath of 9/11 (he'd been parked on the tarmac at JFK Airport in a commercial jet that was suddenly going nowhere) to the fact that he couldn't really click with the iPod, since headphones reminded him of work and being in the studio. He then revealed the surprising holes in his knowledge of Beatles history.

"I'm the world's worst analyst of me," he reasoned brightly. "Beatles fans can tell you exactly what was going on in the 1960s, and I kinda go, Oh yeah, that's right. I know *Sgt. Pepper* was 1967. I know that much."

In many ways, he proved as affable, laid-back, and hey-whatever as I'd imagined he might be. When I'd arrived, he'd instantly seemed to warm to the fact that his interviewer for the day was Scottish (having of course enjoyed a decades-long relationship with the country and its people) and had hung around the studio's buffet table urging me, with typical bonhomie, to try the caramelized vegetables. Yet his head was clearly elsewhere, and a heavy air of *something* hung over him.

Only when he briefly mentioned his second wife, Heather Mills, saying her first name almost under his breath as he admitted that she hadn't quite taken to his penchant for the odd spliff ("She's violently against it"), did I get an inkling that the rumors that the pair's marriage was in deep trouble might be true. The previous day, one of the tabloids had run papped shots of Paul wandering around alone on a break in France. Two days after our conversation, his publicist made the announcement that the pair were to split.

Having done a fair bit of this interviewing thing, I hadn't taken his semidetached state that day as some kind of failure on my part, and it was now clear what had been weighing on his mind. But it made me determined to try to hold his full attention, to ask and say the things that other writers might not dare, if and when we should meet again. Printed encounters with Paul McCartney in recent years had tended to be fairly stiff affairs, with many journalists—entirely reasonably, since I'd suffered from a touch of nerves myself—too intimidated to ask him much beyond the ho-hum or draw him into a spot of lively banter, or even just try to have a good old laugh with him.

Next time, I thought.

The next time arrived sixteen months later, when I was given the opportunity to meet him in his lair, two floors above the reception area of 1 Soho Square, at the offices of MPL, McCartney Productions Limited. This is Paul's comfort zone, the room where he most often chooses to be interviewed—the dark, wood-paneled Art Deco den having been the center of his operation since 1975. In this environment he instantly seemed more relaxed, more focused, very much in control, and virtually unflappable, even when it came to broaching some of the more difficult times in his life.

Outside his office door there was an air of brisk business being done by his staff, of meetings being arranged and schedules being plotted. It was no coincidence, I felt, that this man was a multimillionaire.

Inside, McCartney, settling on a sofa, was surrounded by Willem de Kooning originals and backlit by his neon-piped Wurlitzer jukebox, which contained the old rock'n'roll 45s that were his sacred texts as a teenager. As we talked, he made his way through a cheese-and-pickle sandwich, a spare triangle of which he repeatedly offered to me during the interview. He seemed to be disappointed that I wasn't really keen on it. "Go on," he urged me, for the third time. I gave in and took a bite.

"So this'll be vegetarian cheese, then?" I wondered aloud.

"It's just cheese," said the famed animal-rights campaigner with a shrug, missing the point that I was surprised that he wasn't plumping for the rennet-free variety.

Up close, McCartney looked to have worn pretty well, given the sheer intensity of his past. Only a wrinkling around the lips and his slightly sunken cheeks gave away his age, with his hair more expertly dyed now than the plum shades of his fifties, when—since he's nothing if not a homemade guy—you suspected he was doing it himself. His hazel eyes flashed with a greenish tinge when caught in a certain light. He appeared trim but moaned that he had a bit of a gut.

"You haven't got a belly on you," I said.

"I'm sucking it in, 'cause there's a journalist here," he joked. His cheeks swelled when he laughed, and the years fell from his face, returning the impish Beatle of old.

Most people, from the Beatles' films and his countless TV interviews, have some idea of how Paul McCartney talks. Face-to-face, however, his tone is more earthy, more Liverpudlian, his speech peppered with lovingly delivered swear words.

But interviewing McCartney is a bit like panning for gold. He can be as slippery as a politician, expertly ducking a question and sometimes making you return to it three times before he tackles it head-on. At other points, he begins to drift into old anecdotes you've read or heard him relate dozens of times. In these moments, you're forced to interject to try to steer him gently back toward less familiar terrain.

Sometimes, particularly when he digresses, you feel as if he's growing a bit bored, either by the question or his response to it, and he says "Anyway," quite definitively, urging you to move on. Other times, you suspect this is a handy defense mechanism when he finds the line of questioning too intrusive.

Being a seasoned interviewee, he is well practiced in the art of talk-

ing a lot while giving very little away. John Lennon once sniffily compli-
mented his former bandmate on being "a good PR man . . . about the
best in the world." There remains a fair amount of truth in this, and,
ultimately, it forces you to push McCartney harder to get beneath his
usual surface spiel. You know you're getting somewhere when he emits
an almost exasperated sigh and says, "Look, to be *honest*."

At the same time, perhaps because he is surrounded by reverence
most of the time, he seems to relish repartee, to enjoy measured ribbing.
He is, of course, a man few ever dare to say no to, never mind lightly
poke fun at. But it's clear that he loves getting back in touch with the
rougher, former working-class Macca, who is never too far away.

On this occasion, with a second meeting scheduled for six days later
and in the same location, we were due to talk about the 1970s, an often
tumultuous and uncertain time for McCartney. During our chat he
began to open up more and more, offering a carefully controlled hon-
esty about his trials during the period: the emotional crash he'd suffered
after the collapse of the Beatles; the brutal public bickering that went on
between him and Lennon; the vilification of Linda by press and fans
alike; the troubled benign dictatorship of Wings, a band that seemed to
suffer from a messy, revolving-door membership policy.

"You could never force musicians to do stuff," he told me, "but
you'd *suggest* strongly."

"I imagine you can be quite . . . *persuasive* in your arguments," I
said.

"There were some arguments," he conceded. "But there were arguments in the Beatles, too. It's unpleasant. But it's actually quite a good
thing."

"Was it tough finding musicians who weren't overawed to be working with 'Paul McCartney, ex-Beatle'?" I wondered.

"I don't blame 'em," he replied, deadpan. "*I'm* overawed by me,
Tom. It's true, man. I'm not kidding!" There was a long pause. "No, no,
no, I am kidding," he added with a smile.

At one point I broached the numerous dope busts he'd suffered as
an enthusiastic user of marijuana. Did he feel victimized by the police
in any way?

"A bit, yeah," he admitted.

"It must have been like the coppers were sitting around thinking,
We've got a slack day, boys, let's bust Macca," I said.

"Well, there was a lot of that," he laughed.

"They found plants at your farmhouse in Scotland, they had you in L.A. with a joint on the floor of your car," I went on.

"That's right, yeah." He nodded. "That was planted. The L.A. thing was planted. What it was, by mistake, I ran a red light 'cause I thought, You can do that in America. Which you can. Often you can turn right on a red light. But this had a sign—NO RIGHT TURN—that I'd missed."

"Because you were stoned?" I ventured.

He hesitated, and then his face spread into a wide grin.

"I might have been."

By the end, I realized he hadn't looked at his watch once.

Close to a week later, we met up again. Just inside his doorway, McCartney gestured to me, inviting me into his office as he messed around on an upright bass. "Check out my new bass, man," he said, his fingers strolling up and down its neck. He looked tired, the years showing on his face. It was the end of a long day.

We parked ourselves on his office sofa again, in the same positions we'd assumed the week before. He'd obviously given our previous conversation some thought and seemed keen to play down the soft-drug angle, mainly because he figured it would be seized upon by the papers and twisted out of context.

"This is gonna get picked up by the tabloids," he said. "'Macca Exposé.' I don't wanna go on about it too much."

I pointed out that "Paul McCartney in Weed-Puffing Shock" was hardly revelatory stuff.

"It's all a bit stronger these days, so I don't want to be the one who advocates it," he argued. "You don't want to give some kids the idea 'Well, great, man, let's go do it.'"

"The Beatles got me into dope, actually," I confessed.

"See, that's it," he said. "But there are people these days who can't handle it, and I don't wanna be responsible for any of that."

Firmly, and for the record, he claimed to have completely given up smoking weed himself, partly as a result of his advancing years. "It's a bit befuddling," he laughed. "It's actually more important at my stage of the game to be unfuddled."

He said his friends had noticed how his vocabulary had improved after he'd quit marijuana. "They'd say, 'Wow, your choice of words has really gone up.' Before I'd go, 'It's like . . . y'know . . . it's like . . . y'know . . . *good.*' Whereas now, it's like, 'It's kinda *exceptional.*' You're actually choosing words that fit better, that I know, but I could never remember."

If the public perception of Paul McCartney is pretty much frozen in stone, he sometimes seems to be entirely at odds with it. At one point I mentioned the "Fab Macca" image of him as the irrepressibly chirpy Liverpudlian, gooning for the cameras with his thumbs aloft. To my surprise, this lit his fuse and prompted a sweary explosion of only partly comedic rage.

"I have been chastened by the world opinion on that," he said, his hackles beginning to rise. "You will not actually see me do it."

"Is that right?" I said, not entirely buying this.

"Well, have you seen me do it in the last ten years?" he said.

I admitted I hadn't.

"Because I'm suitably chastened by people saying, 'You shouldn't do that.' It's like fucking school! 'One thing you must not do is put your fucking thumbs up, you twat!' So much of what happens reminds me of school. And I think my attitude's the same as it always was. 'Yes, sir.' Waits till sir has gone out the room and then goes, 'Fuck off!' Y'know, that's what we *really* think. Anyone dares to tell us we're . . . *cunts* . . . is a *twat.* . . . Excuse me, I've just gone all sweary. You said I was Wacky Thumbs Aloft, you see."

"Still," I contended, "it's quite a handy two-dimensional public image to have, isn't it? It kind of conceals the guy who gets annoyed or angry or tells people what to do."

McCartney seemed temporarily thrown.

"Uh, y'know . . . I don't know," he said. "Maybe it is. Like I say, man, I really don't know. It seems natural to me, y'know. I'm not always feeling in that mood. But I am optimistic and want to remain optimistic."

It was in moments such as this that I realized that Paul was not nearly as self-aware as you might expect. Ask him what he himself imagined was the popular image of him, Wacky Macca aside, and he was similarly, and perhaps surprisingly, stumped.

"Oh . . . I don't know, man . . . I don't know . . . no, I don't know."

In many ways, it seems, it's this lack of self-analysis that stops him from going entirely mad. Perhaps if he thought too deeply about the fact that he is "Paul McCartney," he might not be able to function.

One of his more peculiar traits is that he often refers to the Beatles as "they" ("They were the greatest little rock band going") and even talks about himself in the third person. ("If anyone's gonna make a decision," he said, looking from the outside in at the warring in Wings, "it should probably be him.") It's as if divorcing himself from reality allows him to unburden himself of the weight of his legend.

He spoke about not quite believing that he had in fact been in certain situations—such as lining up with the other Beatles for a photo opportunity in Miami in 1964 as Cassius Clay (later Muhammad Ali) pretended to knock them all out—until he was presented with the actual pictorial evidence. He further expressed this sense of unreality in "That Was Me" from his 2007 album *Memory Almost Full,* offering lyrical snapshots of himself playing with the Beatles on the *Royal Iris* ferry on the Mersey, at the Cavern, and on TV shows, while struggling to take it in that he'd actually done all of this.

As time passed, I found myself interviewing McCartney once or twice a year, both for major features for *Mojo* and *Q* and for smaller bits and bobs. The playful approach seemed to work well with him, though he never quite let me forget that I was in his company as a journalist and, ultimately, like any big star burned by the tabloids, he had his misgivings about "reporters."

"But they're not bastards, they're lovable rogues," he joshed, though a touch spikily. "They're just not as lovable as they used to be."

"Is it worse now than it was in the 1960s?" I asked him, perhaps stupidly.

"Well, you know it is," he said. "You don't have to ask me. You're *with them.*"

"I'm not with those bastards," I protested, slightly affronted. "I work for music magazines."

"No, but . . . okay," he said, softening his tack. "You're on the side of the fence that gives you *access* to those bastards."

All the same, one later incident in particular highlighted how he didn't really believe that I was in cahoots with the tabloid scummers. We were going over his experiences of the past few years, taking in the high points and, of course, the low points. It had been only nineteen months since his ugly divorce from Heather Mills.

What was the one thing he'd done in the past decade that he wished he hadn't?

He laughed, a touch edgily. "Oh God, I dunno. Well, I did wish I didn't . . . not really . . . can't think of any."

"There is one obvious one," I said, knowing I was veering into dodgy territory.

"What're you saying?" he shot back, suddenly cool.

"Getting married again?" I said.

He laughed once again, more easily this time. "Well, okay, yeah. I suppose that has to be the prime contender. But I don't wanna down anyone. I mean, these things happen, y'know. It's the ups and downs of life. And it was a pity that it happened that way. But I tend to look at the sort of positive side, which is that I have another beautiful daughter."

Inevitably, perhaps, once it was published, the *Daily Mail* pounced on this quote and reprinted it under the sleight-of-hand headline "Sir Paul McCartney Admits Marriage to Heather Mills Was His 'Biggest Mistake.'" Of course, this was entirely beyond my control, and, through a writer friend, I heard that even though Paul was irked by it, he didn't blame me.

Increasingly, a more informal tone began to characterize our conversations, often conducted via phone when he had half an hour to spare, shooting from somewhere to somewhere in the back of a car in Europe or America. Once I had to wait by the phone for almost an entire dreary week, his publicist telling me that Paul—on holiday at the time and so virtually impossible to pin down—would call me between four and eleven P.M. on any number of given days. Another time, we spoke for ten minutes two days before Christmas and both of us had colds, and it was clear that neither of us was really in the mood.

At the end of one call in the middle of his summer holiday in the Hamptons, he seemed at loose ends and clearly wanted to carry on nattering away, talking about what we each had planned for the rest of the day.

"You know what?" he said, making the rest of *his* day sound a touch more idyllic than mine. "I'm actually going to have a sail on my wee sailboat. It's a nice day here, and it's only four o'clock in the afternoon."

I told him that a long-lens shot had appeared in that morning's papers, strangely enough, of him posing behind a dress hanging on a clothesline. It turned out that he and his then girlfriend, now third wife, Nancy Shevell, had been wandering past a clothes stall when Paul spotted a shifty photographer.

"It's weird, 'cause I saw him and I thought, I bet that's a pap," he said. "And I thought, Nah, I'm being paranoid. But my instincts are too damn good on that stuff and I was right. I sort of went up to him, but he was a coward and he drove off.

"I did say to Nancy, 'D'you know what? Look, it's us having fun on holiday, we're having a laugh.' Y'know, standing behind a dress. I was originally trying to get her to stand behind it to see if it fitted her. So I got behind it and I must admit, as I did it, I thought, He's gonna get this, this'll be the one."

Still, he confessed that on numerous occasions such a laissez-faire attitude to the paparazzi is hard to maintain. He comically fumed that he finds it hard to relax on a beach, lest a concealed snapper grab a few frames of him looking paunchy. He recalled enviously spying another bloke of a similar age on holiday one time. "Just a family man, and his belly was hanging out," he said wistfully. "He didn't give a shit, he's playing with his kids. But I'm looking to see who's in the hotel room with a long lens."

Talking to me on the phone one night in spring 2013, as he rather nervously drove himself to the studio in Los Angeles in "a low-slung sports car . . . I'm used to a big, high, strong SUV," he swung between bursts of annoyance about the intrusions caused by his celebrity and being gently tickled by the notion that he has one of the most famous faces on earth. He broke off our conversation at one point, having been spotted by a fan, to bark under his breath, "Oi! No. Pfff-fucking hell. Everyone's got a camera these days."

At another point he suddenly began killing himself laughing for no apparent reason. "I've got a funny thing happening here, Tom," he explained. "I'm driving along, and right behind me there's one of those buses doing the star tours. I always want to stop and get out and go, 'Hey, guys, how're you doing?' I love the irony of it. They're going around, saying, 'Oh, here's so-and-so, here's so-and-so.' And I'm *right* under their noses, man."

He arrived at the studio and seemed to be having a bit of trouble parking the sports car. "Whoops," he cried out. "I've just clunked me car. Shit. Hold on. It's a lesson in parking—how to not hit things in front of you."

In Los Angeles, against his better judgment, he'll find himself jumping red lights in an effort to escape the paps. "You think, This is dangerous," he said. "It's like a spy chase and you think, Spies get killed doing this. And I didn't do anything."

In New York, more gallingly, he'll try to placate tailing photographers only to have his peace offering thrown back in his face. He'll pull the car over and three or four others will screech to a halt behind him. He'll get out and make them a deal: take your picture, then leave me alone.

"These days, of course, they've even got video cameras," he pointed out, "which is embarrassing 'cause I used to love gritting my teeth and going, 'I hate you but I'm smiling.' So I say, 'Okay, guys, that's it, you've got your picture.' Get back in the car and they just *keep on following*."

"Ever hit a photographer?" I asked him.

"*Nah,*" he said, softly and without any real conviction, before changing his mind. "Well, I have, actually. But it didn't get reported. I got lucky. I think he thought he deserved it.

"But I always remember the famous story that gives you pause for thought, which was Mick Jagger was allegedly in Paris one night and he comes out of a nightclub and there was a photographer. Mick went up to the guy to clock him one. The guy turned out to be into karate. Went *foo-foo-foo-foo-foom*. Got Mick on the floor, *then* took a picture."

Only once did I witness McCartney dealing with photographers first-hand. I was charged with chaperoning him at the *Q* Awards in 2010, where he was picking up an award for the remastered *Band on the Run*. Arrangements had been made for him to arrive at the service entrance at the back of the Grosvenor House Hotel, to save him having to negotiate the red-carpet rat run beloved of artists with a record to plug.

He arrived, with only one security guard in tow, in a car driven by his longtime personal assistant, former Wings guitar tech John Hammel, and good-naturedly elbowed his way through a clot of snappers and fans who had made a hasty dash the few yards down from the gate where the other attendees were shuffling in.

Once I'd ushered him inside and into an anteroom reserved for him by the organizers, he was chipper, if a touch confused—as is sometimes the way up in the dizzy altitudes of the superstar—by the exact nature of the do. "Is this the *Q* Awards or the *GQ* Awards? Are there film stars out there or just musicians?" he asked me, trying on a couple of jackets and seeking my approval and Hammel's before settling on a navy blue number with matching epaulettes.

Ten minutes later followed a bizarre moment when Hammel, the security guy, a couple of the awards organizers, and I marched down the corridors in convoy, like a presidential procession, to show the former Beatle where he could take a leak.

En route, a bloke who claimed to be from *Q* (though I'd never seen him before) stopped McCartney, grabbed his hand, and nervously burbled, "Oh wow, hi Paul, I just wanted to say it's a total honor to meet you," as McCartney calmly and politely responded—as he has doubtless done thousands of times—"Well, thanks, great to meet you, too."

But then the guy wouldn't let go of his hand, continuing to shake it maniacally, visibly tightening his grip. The disbelief began to spread across McCartney's face. From what I've seen and experienced, one of the worst things you can do when meeting a famous person is lose the plot in the manner of a frothing, hyperventilating fan (fan, of course, being short for *fanatic*).

"I'll let you go then," said the bloke, sensing McCartney's discomfort and finally loosening his grasp.

As we continued on our way down the corridor, Paul, in a revealing moment, turned to me, laughing, completely at ease, and said, "That was fucking big of him to let me go, wasn't it?"

An hour or so later, onstage, in front of an assemblage comprising, as he put it, "All the younger bands . . . which is pretty much everybody," McCartney accepted the award for Classic Album for *Band on the Run,* dedicating it to Linda in a characteristically jocular though properly heartfelt speech.

"The Beatles were a pretty hard act to follow, and we were gonna follow them," he said into the microphone, to whoops and cheers. "Linda was getting slagged off for being in my band. *I* was getting slagged off for letting her in the band. This album was quite a struggle to make."

If any word sums up Paul McCartney in the 1970s, it is *struggle.* Another is *escape.*

In essence, he spent the decade struggling to escape the shadow of the Beatles, effectively becoming an outlaw hippie millionaire, hiding out in his Scottish farmhouse before traveling the world with makeshift bands and barefoot children. It was a time of numerous drug busts and brilliant, banned, and sometimes baffling records. For McCartney, it was an edgy, liberating, sometimes frightening period of his life that has largely been forgotten.

When I was discussing this period in depth with him, a notion sparked in my head that led to the writing of this book. For me, a very different figure was beginning to emerge, in sharp contrast to the oft-perceived slightly cozy, head-wobbling national and international treasure who these days opens the Olympics or performs for the queen.

Between 1969 and 1981, Paul McCartney was a man on the run— from his recent past as a Beatle, from his horrendous split from his bandmates, from the towering expectation that surrounded his every move. Behind his lasting image during that period as a Bambi-eyed soft-rock balladeer, he was actually a far more counterculturally leaning individual (albeit one overshadowed by the light-sucking Lennon) than he was ever given credit for—freewheeling in his hippiefied way, taking to the road with a "bunch of nutters" for an impromptu, disorganized university tour with the proto-Wings, viewing the world though perma-stoned eyes, and defiantly continuing to flip off the authorities the world over who sought to criminalize him, all the while adopting a shrugging, amused attitude to it all.

These days he marvels at a photograph taken of him carrying the naked infant Mary through Dublin Airport in the early 1970s ("I could not imagine that now"), yet he is still slightly disbelieving of the Victorian attitudes that prompted the staff of an exclusive country club in Lagos, during the making of *Band on the Run,* to require him to put swimsuits on his nude, pool-diving children. "I'm going, 'You're kidding? They're aged *nothing.*' "

If there was one key insight that struck me during my conversations with McCartney and the research and writing of this book, it was his eccentricity, which often gets lost behind his deceptive façade of straightness. As his devoted 1970s Wings sidekick Denny Laine told me, "Paul *is* a bit eccentric, and whatever he wants he usually gets."

This eccentricity is perhaps the key to everything—from the release of the bewildering "Mary Had a Little Lamb" single, to his 1972 European tour in a gaudily painted open-topped bus, to the beautifully dreamy, softly psychedelic U.S. No. 1 single written about his uncle Albert, to his incarceration in Japan in 1980 after attempting to sneak half a pound of marijuana into the country.

In this way, *Man on the Run* sets out to tell the tale of a man living outside normal society and, for better or for worse, acting on his own tangential whims, during a chaotic and fascinating period of his life.

Back in the late 1960s, much to Lennon's delight, his Beatle bandmate had come up with the idea of recording a wholly experimental album entitled *Paul McCartney Goes Too Far.* While that never came to pass, in many ways, in the 1970s, Paul McCartney did go too far, and not always in the right directions.

"You have to be honest about your past," he confessed to me at one point. "I was such a daring young thing. We were on this wacky adventure."

MAN ON THE RUN

1

ON THE RUN

Your first solo album, McCartney. *You recorded that at home, in secret, in the midst of all of your wrangles with the Beatles.*

Yeah. It was really . . . kind of . . . therapy through hell. It was one of the worst times of my life.

H E KNEW HE WAS IN TROUBLE the morning he couldn't lift his head off the pillow. He awoke facedown, his skull feeling like a useless dead weight. A dark thought flashed through his mind: if he couldn't make the effort to pull himself up, he'd suffocate right there and then.

Somehow, as if it was the hardest thing he'd ever done, he summoned the energy to move. He flipped over onto his back and thought, Jesus . . . that was a bit near.

Day by day, week by week, his condition had been steadily worsening. His often sleepless nights were spent shaking with anxiety, while his days, which he was finding harder and harder to make it through, were characterized by heavy drinking and self-sedation with marijuana. He found himself chain-smoking his unfiltered, lung-blackening Senior Service cigarettes one after another after another.

Later, he would look back on this period and tell everyone that he'd almost had a nervous breakdown. From the outside, there appeared to be no "almost" about it.

For the first time in his life, he felt utterly worthless. Everything he had been since the age of fifteen had been wrapped up in the band. Now, even though he couldn't tell the world, that period of his life was almost certainly over.

It was as if he'd suddenly and unexpectedly lost his job, been made entirely redundant. He was twenty-seven and of no use to anyone anymore. Even the money he'd earned up to this point was no comfort, made no real difference. This was an identity crisis in extremis: who exactly was he if he wasn't Beatle Paul McCartney?

On the mornings when he forced himself to rise, he'd sit on the edge of his bed for a while before defeatedly crawling back under the covers. When he did get out of bed he'd reach straight for the whiskey, his drinking creeping earlier and earlier into the day. By three in the afternoon, he was usually out of it.

"I hit the bottle," he admits. "I hit the substances."

He was eaten up with anger—at himself, at the outside world. He could describe it only as a barreling, empty feeling rolling across his soul.

Out of work and with nothing to distract him, he was tormented by ghosts from his past; they would rise up, whispering in his head, telling him that, in spite of everything he'd achieved, they knew he'd never really amount to anything. That he should have found a proper job in the first place, just as they'd always said.

He realized that up until this point he'd been a "cocky sod." And now there was this: the first serious blow to his confidence he'd ever experienced. Even when he was fourteen and the complications from a mastectomy had suddenly taken his mother's life, he had understood that this horrific event had been beyond his control. Somehow, now, in the depths of his muddied thinking, he was starting to believe that everything that was happening was nobody's fault but his own.

His wife of less than a year later said she had felt the situation was "frightening beyond belief." Within a matter of months, her new partner had gone from being a sparky, driven, world-famous rock star to a broken man who didn't want to set foot out of their bedroom. But even if Linda was scared, she knew she couldn't give up on Paul. She recognized that her husband was sinking into emotional quicksand, and she knew that it was down to her alone to pull him out before he went under for good.

"Linda saved me," he says. "And it was all done in a sort of domestic setting."

It had been two years since they'd first met, at the Bag O' Nails nightclub in Soho, four days later being seen deep in conversation at the press launch for *Sgt. Pepper*. It was only a year since they'd managed to float unnoticed together through the streets of New York (where, in Chinatown, he had comically tried to pull her into a temple offering Buddhist weddings) before flying from coast to coast, landing in Los Angeles and disappearing for days into a bungalow at the Beverly Hills Hotel. It was still only six months since they'd giggled their way through their wedding ceremony at Marylebone registry office in London, amid a fog of seething female jealousy that seemed to spread across the world.

He had been the last single Beatle, the one seen about town, haunting the clubs and hanging with the artsy crowd. She was the American single-mother divorcée who had earned some renown as a rock photographer and who had apparently had flings with Mick Jagger and Jim Morrison. To Paul, Linda appeared deeper than the frothy, starry-eyed girls who tended to flock around him, less buttoned-up than his then paramour, the actress Jane Asher.

Linda would take Paul out on long drives, saying, "Let's get lost" in her drawly, spacey way, showing him a new kind of freedom. She had surprised him by telling him, "I could make you a nice home."

Now it was the autumn of 1969, and the McCartneys were in Scotland, "hiding away in the mists," as Paul puts it. They had escaped here, far from London and the heavy weather of intra-Beatle feuding that refused to lift.

But High Park Farm was no rock-star country pile. Paul had bought the run-down farmhouse, set on a hill overlooking Skeroblin Loch amid 183 acres of rough Scottish landscape, back in June 1966, the year he became a millionaire. His accountant had suggested that McCartney invest in property to wrestle some of his earnings away from the clutches of Harold Wilson and his Labour government's painful 95 percent taxing of high earners.

The ever frugal Paul, of course, leaped at such an opportunity, picking High Park Farm out of the reams of property documents his accountant sent him. The asking price was a not insubstantial £35,000, more than ten times the cost of the average family home in the mid-1960s. It was, says Paul, "wee," consisting of only three rooms: a bedroom at either end separated by a combined kitchen and living area. The hole in the roof of the farmhouse was included in the deal.

But it was another eighteen months after the purchase, in December 1967, before Paul, with Jane Asher in tow, made the trip north to check out his new investment. High Park was set more than a mile up a bumpy dirt path, and visitors unprepared for the terrain would moan that the drive would virtually wreck their offroad-unworthy vehicles.

The sorely neglected property was in a wild and windswept location, fourteen miles from the southern tip of the remote Kintyre Peninsula, in Argyll. Three miles west of the hill lay the six-mile sweep of beach at Machrihanish Bay. A five-mile drive southeast down the A83 sat the small fishing port of Campbeltown and the closest amenities.

At the tail-end of 1967—equally the Beatles' annus mirabilis and their annus horribilis (the marvel of *Sgt. Pepper,* the paralyzing shock of Brian Epstein's death, the trials of *Magical Mystery Tour,* and the sense that nothing would ever be the same again)—McCartney tried to make High Park habitable on a characteristically thrifty level.

He dispatched Beatles gofer Alistair Taylor into Campbeltown; Taylor returned with a secondhand Formica table and chairs, an electric stove, and a couple of beds. The pair fashioned a sofa out of a pile of Sharpe's Express wooden potato boxes, with an old mattress found in the barn folded over the makeshift frame.

After his split from Asher, Paul first went back there with Linda in November 1968. The eldest daughter of the moneyed New York Eastman family had immediately fallen in love with the place and the idea of roughing it in this remoteness—no hot water, mice and rats in the walls and all—but had suggested to Paul that they do the place up a bit. It was a notion that hadn't even occurred to the airy McCartney.

She encouraged him to pour a cement floor in the kitchen, an improvement over the wooden planks laid over the bare earth. He began making a table to replace the flimsy Formica one. He scaled a ladder and climbed onto the roof to fix its hole, Linda soundtracking his handiwork by spinning the newly released *Tighten Up* reggae compilation LPs.

If you had walked through the door of the farmhouse in the latter months of 1969, according to Paul, you'd have seen "nappies, bottles, musical instruments, me and Lin, like a couple of hippies. . . . It wasn't sort of dirty, but it wasn't clean."

High Park wasn't entirely cut off from civilization, though it certainly had that feel. Linda in particular romanticized this notion, imagining that the McCartneys were living in another era, as if they were pioneers in this isolated place. She loved the fact that they were, as she fancifully saw it, "at the end of nowhere."

As the months passed, Paul and Linda grew into their rural personas. At Christmas, he bought her twelve pheasants; she bought him a tractor, which he used to plow a vegetable patch, where they grew parsnips, turnips, potatoes, green beans, runner beans, and spinach.

Their acreage was home to 150 to 200 sheep, which Paul learned to clip using hand shears, after which they sold the fleeces to the Wool Marketing Board. Already leaning toward vegetarianism, they balked at the notion of killing their lambs, although they were forced to send some off to market when the numbers grew too high. They tried to separate the ewes from the rams, but sometimes one of the male sheep would enthusiastically spring over the fence. In time, they had six horses, including the retired racer Drake's Drum, bought for Paul's father, Jim, and a former winner at Aintree, alongside Honor (Paul's), Cinnamon (Linda's), and three ponies, Sugarfoot, Cookie, and Coconut.

Revving up a generator, Paul put together an ad hoc four-track recording facility in High Park's rickety lean-to, which he named Rude Studio. It was in here, gently encouraged by Linda, that his songwriting slowly began to return to him, as he effectively used music as therapy to alleviate his depression. "She eased me out of it," he remembers, "and just said, 'Hey, y'know, you don't want to get too crazy.'"

Paul shied away from admitting that there was a strong autobiographical element to some of these new compositions, but his protestations rang hollow. The lyrics of "Man We Was Lonely" speak of how his and Linda's self-imposed exile was not as idyllic as it outwardly seemed, that their spirits had been low, but, under the comfort blanket of domesticity, their positivity was returning.

"Every Night," a song he'd first begun messing around with during the *Let It Be* sessions, was more confessional still—its singer painting a grim picture of a routine involving getting wasted and struggling to drag himself out of bed. The chorus, as was increasingly becoming a McCartney trait, pledged his devotion to Linda. As a song, it was a deceptively breezy affair. While elsewhere Lennon was screaming his pain, it was typical of McCartney to mask his with melody. Only if you listened closely would you really be able to detect the songwriter's anguish.

As Paul seemed to stabilize, the McCartneys settled into a daily routine, riding their horses across the land or taking sheepdog Martha for long walks. They drove into Campbeltown in their Land Rover, which they'd nicknamed Helen Wheels, the Beatle becoming a regular sight wandering around in his Wellies and sheepskin-lined brown leather jacket. In the evening, he would light the fire while Linda cooked, and then Paul would step into Rude to work on songs. At night, they would cuddle up, get stoned, and watch TV. "We were not cut off from the world," said Linda. "We were never hermits."

In addition, to playfully distract Paul from his troubles, there were the children to look after: the newborn Mary and Linda's child from her first marriage, shy Heather, only six. For the kids, High Park was a cross between a playground and a junkyard. As soon as she began to walk, Mary was free to toddle outside, through its abandoned gypsy encampment–like clutter of scrap wood, sheets of corrugated iron, and teetering log piles (noting incredulously as an adult that she'd effectively been brought up in a "lumber yard").

It was a messy scene but, for McCartney, one filled with increasingly frequent spells of happiness. Nevertheless, in a corner of his mind, knowing that there was a Beatles-shaped storm brewing back down in London, Paul was still plagued with unease.

It didn't help that everyone was arguing about whether or not he was dead.

The rumor had first circulated among the bloodshot-eyed student populace of Drake University in Iowa, around the time McCartney had first holed up in Scotland. The signs were all there if you cared to dig "deep" enough, to stop just rolling joints on the covers of Beatles albums and decipher the hidden messages in the artwork and between the grooves. The students listened to Lennon's daft murmur of "cranberry sauce" in the fade-out of "Strawberry Fields Forever" and imagined it to be "I buried Paul." They would spin *The White Album* backward with an index finger and convince themselves that a voice could be heard saying, "Turn me on, dead man."

In many ways, the Beatles had brought this upon themselves. In their touring absence and with their increasingly cryptic music, they had laid playful clues and red herrings: with the opening lines of "Rain" played backward at the end of the song; with the garbled, wonked-out voices locked in the play-out groove of side 2 of *Sgt. Pepper*; with Lennon's head-game assertion in "Glass Onion" that the walrus was Paul.

"We'd done them for fun, just for something to do," says Paul, in admitting the Beatles' surprise that their penchant for japery was taken so seriously. "Then everyone analyzed them and we thought, *Ah*. We were completely oblivious to all those other 'hidden' messages."

That was until the clueheads began to air their tangential theories. September 16, 1969, saw the first piece, in the Drake University student paper, under the tantalizing headline "Is Paul McCartney Dead?" A week later, the *Northern Star*, the campus rag of Northern Illinois University, went one better: "Clues Hint at Possible Beatle Death."

A student identifying himself only as Tom called Detroit DJ Russ Gibb to inform him of the rumors. Listening in, a college writer named Fred LaBour decided to turn prankster, taking it upon himself to "kill" McCartney, adding arm upon leg to the growing myth. Two days later, the *Michigan Daily* printed his fabricated revelations under a more contentious banner: "McCartney Dead: New Evidence Brought to Light." The rumor spread countrywide when Roby Yonge, on his networked show from WABC in New York, discussed the theories on the air in the small hours, when the stoned were at their most receptive.

It all made sense to the herbally enhanced mind, of course, and somehow an elaborate backstory began to emerge. Instead of, as the real tale went, having suffered a chipped tooth and badly cut lip in a moped accident in Liverpool in December 1965 (Paul had been "looking at the moon," hit a rock, and gone flying over the handlebars), McCartney had stormed off from a Beatles session at Abbey Road on November 9, 1966, in a huff, following an argument with the other Beatles, and crashed his Aston Martin, decapitating himself. The panicked band had subsequently replaced him with a doppelgänger, the winner of a secret Paul McCartney look-alike competition, a Scotsman named William Campbell, who was then given plastic surgery to render him identical.

There were other clues, apparently. The palm of a hand held above McCartney's head on the cover of *Sgt. Pepper* was a mystical sign of death (it wasn't). Paul was barefoot in the "funeral-procession" zebracrossing cover shot of *Abbey Road* to indicate that he was a corpse (the duller truth being that it had been a hot August day, he'd been wearing sandals, and he'd slipped them off). The license plate of the white Volkswagen Beetle in the background of the image that ended with "28IF" was symbolically stating the age McCartney would have been had he survived the rumored accident (in fact, photographer Iain Macmillan had attempted to have the car towed out of the shot). The word *walrus* was Greek for "corpse" (it isn't). The "one and one and one is three" that Lennon sang about in "Come Together" referred to the surviving Beatles (rather than being just a throwaway line in a surreal, pinballing lyric). Paul is facing away from the camera on the back cover of *Sgt. Pepper* because the image in fact shows William Campbell, hiding his surgical scars (although that didn't explain why he is shown facing forward on the front cover). And on and on and on it fantastically went.

By November, the story had made it to the pages of *Rolling Stone*, albeit in a piece with an eyebrow-raised, slightly mocking tone. Nevertheless, Beatles publicist Derek Taylor soon found himself having to fend off calls from reporters the world over. And still the rumor persisted, not least when Dr. Henry Truby of the University of Miami studied three pre- and post-1966 recordings of McCartney singing and rather vaguely stated that he couldn't conclude that they were definitely the work of the same person.

But even for its chief propagator, the whole affair was getting out of hand. Fred LaBour was invited to appear on TV in California in a mock trial where he would present evidence to back up his claims. Before the recording, however, he confessed to the show's host, lawyer F. Lee Bailey, that he had made the whole thing up. It was too late, pointed out Bailey. They would have to go with it, to air the legend.

Finally, Paul issued a statement through the Beatles' press office. "I'm alive and well," he said. "But if I were dead I would be the last to know."

Of course, maddeningly, it was such a ridiculous myth that it was almost impossible to disprove. It hinged on McCartney somehow managing to prove that he was who he said he was. But even if he underwent and passed a fingerprint test, the naysayers could crow that it was all down to forgery and conspiracy.

Given McCartney's distinctive voice, features, and physical demeanor, the Paul Is Dead fiction was of course absurd. In London, even his longtime barber was forced to respond to a New York radio reporter's probing by saying that the last time he'd cut Paul's hair, a flaw in his part had still been there.

In the end, it came down to one simple, rumor-puncturing question: if this impostor William Campbell had managed not only to win the McCartney look-alike competition but had also gone under the plastic surgeon's knife, learned to sing like Paul, and written songs of the caliber of "She's Leaving Home" and "Hey Jude," why would he or any of the other Beatles have left a trail of clues to blow his cover?

More tickled than annoyed, and mindful of Mark Twain's famous quote, after the publication of an erroneous obituary, about the rumors of his death being greatly exaggerated, McCartney was aware that there might be a positive, publicity-friendly angle to all of this. It couldn't do the just-released *Abbey Road* any harm, and in the end the rumpus sent its sales rocketing skyward, making it the biggest-selling Beatles album in the United States since *Sgt. Pepper.*

Nevertheless, dying, as McCartney now jokes, "wasn't easy . . . it took a lot out of me."

It also drew the unwanted attention of the press directly to the door of High Park. The first journalist to make the long and difficult journey from London to Scotland and out to the Kintyre Peninsula was dogged *Daily Express* pop scribe Judith Simons, who in the past had interviewed the Beatles on many occasions.

The trek was clearly more arduous and involved than the writer had expected, since she showed up at night, in the dark, timorously knocking on the door of the farmhouse. Paul, who considered Simons "a little sweetheart," wasn't particularly irritated by her intrusion; instead, he was quietly impressed by her tenacity and bravery.

"She was totally scared shitless of being in the middle of this place," he says. "I mean, there were no lights on the road." Still, he remained vague and nonplussed when Simons started firing what he viewed as wholly trivial questions at him. "She was just asking me about some story. I'm saying, 'What can I tell you?'"

In truth, Paul had stopped doing interviews because he still felt far too exposed and emotionally raw. There was one question he dreaded above all others: "Are you happy?" In his precariously balanced state, it would almost make him burst into tears.

Nevertheless, as time went on, his patience began to fray, resulting in eruptions of other emotions entirely. When a pair from the London offices of the U.S. magazine *Life*—writer Dorothy Bacon and photographer Terence Spencer—flew to Scotland, schlepping all the way to High Park to get a reaction about the death rumors, McCartney's anger boiled over.

It was a Sunday morning in late October and Paul, unsurprisingly, was still in bed. The *Life* duo had cannily assumed that this would be a good time to catch the McCartneys at home and that their journey was less likely to be hindered by interfering local farmers. Intrepidly, they hoofed up to High Park from the main road, trudging across the fields for close to an hour.

Arriving at the door of the farmhouse, Bacon knocked. Paul, having got up as soon as he realized what was going on outside, jerked the door open, a bucket of slop from the McCartneys' rudimentary kitchen in one hand. He was unshaven, his hair an early Beatles mop top grown out and gone pineappleishly unkempt. His face was beet red with fury. Spencer raised his camera to take a shot.

"I threw the bucket at him," Paul says. "It was nearly the cover of *Life*."

The bucket flew past the photographer's head, but Spencer had got the shot and Paul knew it. Enraged, he stepped forward and punched the snapper on the shoulder. Having covered six wars and experienced nothing in the way of physical violence until faced with a raging Beatle, the startled Spencer said to Bacon, "I think we've run out of our hospitality." The pair turned tail and quickly marched away.

Alone, calming down, Paul reflected on what had just happened. He'd utterly lost his cool, and now the photographer definitely had a shot of him looking furious and demented. Ever the PR man, Paul realized he had to try to mend the situation if the shot wasn't to appear on the cover of *Life* and in the world's papers thereafter, making him look like a lunatic.

Bacon and Spencer, meanwhile, were shaken but happy enough: they had pictorial proof that McCartney was still alive.

As they made their way back down the farm track, the McCartneys'

Land Rover, with Paul, Linda, and the kids inside, pulled up behind them. Spencer was initially afraid, saying to Bacon, "For God's sake, be careful, because that man is mad."

But it was an altogether more amiable and contrite Paul who emerged from the Land Rover, apologizing, proffering a handshake, and offering, in return for the roll of film containing the offending snap, to give a short interview and, albeit still reluctantly, to have his photograph taken with the family.

"We agreed to pose on the Land Rover," he remembers. "But I was definitely not in posing mode."

A slightly haunted-looking image of the McCartneys made the cover of *Life* dated November 7, 1969, along with the accompanying splash "The Case of the 'Missing' Beatle: Paul Is Still with Us." In the shot, one of two that would illustrate the piece, Paul appears bed-headed and morning rough, his left arm curled protectively around a wind-blown Linda, his right cradling baby Mary, as in front of him, Heather, perhaps sensing her parents' hostility toward these unannounced visitors, wields a walking stick like a club. In the second, the family is arranged on the front bumper of the Land Rover, Paul trying to appear upbeat, raising his hand in a friendly, open gesture as Linda nuzzles his neck.

In the interview, he addressed the Paul Is Dead rumors. "It is all bloody stupid," he said. "Perhaps the rumor started because I haven't been much in the press lately. I don't have anything to say these days. I am happy to be with my family and I will work when I work. I was switched on for ten years and I never switched off. Now I am switching off whenever I can. I would rather be a little less famous these days.

"The people who are making up these rumors should look to themselves a little more," he went on. "They should worry about themselves instead of worrying whether I am dead or not.

"I would rather do what I began doing, which is making music. But the Beatle thing is over. It has been exploded, partly by what we have done, and partly by other people.

"What I have to say is all in the music," he concluded. "If I want to say anything, I write a song. Can you spread it around that I am just an ordinary person and want to live in peace? We have to go now. We have two children at home."

Upon publication, the piece appeared to lay to rest the ghosts of the

Paul Is Dead furor, although in some heads the doubts and conspiracies rumble on to this day.

One crucial point was completely missed, however: the fact that Paul had let slip that "the Beatle thing is over." *Life* had in fact got the world exclusive that the former Fabs had secretly imploded. But, amid all the fuss, no one even noticed.

In private, the Beatles had fallen out and fallen apart, prompting McCartney's state of panic and depression. As if to spotlight the emotional distance and physical remove of the four former friends, each was filmed separately with their respective partners for the promotional clip for "Something," Apple managing director Neil Aspinall having traveled to High Park to shoot the jokey, smoochy segments featuring Paul and Linda.

The critical episode in what Lennon called the "slow death" of the Beatles had come at a meeting at Apple on September 20, 1969. Three of the band members (George Harrison was away, his mother having just been diagnosed with cancer) had convened at the office to ink their names on a new deal with Capitol Records, their label in the United States and most other international territories. The deal had been hammered out by Allen Klein, a hate figure to Paul, who represented the others, while McCartney had divisively chosen to be looked after by his new in-laws, father-and-son lawyer team Lee and John Eastman. A touch gallingly for Paul, the contract Klein had brokered carved out an impressive 25 percent royalty cut for the Beatles, the highest of any recording artists in the world.

On the day, in the preamble to signing the deal, a self-consciously babbling Paul attempted to rah-rah-rah his downbeat colleagues into trying to recapture their fire. He suggested that they could perhaps do this by way of a tour of small clubs, where the band—who had last performed for a paying audience more than three years before—could turn up unannounced or billed under a pseudonym (he proposed Rikki and the Redstreaks). He argued that this might prop up their sagging confidence in their live abilities and help them get back in touch with who they were.

"I think you're daft," a scowling Lennon abruptly informed McCartney, before announcing, "I'm leaving the group. I want a divorce."

Following this jaw-dropping declaration, the three signed the contract (which would, in any case, ensure that they earned far more from
their future record sales, whether or not they stuck together) "in a bit of
a daze," according to Paul. All involved would look back on this as
being the moment when the illness that had been affecting the Beatles
finally became terminal.

As he would later attest when the press and fans cast him as the
pantomime baddie in the drama of the Beatles' separation, Paul was
actually the only member who up until that point hadn't previously
walked out on the band. Ringo, feeling like an outsider and, worse, a
musician of dwindling talent, had announced during the sessions for
The White Album, in the summer of 1968, that he was quitting. On his
return from a cooling-off-period holiday in Sardinia, he walked into
Abbey Road to find the studio festooned with flowers to celebrate his
return.

George, meanwhile, had stormed out of the rehearsals for *Let It Be*
in the cold environs of Twickenham Film Studios during the Beatles'
winter of discontent in January 1969. Harrison, who would later gripe
that McCartney had treated him with a "superior attitude" for some
years, had bitterly argued with Paul over the guitar part for "I've Got a
Feeling," as seen in the final cut of the painfully candid documentary.
On the day he walked, however, he had been battling with Lennon over
a matter long since forgotten, though serious enough to enrage both
sufficiently that they ended up trading blows.

After Harrison's departure, the Beatles spent the rest of the day rehearsing without him. That afternoon, with a significance that can't
have escaped anyone, Yoko Ono took over George's position and began
wailing into his microphone. The others reacted—Lennon with enthusiasm, McCartney and Starr in frustration—by erupting into an accompanying barrage of feedback and thunderous drumming.

George, of course, returned to the band a week later, though the
schism between him and Paul was now even wider, if papered over for
the purposes of band morale.

In the aftermath of the ultimate Beatles split, the wives would
take the blame. But it was Allen Klein, rather than Yoko Ono or Linda
McCartney, who broke up the Beatles.

Klein walked into the Beatles' world like something from a bad cartoon, a squat, cigar-sucking caricature of a Jewish showbiz manager.

The New Yorker divided and conquered John, Paul, George, and Ringo when they were lost and insecure and lacking in impetus and direction. He was also a master of casual intimidation; in one meeting in the Apple boardroom, he smirked at Lennon while nonchalantly brandishing a hammer.

He had served his apprenticeship as an accountant at an entertainment firm before moving into management, initially handling 1950s crooner Bobby Darin. But Klein's special skills soon became apparent: meticulously auditing accounts and sniffing out discrepancies and, later, prying enormous advances from record companies. He had pulled off something of a coup by securing $1 million for American soul singer Sam Cooke. More significantly, however, in 1965, the Rolling Stones had appointed Klein as their business manager and he'd renegotiated their contract with Decca, resulting in a record-breaking $1.25 million advance that wouldn't have escaped the attention of the Beatles.

It was Lennon who first became captivated by Klein, before convincing Starr and Harrison that this mouthy character could plug the holes in their business affairs. McCartney was not so sure. He'd already put forward Lee Eastman as a possible candidate for, if not exactly Beatles manager, then at least some form of financial controller for Apple. "But they said, 'Nah, nah, he'd be just too biased for you and against us,'" Paul says. "Which I could see."

Significantly, Eastman had informed McCartney about the shady flipside of Klein's reputation in America. At the point when Klein first approached the Beatles, he had just been investigated for both insider trading (he was in fact cleared, though he immediately changed his company name from Cameo-Parkway to ABKCO) and tax evasion.

Then Paul received a letter from Mick Jagger, pointedly warning him, through his own bitter experience—the New Yorker having managed to con the Stones into signing over their hits up to that point to his company—about getting involved with Klein. Paul, feeling that at last he had someone to add weight to his serious misgivings about the manager, invited Jagger to Apple to meet the others and explain his feelings about Klein. McCartney remembers the Stones' singer backing down when faced with all four Beatles: "He said, 'Well, he's all right if you like that kind of thing.' He didn't say, 'He's a robber.'"

The bad feelings festering among the Beatles came to a head one night when George, John, and Ringo turned up at Olympic Studios during the *Abbey Road* sessions with Klein in tow. The three informed Paul that he would have to sign the ABKCO management agreement right there and then, as Klein had to report to his board. McCartney refused to put pen to paper, pointing out that it was Friday night anyway and, since Klein was "a law unto himself," the board theory didn't wash. The others then told McCartney that Klein was asking for 20 percent of their future earnings. Paul, enraged, insisted that Klein would take 15, since the Beatles were, with no little understatement, "a big act." The three accused him of stalling and walked out of the studio.

On May 8, 1969, John, Ringo, and George signed the ABKCO agreement. Only three days before, the Beatles had begun recording Paul's melancholic and resigned "You Never Give Me Your Money," a barely disguised attack on Klein. McCartney remembers that Lennon, perhaps typically, appreciated the twisted humor of the lyrical gesture.

But now, no one could even laugh about where the Beatles had ended up. "It was," Paul says, "just fucking awful."

McCartney greeted the dawning of the 1970s back in London in his St. John's Wood townhouse at 7 Cavendish Avenue, within walking distance of Abbey Road. Here, Linda and Heather, still relative newcomers to England, attempted to fit back into London life.

For Linda it was a frequently claustrophobic experience, thanks to the often bitter and vicious attentions of the feral girl fans who stalked her every time she stepped outside the house, tried to trip her, or, if she was in a car without Paul, hammered on its roof and lobbed abuse at her. They scrawled messages on the walls outside: "Fuck Linda." They broke into the house and stole her photographs. They mailed her cruel letters and parcels containing human turds.

For Heather, naturally reticent and in possession of an incongruous American accent, life at Robinsfield, the local private primary school in which the McCartneys had enrolled her, was equally tough. She found it hard to make friends and often appeared sad and isolated, a situation only made worse by her elongated breaks from school as she traveled with her mum and soon-to-be adoptive dad, in an arrangement that would become looser as the decade progressed.

At the time, the McCartneys professed a wholly laid-back attitude toward their child's education. "I leave Heather to herself pretty much," said Linda. "I'm not interested in breathing over her shoulder."

"I'm not fussy about education," said Paul. "Linda's not very well educated. I know a lot of people who aren't and they're still really great people. So I don't place very heavy emphasis on it."

For Paul, returning to the capital from Scotland made him quickly realize that the destructive animosity that had set in among the Beatles was, if anything, beginning to intensify.

Business woes aside, there was still the matter of the unreleased tapes of the troubled Twickenham sessions (which had been transplanted to Apple Studios in Savile Row upon Harrison's return to the group). Throughout 1969 and into early 1970, two intensive attempts were made by producer Glyn Johns to boil down the hours of unvarnished, often sloppy takes—inspired by the bare-bones live jams of the Band—into an album that deserved to be released under the Beatles' name.

Test acetates had been found lacking in one way or another, although a mocked-up sleeve had been designed for the planned album, to be named *Get Back*. It featured the Beatles assuming the same positions and poses they'd adopted on the balcony of EMI's Manchester Square offices for their *Please Please Me* debut album six years earlier, the four now decidedly hirsute, with Lennon the most dramatically changed of all.

Back in Beatles headspace, Paul sat in a room at Cavendish Avenue and, with fresh ears, reviewed the results of the second version of the *Get Back* LP. To his mind, the music was stark, unadorned, frighteningly bare, but ultimately thrilling.

Klein, meanwhile, bluntly deemed it "a crock of shit" and conspired with Lennon to bring in Phil Spector, who had just overseen the rousing production of "Instant Karma!," to rework the tapes. Unbeknownst to McCartney, Spector booked studio time in March and began slathering strings and brass, fairy-tale harp and *aaahing* choir onto "The Long and Winding Road," making it sound hopelessly corny, like a BBC orchestra backing Engelbert Humperdinck.

At this stage, however, Paul remained unaware of this development, his thoughts somewhere else entirely. Secluded in his music room at Cavendish Avenue, McCartney began recording his first solo album, without the knowledge of the others. He wheeled a stove-sized four-track machine from Abbey Road into his home and, free of the emotional and artistic complications of the Beatles' most recent sessions, began to play, in the childlike sense of the word.

"It was very liberating," he says. "But very necessary at that time, 'cause otherwise, I wouldn't have anywhere to go to get away from the turmoil." In these solo sessions, it became clear to Paul that treating his music as therapy was yielding positive results: "It's a bit like after an operation, where you want to rest but you've got to push it."

He was able to record entirely alone, and even without a recording engineer, thanks to a device built by an Abbey Road technician that allowed him to plug directly into the back of the tape machine. He muffled boomy tom-toms with towels or simply moved the cymbals farther away from the microphone if they sounded too loud and splashy on the recording. "It was brilliant, actually," he says of this unfussy approach. "You're talking pure sound."

When it became clear to him that he would have to step outside his house to finish the recordings, Linda booked time for him at Morgan Studios in Willesden, northwest London, under the name Billy Martin, making explicit the necessity for secrecy.

Inside Morgan, the troubles of the outside world seemed to evaporate, as noted by the facility's house engineer, Robin Black. "You would never have guessed that he had any problems at all, quite frankly," he says. It was "like a holiday," according to Paul. He and Linda would even turn up with a packed lunch: "We'd take some sandwiches and a bottle of grape juice and put the baby on the floor."

The sense of fun and games spilled over from Cavendish Avenue and into the Morgan sessions. One day, inspired by a TV documentary he'd watched the previous evening about the Kreen-Akrore tribe of the Brazilian Amazon region, Paul fashioned a slightly daft ethno-rock instrumental of the same name. Feeling that something was lacking from the track, he disappeared for an hour and returned from Harrods with a longbow-and-arrow set, which he fired at a target to add percussive effects to the recording. "I had microphones the whole way across the studio," says Black, "to try and capture the sound of the release of an arrow and the swish and the thud as it hit the target."

Homemade and handmade, the resulting album, *McCartney,* was less the grand launch of his solo career and more an insight into Paul's creative practices, a precursor to the lo-fi recordings that would be in vogue decades later. But without the critical input of the other Beatles or George Martin, McCartney's creativity ran rampant, and to many the record seemed too random and sketchy, especially coming after the polished *Abbey Road*. In many ways, the freedom and playfulness resulted in Paul's quality control slipping. For every track with the sophistication of the dreamlike and nostalgic "Junk" or the gold-standard McCartney ballad "Maybe I'm Amazed," there was the cloyingly simple snippet "The Lovely Linda" or the throwaway one-man jam of "Oo You."

But before the listening public even had the opportunity to make up their minds about Paul's first solo effort, it was to provoke an almighty ruckus.

Ringo Starr stood on the doorstep of McCartney's house at Cavendish Avenue, unaware that he was about to precipitate the end of the Beatles. His tricky diplomatic mission, which he had chosen to accept in his role as the chirpy drummer, was to convince his increasingly estranged bandmate that there was an unacceptable clash of release dates between the long-delayed *Get Back*—now renamed *Let It Be*—and Paul's freshly minted eponymous solo album, which was due to be issued only a week before.

With him, he had a letter, dated March 31, 1970, handwritten by John Lennon and cosigned by George Harrison. It read: "Dear Paul, We thought a lot about the Beatles and yours [*sic*] LPs—and decided it's stupid for Apple to put out two big albums within 7 days of each other. So we sent a letter to EMI telling them to hold your release date 'til June 4th (there's a big Apple-Capitol convention in Hawaii then). We thought you'd come round when you realized that the Beatles album was coming out on April 24th. We're sorry it turned out like this—it's nothing personal. Love, John and George."

Paul—his patience already strained, his temper on a hair trigger—invited his friend inside and very quickly absorbed this information. Then he erupted.

"I told him to eff off," Paul says. "Everyone, to my mind, was completely treating me like dirt. It was kind of like 'We're the big guys, we're the grown-ups.' And I said, 'No way, man. Get out.'"

Ringo swiftly departed with the sound of Paul's fury ringing in his ears. McCartney refused to budge, and his solo album was released on April 17, 1970, forcing *Let It Be* back another two weeks, to May 8.

That was the moment when Paul McCartney finally gave up on the Beatles, the point where he mentally quit the group. Interview-phobic as he was at the time, when it came to promoting *McCartney,* Paul side-stepped face-to-face encounters by inserting a press release–cum–self-interview with the review copies of the album.

In the mock questionnaire, however, he sounded sulky, revealing more of his unhappy state of mind than perhaps even the most probing interviewer might have been able to. Was it true that Allen Klein and ABKCO weren't to be involved in the manufacturing or distribution of the new album? Not if Paul could help it. Was he planning any new records with the Beatles? No. Due to "personal differences, business differences, musical differences." Did he see himself writing songs with John in the future? No. What were his plans now? "My only plan is to grow up," he wrote.

Not that anyone could tell from the tone of the pseudo-interview, which was ill-tempered and childish. Later, McCartney said it made him shudder to look back at it.

The news exploded across the front pages of the world's newspapers. The *Daily Mirror* in Britain, on the morning of April 10, 1970, was the first to break the news of the band's split, with the unfussy words "Paul Quits the Beatles." In the days that followed, a wave of outrage began to build, with fans and reporters alike stunned that McCartney would dare to walk out on their beloved Fabs. Lost in the roar was the fact that at no point in the "interview" had McCartney actually stated that he was walking out on the band.

Overwhelmed by the reaction, Paul thought, "Christ, what have I done?," as he vainly attempted to backpedal. Forced to break his year-long British press silence, he asked Derek Taylor to arrange an interview with a trusted journalist, Ray Connolly of the *London Evening Standard*. The pair met for lunch, along with Linda, at a packed seafood restaurant in Soho. It was apparent that Paul was desperate to set the record straight.

"It was all a misunderstanding," he protested. "I never intended the statement to mean 'Paul McCartney Quits Beatles.' I didn't leave the Beatles. The Beatles have left the Beatles, but no one wants to be the one to say the party's over." He went on to spend much of the remainder of the interview venting and moaning: about Klein, about the previous flounce-offs by Ringo and George, about how John had demanded a divorce from the Beatles, about how this "trial separation" wasn't working.

If Paul was trying to redirect the finger of blame toward John, that suited Lennon fine, since he was fuming that Paul had broken the news. John had in fact told Ray Connolly the previous December that he had left the band but had asked the writer not to print the story, since Klein didn't want the news to leak until after the release of *Let It Be*.

Now, of course, Lennon was furious that McCartney had beaten him to it. Ray Connolly would later wonder whether Lennon had attempted to set him up with a "Beatles Split" exclusive, figuring the journalist wouldn't be able to resist printing it and that John could shrug and walk away from the band, blaming the writer for letting the cat out of the bag.

McCartney, meanwhile, now viewed Klein with out-and-out contempt. On April 14, 1970, he wrote the manager a flinty letter, addressing what he saw as the vandalizing of "The Long and Winding Road," informing him that "in future no one will be allowed to add to or subtract from a recording of one of my songs without my permission," though only going as far as to insist that the orchestration be toned down. Menacingly, though, he ended with a threat: "Don't ever do it again."

But Klein was no pushover. For the U.S. release of *McCartney,* he further incensed Paul by taking out ads in *Rolling Stone* provocatively proclaiming that the album was being released by Apple, "an ABKCO-managed company." The battle, it seemed, was on.

In the fallout, the McCartneys once again ran away to Scotland. But Klein continued to haunt Paul. He would appear in Paul's dreams as a demented dentist, chasing after him with a hypodermic needle, determined to, as he imagined, "put me out." When McCartney confessed his fears to those close to him, they laughed. "No," Paul insisted, "it's really fucking scary."

For the first time in his life, he noticed gray in his hair. He gritted his teeth and read the music-press reports of how he had apparently betrayed the other Beatles and about how, vain and reclusive, he was "sitting up in Scotland, looking into his mirror, admiring his own image."

It drove him back to the bottle. One evening, in front of his wife, Lee Eastman, and another unnamed guest, Paul began swigging whiskey and jabbering, mumbling repeated phrases to himself: "Fuckers . . . fucked me up . . . fucking carve-up."

Eventually Linda led him to bed. Again, it was down to her to straighten out her husband's head. "If I'd been doing that on my own," Paul says, "I'm not sure I'd have got out of it."

Come summer, Lennon and McCartney entered into an odd correspondence, in an attempt to untangle the legal binding of the Beatles. First, Paul sent a twelve-page document to his bandmate, listing his many dissatisfactions. The gist was: "I want to leave." John artily responded with a photograph of himself, upon which he'd drawn a speech bubble containing the words "How and why?" Paul wrote back saying he wanted the band's partnership to be officially dissolved because there was no partnership left. John sent him a curt postcard: "Get well soon. Get the other signatures and I will think about it."

The words "I will think about it" unsettled Paul. For the first time, he considered the sickening notion that he might have to resort to legal action. It was something that had already occurred to Lee Eastman, the sixty-year-old legal veteran, music publisher, and expert in copyright law. Eastman had a reputation as a strong-headed negotiator himself and had already lost his composure in meetings with Klein. In June, he wrote an official letter to his adversary seeking the dissolution of the Beatles' partnership. Klein didn't reply. Eastman read the signs and understood that this had all the makings of a dirty fight.

For their part, the other Beatles had one important reason for being distrustful of McCartney and the Eastmans. During the divvying of the Beatles' business affairs between the two New Yorker factions, Lee Eastman had furtively advised Paul to buy up extra shares in the band's publishing company, Northern Songs, in an effort to strengthen his bargaining power. Upon his discovery of this, Lennon flew at Eastman, attempting to thump him.

Amid all of this viciousness and spite, a touch ludicrously, U.S. promoter Sid Bernstein chose this moment to publicly offer the Beatles

$1 million to perform at a music festival in Holland in August 1970. If at that time it seemed to McCartney that a reunion had never been less likely, in fact it wasn't quite as ridiculous a concept as it appeared.

Suddenly concerned that he had inadvertently slit the throat of his golden goose, in October Klein was behind a sneaky attempt to bring the band back together, when he tried to trick McCartney into returning to the fold. He instructed John to call Paul and say, "We're recording next Friday, are you coming?" Dutifully, John did just that, having been advised by Klein that any signs of détente might limit Paul's powers in being able to legally extricate himself from the group.

Paul simply didn't show up. The three others then proceeded to work on a song called "Early 1970," sung by Ringo and set to become the B side to his subsequent single, "It Don't Come Easy." The loping, lighthearted number addressed each of the other Beatles in the first three verses, before mocking Ringo's own musical limitations in the final stanza. In the opening lines, concerning Paul, Starr noted that his estranged friend not only lived on a farm but, in addition, apparently had "plenty of charm."

If it was any kind of serious attempt at reconciliation, it was too little, too late. That same month, the McCartneys traveled to New York to "get away from everything," not knowing that both Harrison and Lennon were coincidentally to be in the city at the same time.

While there, John arranged a meeting with Paul. McCartney canceled, and Lennon later claimed that he hadn't planned to turn up anyway. Paul and George did meet, however, though their conversation quickly turned argumentative. McCartney stressed that he wanted off Apple. "You'll stay on the fucking label," Harrison hissed, before reflexively adding, "Hare Krishna."

And so McCartney's mind was set, even if, torn and procrastinating, he let the situation drift on for another couple of months before making his final move.

That December, back in Argyll, on a bright, cold day, McCartney stood high on a hill overlooking Skeroblin Loch, at the end of a long walk and a deep conversation with Lee Eastman, in which, Paul says, "we'd been searching our souls." There was no other way, he concluded.

Surveying this peaceful scene, he decided that it was time to sue his bandmates, to legally kill the Beatles.

2

ACROSS THE WATER

Taking the other Beatles to court must have been a huge, difficult decision for you to make.

It was just something I knew I had to do. I could not let Allen Klein get away with it. I just knew that very clearly. And unfortunately, nobody else did. You've got to imagine yourself in my position then. Being, in my mind, the only person without the blindfold on.

THREE DAYS INTO THE NEW YEAR OF 1971, the SS *France* pulled out of Southampton harbor, en route to New York, with the McCartneys aboard. Unusually for Paul, visibly reflecting his desire to be distanced from the "straights" he was forced to share the luxury ocean liner with for six days, he spent much of the voyage sporting dark glasses.

This starry behavior disgruntled one female passenger in particular, who was affronted by the singer walking into the dining room one evening without first removing his shades. She duly accosted him, saying, "Take your sunglasses off. Elizabeth Taylor is on this boat and she doesn't wear them."

In response, Paul accurately pointed out, "Well, I'm not Elizabeth Taylor."

McCartney was intent on putting some miles between himself and the legal ructions beginning to rumble back in London. Effectively, this trip to the States would find him, for a limited period, in self-imposed exile.

On the final day of 1970, he had filed to dissolve the Beatles & Company, listing his three estranged friends as defendants. There were still almost seven years left to run in the ten-year partnership agreement that the four had signed together in April 1967. In the light of the recent aggravations, however, McCartney couldn't bear the prospect of every financial or creative move he made having to be filtered through the clogged Beatles bureaucracy.

At the same time, he also sought to have a receiver for Apple appointed, to run the label until the dispute was settled, and asked that Klein be charged with the mismanagement of Apple funds, since McCartney claimed not to have had accurate accounts from the New Yorker for either Apple or the band's partnership. Access to the band's recent income, totaling nearly £4 million, was accordingly frozen.

From here on in, no one could get their hands on any of the money earned in the name of the Beatles.

To Paul's way of thinking, Klein had ripped off the Rolling Stones, and the Beatles were next. "I was the lone voice," he says. "It was really painful, but I knew I had to take a stand."

Compounding the agony, John and Paul's feud was intensifying and, worse, going public. Lennon fired the first shot in the press war, lambasting McCartney in his lengthy, Beatles-demolishing *Rolling Stone* interview, published in two parts early in 1971.

It caught John in a coarse, purgative mood. Far from being adorable mop tops, the Beatles, he said, were "the biggest bastards on earth." He even took a dig at the mild, inoffensive George Martin, dismissing the producer's crucial role in the band's development. But, of course, he spewed most of his bitter rage in the direction of McCartney.

Paul had elected himself bandleader after Brian Epstein's death, Lennon said, but in the end McCartney had only led the Beatles round and round in circles. Eventually, Lennon began to think of his role in the band merely as a day job. Paul would toss him a guitar solo on Beatles records only when he was feeling "kindly" or guilty that he'd commandeered the A side. The other Beatles had grown sick of being merely sidemen for McCartney.

If you believed, as many of his critics did, that Paul was casually domineering by nature, there was a ring of truth to all of this.

But then Lennon twisted the knife: the *McCartney* LP was "rubbish." The *Let It Be* film had been "set up by Paul, for Paul." McCartney had fallen for the Eastmans' "bullshit" because he was hopelessly entranced by this "East Coast suit . . . with Picassos hanging on the wall." They were cut from the same cloth, anyway, Paul being "all form and no substance." Now, Lennon seethed, McCartney would only talk to the others through lawyers because his attitude was "I'm going to drag my feet and try and fuck you."

Lennon's rant blindsided McCartney and, privately, it began to further deplete his already pitifully low self-esteem. Paul sat down and pored over every sentence, thinking maybe Lennon was right; maybe he was this horrendous, vain, pigheaded, self-serving bastard. He voiced these thoughts aloud: "He's captured me so well," he said. "I'm a turd."

Again, Linda tried to talk her husband out of his black fug, saying, "Now, you know that's not true." But Paul was wary of being drawn into a public battle with the merciless, acidic Lennon. Beyond worrying about merely losing face, he feared being humiliated: "He'd do me in."

In New York, Paul kept his head down, scruffy-bearded and dressed down in a combat jacket and jeans to look "like any junkie on the street." One night, he and Linda rolled up to the Apollo, in Harlem, to check out the talent show. As usual, they arrived late, and Linda had to sweet-talk the doorman into letting them in. At the tail end of an era violently stirred by the Black Panthers, they were the only two white faces in the theater, blithely assuming that they would be safe in the crowd.

Elsewhere, paranoia was in the air. As a father, Paul worried about his kids being photographed by fans or, unthinkably, kidnapped, and tried to maintain as low a profile for his family as for himself. At the same time, there remained an oddness to his behavior. One New Yorker Beatles fan, Libby Fields, claimed to have discovered a rumpled-looking McCartney very early one morning, spaced out and jaded, in his army fatigue jacket, sitting on a bench in Harlem's Marcus Garvey Park. Shocked by his demeanor but thrilled to have this surprise one-to-one with even an apparently down-and-out Beatle, she asked him if he could wait five minutes while she ran home to grab her camera.

"Why not?" said Paul. "I'm not going anywhere."

———

A week into January, drummer Denny Seiwell, booked for a nameless demo session, turned up at an address in an unsettlingly seedy area of Manhattan, on Forty-third Street between Ninth and Tenth Avenues. Immediately, he felt something was not right: the building looked burned out and appeared to have no electricity.

Through the open door of the lobby he saw a guy sitting at a desk. Seiwell tentatively asked, "Is there something going on?" The doorman nodded and gestured: "Yep, down there." Seiwell felt uneasy but made his way downstairs. There, in the damp, dilapidated basement, to his relief and surprise, he found Paul and Linda, sitting beside a battered old hired drum kit.

"They said, 'Do you mind playing for us?'" says Seiwell. "And I just went into Ringo on the tom-toms." His playing aside, the drummer scored extra points for not being thrown by the idea of performing for a Beatle. "I was young, and I don't mean to sound egotistical, but I knew I had something good. I felt like I deserved to be in there."

Two days beforehand, New York session guitarist David Spinozza had found himself auditioning for Paul in a filthy loft on Forty-fifth Street. Linda, now acting as day-to-day organizer for Paul, had called the guitarist, introducing herself as Mrs. McCartney, before vaguely asking him if he would like to meet her husband. The much-in-demand Spinozza copped something of an attitude straightaway, playing hard to get and forcing the cagey Linda finally to name Paul. "Like I'm supposed to know Paul McCartney was calling my house," he huffed.

After the audition, the guitarist got the gig and was asked if he was available to work five days a week for the next six weeks. He said he wasn't but that he could manage two days a week. And so began the loose, three-handed recording sessions, featuring McCartney, Seiwell and Spinozza, for what would become *Ram*.

While the album was to be credited to Paul and Linda McCartney, Spinozza confirmed—their increasingly accomplished and characteristic harmonies aside—that the latter's input was minimal. The sessions at Phil Ramone's A&R Studios, on West Forty-eighth Street, were markedly clean and efficient: McCartney and the two session men working regular hours, with no imbibing of alcohol or dope, usually knocking off late in the afternoon. Emphasizing the McCartneys' growing attitude that they were a traveling musical family, Linda and the kids were always present, even on the rare occasions when a session dragged on until four in the morning.

During the making of *Ram,* Seiwell and McCartney grew closer and closer. "I'd never seen that kind of talent before," says the drummer. In this setting, far from London and the battling Beatles, working with musicians paid to follow his every musical instruction, Paul was at last free to let his creativity flourish without argument or interference. For the time being, this arrangement was highly productive, McCartney directing the musicians through song after song, great take after great take. To Seiwell's ears, one standout number, "Another Day," about the mundane daily routine of a female office worker, set against a dreamy, hooky acoustic-guitar-strummed backing, sounded like "Eleanor Rigby" transported to inner-city New York.

But while the sessions were creatively successful, Seiwell remembers that the money deals with the musicians were done, in a foreshadowing of the troubles to come, purely "on a hippie handshake."

Sorely disrupting the creative flow, on the other side of the Atlantic there was the tangled mess of the Beatles' legal affairs still to unravel. On February 19, 1971, a Friday, Paul stepped back into the eye of the storm, gently shoving through the crush of reporters outside the High Court in London for the first day of the case to settle the dispute in the partnership. Even if it was weighed down with negativity, there was still the thrill of a Beatle-styled happening in the air.

John Eastman had insisted that Paul appear in court every day wearing a suit and tie. McCartney initially protested, until he was reminded of exactly what was at risk. If Allen Klein and the other Beatles retained control of the band's interests, McCartney would effectively wind up bound to Apple or, cripplingly, to ABKCO.

Paul turned up for the first day in court in the dark gray Tommy Nutter–designed suit he'd worn on the cover of *Abbey Road,* matched with an open-necked shirt, in a minor show of defiance. Conforming to the point of wearing a tie, he told his brother-in-law, would feel like "humiliation." Though his hair was trimmed, his bushy beard remained, signifying his recent rough times and his desire to shield himself psychically.

In tow was Linda and Paul's counsel, David Hirst. The McCartneys settled into the second row, facing the judge's bench, with Hirst directly behind and, two rows farther back, Klein, in his trademark brown turtleneck sweater, along with his legal team. Paul shot a blank stare at the New Yorker and then turned away.

In a prelude to the proceedings, there was a moment of lightness to lift the tension. The court attendant whispered to Paul that he expected the imminent arrival of John and Yoko, since it was unlikely that they would be able to resist turning up. Paul bet him two shillings that they wouldn't show, and won. None of the other Beatles would make an appearance during the twelve-day period in which the case lumbered on.

Facing the judge, Sir Blanshard Stamp, Hirst set about dismantling Klein's professional character—a task made far easier by his opening announcement that the manager had been convicted of ten tax offenses by a New York jury only three weeks before. "It has obviously not enhanced Mr. McCartney's confidence in Mr. Klein," Hirst pointed out dryly. He further argued that Klein couldn't be trusted to look after the partnership and its assets, and he accused Klein of having overpaid himself in commissions.

McCartney sat before the judge, using body language as a weapon, shaking his head sadly every time an erroneous statement was read out by Klein's defense. Then, having made this first-day appearance, he disappeared to New York once again.

On day two, Klein's counsel, Morris Finer, declared that Klein had effectively saved the Beatles from bankruptcy and contended that the current partnership could be advantageous to McCartney since, under the arrangement, all four Beatles shared in the profits of one another's solo records. Harrison's "My Sweet Lord," he pointed out, had earned nearly £1 million, close to twice what Paul's solo releases in 1970 had brought into Apple. "No one is getting at Mr. McCartney on this," he stressed.

On the third day, the affidavits from the other Beatles were read out. Lennon's was long and, in places, persuasive. He didn't agree with Paul that the Beatles had begun to drift apart after their touring days ended, in 1966. In fact, he claimed, they had argued more on the road, and since then had got on better and were regular visitors to one another's homes. The Beatles were, however, he admitted, largely clueless about business, which was why Apple had become a hopeless mess.

Klein, Lennon reckoned, was "certainly forceful to an extreme, but he does get results." John said he had brought in Klein to clear out the "hustlers" and "spongers" responsible for the hemorrhaging of Apple funds. Further, he claimed that he had initially only wanted Klein to be his personal manager and that he hadn't tried to force him on the other Beatles. He concluded by declaring that Paul was acting "selfishly and unreasonably."

Harrison was clearly keen to air his grievances, too. The major rift within the band had been between himself and Paul. Since George had walked out of the Twickenham *Let It Be* sessions, however, Paul had treated him more as a "musical equal." This, he reasoned, showed that an intra-Beatles argument could be beneficially resolved. He had been stunned by Paul's legal letter seeking to dissolve the partnership: "I still cannot understand why Paul acted as he did."

Ringo's statement at first flattered Paul, calling him "the greatest bass guitar player in the world," but went on to say that McCartney was also "determined. . . . He goes on and on to see if he can get his own way." This, the drummer argued, had led to musical disagreements, even if these often proved to be the grit that produced the pearls. In December, he said, Paul had apparently agreed to sit down for an air-clearing meeting with the other Beatles in January, and so the writ had shocked the drummer.

"Something serious, about which I have no knowledge, must have happened after Paul's meeting with George at the end of December," Ringo reasoned, apparently entirely unaware of the damage the guitarist had done by angrily telling McCartney he would make him stay on the label. Starr ended on a positive note, however, saying that he hoped that "all four of us together could even yet work out everything satisfactorily."

On day four, Klein launched his defense in an affidavit read out to the court, pointing out that he had vastly improved the Beatles' financial affairs. In 1969 their earnings had doubled; in 1970 they had increased fivefold. He then griped that "Mr. McCartney has made attacks on my commercial integrity."

One of Paul's chief grievances was that Klein had sold the rights to the *Let It Be* film to United Artists without his approval. Klein argued that the sale had "made an absolute fortune for all four Beatles." In this way, he was virtually holding up his hands and admitting he was a music-business hustler, while pointing out that all four Beatles were better off as a result. This was, of course, undeniable: Paul had profited from the deals Klein had made. "McCartney has accepted the benefits," the manager stated, "which I have negotiated in that capacity."

A week into the proceedings, on February 26, Paul returned to the court, entering the witness box. He rejected Lennon's earlier claim, in his statement, that the band "always thought of ourselves as Beatles, whether we recorded singly or in twos or threes." He quoted, almost as evidence, the fact that in the mantra-like "God," from the *John Lennon/ Plastic Ono Band* album, released two months earlier, his former bandmate had listed all the things he no longer believed in, the final one being, simply, "Beatles."

He then tried to undermine Lennon and Klein's relationship. In a phone conversation Klein had apparently told Paul that John was angry with him only because "you came off better than he did in *Let It Be*." In the witness box, McCartney stirred the situation further, saying Klein had also warned him that Yoko was "trouble. . . . She's the one with ambition." Openly and brazenly playing an intra-Beatles mind game, in a court of law, he disingenuously said that he'd wondered what John might make of this.

The main problem, as he saw it, was that when the Beatles signed the 1967 agreement, none of them had really considered the wording. Spotlighting his apparently guileless attitude to business, Paul said he always thought that he could just walk away from the deal at any point. In response to his colleagues' bewilderment when it came to his current legal action, he stated that his reasoning behind it was simple: the Beatles had broken up. In his mind, there could be no partnership if there was no band.

When summing up, David Hirst, for McCartney, said there were four major factors to their argument that the 1967 contract was unworkable: its assets were in jeopardy, one partner was being excluded, there existed a "lack of good faith towards a partner by other partners," and the likelihood was that a dissolution was inevitable.

Morris Finer, for Klein and the other Beatles, rather poetically accused Paul of living "in a world where everyone is either a seraphim or angel, ape or viper." Moreover, he asked the judge not to grant a receivership order, since this would trigger the band's business organization descending further into "chaos."

McCartney's lawyers, having sifted through a three-foot-high pile of Beatles- and Klein-related documents, finally showed their hand. Hirst produced a check from Capitol to Klein for £852,000. The manager had of course increased the Beatles' U.S. royalty rate from 17.5 percent to 25 percent, contractually entitling him to a fifth of the 7.5 percent rise. But this was a commission for a fifth of the band's entire cut. Paul argued that Klein had invoiced for at least £500,000 more than he should have. "We couldn't send him to jail for that," he later said, "but at least we could get a judgment."

On the ropes, Klein's team cited a letter from the other three Beatles, dated January 1970, that seemed to rubber-stamp this new commission agreement. McCartney's team rightly argued that his former bandmates weren't allowed to alter management terms without his permission. Justice Stamp instantly backed them, denouncing Klein's protestations as "the prattling of a second-class salesman."

After all the debate and deliberation, on March 12, 1971, Justice Stamp granted McCartney's request for a receiver to oversee the band's interests "pending a permanent fix."

James Spooner, a City-based chartered accountant, was appointed to oversee the Beatles' business affairs. Later, as he dug deeper into the paperwork, he discovered a different partnership agreement that appeared to have Paul's signature on it. He concluded that it was a forgery, which was a distinct possibility, given that through years of signing countless records, the Beatles had successfully learned to copy each other's signatures. "It was a very crooked piece of paper," Spooner noted.

Whatever the truth behind this strange postscript to the whole chaotic affair, McCartney had unequivocally won the first crucial round in the Beatles' legal battle, even if he now found himself hated by the press, the fans, and the other band members.

"There was a lot of hostility going around," he says now. "But I had to do that to not let Allen Klein own the Beatles. If I hadn't done it, everything we'd ever done would've just gone down the drain. A few years later, they all recognized that."

That was to be some way into the future, however. The day the verdict was announced, according to the eyewitness accounts of the constant scrum of fans outside Paul's house, John, Ringo, and George turned up at Cavendish Avenue in Lennon's white Rolls-Royce.

Lennon emerged from the car with two bricks, scaled the wall, and, reverting to the furious teenage teddy boy who used to wreck phone boxes in Liverpool, smashed McCartney's windows.

Meanwhile, Paul was three thousand miles away, back in New York. Three days after the end of the court case, with the recording of *Ram* completed, he flew to the West Coast with Linda and the girls to oversee its mixing in Los Angeles. For the duration of their stay the family rented a Santa Monica beachside house, owned by the Getty family. Their routine quickly began to resemble a working holiday: leisurely laps in the pool while listening to Linda's reggae records, lengthy dinners in hip restaurants on Ocean Park Boulevard.

In his final act of Beatle duty, Paul attended the Grammys with Linda, padding up to the podium to pick up the award for Best Original Score for *Let It Be* from, a touch surreally, famously swaggering Western screen legend John Wayne. As the McCartneys left, a reporter asked Paul if he was planning to do any recording while in Los Angeles. Paul, in a line that sounded prefabricated, said, "I have a knife and fork and I'm here to cut a record."

Whereas the New York leg of the album had been cleanly and successfully marshaled, the Los Angeles sessions were fueled by dope. Paul would usually arrive in midafternoon, spark up a joint, and then tinker around endlessly. This mood of stoned whimsy extended to the album's artwork, which features a black-and-white shot of McCartney manfully handling the horns of a blackface sheep on the Scottish farm, framed by crude felt-tip scribbling in yellow, purple, green, and red. The inner art was similarly childlike, incorporating photos of Paul and Linda and images of horses (real and drawn) into a purposely rough-cut collage with slightly bizarre found elements: grass from the garden, a few strands of human hair.

Upon the release of *Ram,* in May 1971, keen artwork scanners soon found on its back cover what they assumed to be an oblique jibe: a nature photography library shot of two beetles copulating. This was interpreted in various ways: fucking Beatles, fuck the Beatles, fucked by the Beatles. Paul insists that its inclusion was purely accidental. "It was just a funny shot," he protests. "A photograph of two beetles shagging. I mean, that *had to* get on the cover. Then afterwards, you go, 'Oh, but they were beetles.' To me they were just a couple of little ladybirds or something. I swear to God I didn't think about that. The thing is, whatever you do gets interpreted. And I don't see half of it coming."

Less considered still was a strange promo disc sent out to the press and radio stations to publicize the album, entitled *Brung to Ewe;* it featured a sound collage of sheep noises, nonsensical snatches of dialogue between Paul and Linda, and in-jokes over snippets of the album's songs. Recurring throughout was a gospel number, "Now Hear This Song of Mine," that hadn't even made it onto the record. Those in the music industry who heard it were slightly baffled: rather than summoning the spirit of Beatleish playfulness, it sounded like a lot of stoned rambling.

Nevertheless, although not viewed as such at the time in many quarters, given the Olympian expectations of the solo Beatles, *Ram* was something of a marvel. Really the true successor to *Abbey Road,* in its baroque detail and flights of imagination, it was variously funny, daft, touching, and knowing. It was also deliberately eventful in its structure, featuring songs within songs and unexpected dips and turns.

"I tried to avoid any Beatles clichés and just went to different places," says Paul. "So the songs became a little more episodic or something. I took on that kind of idea a bit more than I would've with the Beatles. I suppose I was just letting myself be free. So if I wanted to do 'Monkberry Moon Delight' with 'a piano up my nose,' then I figured, that'll be okay."

The unlikely U.S. No. 1 hit "Uncle Albert/Admiral Halsey" spotlighted the new McCartney method: its trippy sentimentality gives way to rain and vocally impersonated ringing telephone effects before restlessly tempo-shifting upward through its lengthy coda. Elsewhere, Beach Boys references abounded, not least in the ornate arrangement of "Ram On" and the multivoiced teenage swoon of "The Back Seat of My Car."

Artwork aside, *Ram* also seemed to be carefully mined with lyrical digs at Lennon and the other Beatles. McCartney insists that the apparent potshots in "3 Legs," particularly the parts where he laments being betrayed by a former friend, were misinterpreted: "That was just kind of a joke blues song in my mind."

"Too Many People," though, was directed squarely at the "preaching practices" of John and Yoko. "I felt that was true of what was going on," says McCartney. " 'Do this, do that, do this, do that.' " If there was dark anger at the heart of *Ram*, however, it was deeply hidden. Even the song's opening words, "Piss off," were veiled by a weak pun.

"It's actually 'piece of cake,'" Paul says, "which was thinly disguised as 'piss off, cake.' And, hey, come on, how mild is that? It's not exactly a tirade." The withering put-downs of "Dear Boy," meanwhile, were penned not with any of the Beatles in mind but for Linda's first husband, Mel See. In it, the singer derided See for not recognizing the wonders of the now Mrs. McCartney, who, Paul further admitted in the lyric, had emotionally revived him when he was low.

If relatively slick compared to its scrappier predecessor, *Ram* made it only to No. 2 in the United States, where *McCartney* had reached No. 1, though it topped the albums chart in the United Kingdom. Critics on both sides of the Atlantic, however, were unkind, verging on brutal. *Rolling Stone*'s review was particularly vitriolic, loftily claiming, "*Ram* represents the nadir in the decomposition of 1960s rock thus far . . . so incredibly inconsequential and monumentally irrelevant." *Melody Maker*, meanwhile, struck a nerve: "It must be hell living up to a name. . . . You expect too much from a man like McCartney."

Asked about *Ram*, Lennon admitted that he liked the beginning and end of "Uncle Albert/Admiral Halsey" but griped that the rest of it "just tripped off all the time." Ringo, quizzed about the record elsewhere, came across as bitter and hurt with regard to Paul. "I don't think there's one tune on *Ram*," he said. "I just feel he's wasted his time. He seems to be going strange. It's like he's not admitting he can write great tunes." The fact that, in May, Paul and Ringo had hung out together at Mick Jagger's wedding to Bianca in Saint-Tropez—the first time they'd socialized since the Beatles split—seemed to have no bearing on the drummer's negative feelings.

For McCartney himself, *Ram* was an entirely successful endeavor, both creatively and commercially, if not critically. In the end, by driving on his post-Beatles career, it served its purpose, as suggested by its determined, dual-meaning title: "It meant," he pointed out, ". . . ram forward, press on, be positive."

If McCartney's ongoing process of creative therapy now found him with his head happily back up in the musical clouds, where it had been

during the best times with the Beatles, it wasn't long before various realities began to drag him back to earth once again.

In April 1971 came the word that Klein and the other Beatles weren't
going to appeal against the court's judgment and had decided to grant
McCartney his freedom from the partnership. But, with most of his
money still tied up in Apple, Paul was suddenly faced with financial
embarrassment. On the last day of March, the newly formed McCartney Productions Limited submitted its first annual accounts for the period 1970 to 1971: £3,017 incoming, £5,417 outgoing, resulting in a
deficit of £2,400.

Day to day, the McCartneys were actually living on the money
Linda had earned as a photographer in New York, before she met Paul.
As a kept husband, McCartney used to joke to his wife that at least one
of them was keeping them afloat.

But in December 1970, before announcing that he was to sue the
other Beatles, Paul had tried to make a business maneuver that, depending on your perspective, was either prescient or crafty. He had asked for
there to be a further definition of the terms of his contract with Northern Songs—the company formed by Brian Epstein, the Beatles, and
music publisher Dick James in 1963, which owned the rights to all of
the group's songs and which James had sold in 1969 to media magnate
Lew Grade's Associated Television, without first consulting the Beatles.
McCartney was arguing that the deal shouldn't cover any material he
wrote with anyone other than John Lennon.

Now, with *Ram*, he was claiming that seven of its fourteen tracks
were straight fifty-fifty co-writes with Linda, despite the fact that she
wasn't a recognized songwriter. Grade, perhaps understandably, thought
he was being swindled and that Paul was underhandedly trying to claw
back some of his songwriting royalties to McCartney Productions.

This, of course, was reasonable, but tough to prove. Only those in
the room when the songs were being written, Paul and Linda, knew
exactly who was responsible for what. "If my wife is actually saying,
'Change that,' or 'I like that better than that,' then I'm using her as a
collaborator," Paul reasoned. In the event, an entirely unconvinced
Grade slapped the McCartneys with a lawsuit for an arbitrarily round
$1 million, in a dispute to be settled, in a wholly unorthodox fashion, a
little further down the line.

———

As the spring of 1971 turned to summer, the strangeness that came with Paul's extraordinary fame began to creep back into the McCartneys' lives. In June, an odd-looking parcel addressed simply to "Paul McCartney" was delivered to the BBC's Bush House in London's Aldwych. Suspecting it to be a letter bomb, the staff there immediately called in the police. Once carefully opened, the package was revealed to be a gift of wineglasses and crockery from a fan, ahead of Paul's upcoming twenty-ninth birthday, along with a letter that said "I love you" in Spanish.

Other, more determined devotees would sometimes make the long pilgrimage to Argyll, since it was no secret now that the McCartneys spent much of their time near Campbeltown. The neighbors would sometimes be shocked to find a frazzled-looking hippie peering through their windows, mistaken about which house was Paul's. Once the McLean family, who lived nearby, found five longhairs hiding in their shed, claiming they had merely wanted to practice yoga in the vicinity of the supposed McCartney aura.

More worryingly, a young girl, a Mormon from Utah, had taken to camping on the edge of some woods just beyond the boundary of High Park, so that she could get close to Paul without trespassing on his land. The McCartneys often saw her, partially hidden by the trees, watching them through binoculars. One day in the summer of 1971, Paul apparently snapped and, according to the girl, came out of the house, drove toward her in his Land Rover, and angrily emerged, shouting and swearing.

The girl claimed that she couldn't remember much of what happened next, except that in the aftermath, her nose was bleeding. The implication, obviously, was that McCartney had assaulted her, which Paul denied. "I have been asking her politely—pleading with her—to leave me and my family alone," he stated. "She refuses to recognize that I am married with a family."

The greater solution to all of this was simple, if expensive, and required much in the way of patience. Now, whenever any of the McCartneys' neighbors put their properties on the market, Paul snapped them up. In time he became the owner of two other nearby farms, Low Park and Low Ranachan, using the barn of the latter as a makeshift rehearsal space. Acre by acre, Paul bought back his privacy.

That summer, in the light of the pressures of the first half of the year, the McCartneys decided to escape farther into Scottish solitude by taking a trip to Shetland. "We just took off in the Land Rover," Paul says. "We piled everything in the back, kids and us in the front, dogs in the back, too. The potty on top of everything and off we went."

The McCartneys drove to the small port of Scrabster, on the northeastern coast of Scotland, with the notion of taking a ferry to Orkney, from where they could fly on to Shetland. But the plan was thwarted when, two cars ahead of them, the announcement came that the ship was full. Still determined, Paul began inquiring around the harbor about the possibility of hiring a fishing boat, romantically fancying that it might involve giving the skipper a salmon or a bottle of whiskey.

Rousing from his slumber the Shetland-sweater-wearing captain of a modest vessel named the *Enterprise,* Paul successfully offered him £30 to take the McCartneys aboard. The kerfuffle involved in getting all of the family's stuff on the boat at low tide, including gently easing sheepdog Martha down in a net, drew a crowd to the quayside. As Paul and Linda and the girls and the dogs pulled out of the harbor on their rented craft, the locals cheered and waved them off.

Once they were into their voyage, passing around beers, the choppy waters ensured that the McCartneys began feeling green around the gills. The baby Mary was the first to be sick, quickly followed by Linda. Paul manfully gripped the mast and tried to hold back his nausea. Soon, it became obvious that this wasn't going to be possible. The skipper, George, gestured toward the fishing baskets, saying, "Do it in there!"

And so, far from the luxuries of the SS *France* six months earlier, there at the edge of the world, Paul leaned over and threw his guts up.

3

KNEE-DEEP IN THE RIVER

McCartney *and* Ram *weren't the first records of yours that Linda appeared on, were they?*

No. She sang backups on "Let It Be." She'd done a real good job. I'd just taken her in the studio quietly one time and said, "We need a high note on the top of the chorus." She just went bang, hit it. Great, y'know.

PICTURE THE SCENE, HE ASKED HER. Imagine us standing behind a curtain and it parts to reveal a waiting, expectant audience.

"Would it completely freak you?" he said.

She suspected it might, but she was at least up for finding out whether or not it did.

The McCartneys were in bed one night when Paul first floated the idea by Linda: "Do you think you could handle being in a band?"

"He made it sound so glamorous," she said, "that I agreed to have a go."

Everything else aside, as he pointed out, if she decided not to come on the road with him, it would curb the family's self-fashioned lifestyle as "roving hippies." This, it seems, sealed the deal.

In the days and weeks that followed, Paul began to map out the basic piano chords for Linda, in her new role as keyboard player. Fourteen years earlier, he'd done something similar with John: shown him how to retune his guitar from the banjo standard taught to Lennon by his mother, Julia, and demonstrated how to reposition his fingers to play rock'n'roll shapes.

With Linda, though, Paul didn't display as much in the way of tolerance or enthusiasm. "He has no patience," she moaned. "I had to learn it myself. The few things he'd show me, if I didn't get it right, he'd get really angry. So I said, 'Like, forget it.'"

Paul's frustration with Linda's lack of natural musical ability aside, there was a part of McCartney that was tempted to indulge in the current vogue for the supergroup. In his mind, he saw himself surrounded by Eric Clapton, John Bonham, Billy Preston—even, in a parallel, ideal world, John Lennon.

But then he cast his mind back to how the Beatles had begun and the camaraderie that couldn't be faked with a bunch of "name" musicians. "All I thought was, How do you start a band?" he says. "Well, you start with nothing and you just learn and you improve. The idea was to get a bunch of mates together. I wasn't interested in putting it together professionally."

Elsewhere, penniless and sleeping on an old mattress in the back room of his manager Tony Secunda's office in Mayfair, Denny Laine was about to get the call that would reroute the next ten years of his life. The Birmingham-born former singer with the Moody Blues, front man of their yearning 1964 hit "Go Now," was on the skids, his life after quitting the band now the slightly desperate one of the nearly-but-not-quite-successful musician.

Laine had gone on to form the proto–classical/rock cross-pollination act the Electric String Band, whose performance at the Saville Theatre in June 1967, supporting Jimi Hendrix, had been witnessed by McCartney three days after the release of *Sgt. Pepper.* In time it proved too expensive for him to keep such an ambitious project on the road, particularly after, comically, the tapes of the band's third single were lost in the mail on the way to their own record label, Decca.

The apparently luckless Laine drifted to Spain; in Andalusia, he lived with Gypsies, rented an artist's hut next to a pigsty, and learned flamenco guitar. Returning to England in 1969, he formed the unfortunately named Midlands supergroup Balls, which quickly disintegrated. Feeling sidelined by Secunda after the manager turned his attentions to his new charge, soon-to-be superstar Marc Bolan, Laine was half-considering a solo career when McCartney phoned him, mooting the idea of a band.

"I was needing the money, really," Laine admits. "But I wouldn't have just gone out and done anything, either. So when I got the call from him, it was like, Oh, this is gonna be fun. I know Paul, I know I can make some dough eventually in doing this, and I'll be back to doing what I like doing."

McCartney and Laine already knew each other, from the days when both the Beatles and the Moody Blues were managed by Brian Epstein's NEMS outfit and rode tour buses together. Reconnecting now, Laine sensed a surprising nervousness in the newly ex-Beatle. "I think his confidence was a little bit in question because, trying to follow the Beatles, what are you gonna do?"

Paul was certainly looking for a vocal foil to replace Lennon, if not exactly a songwriting partner. "Just a fellow vocalist so we could harmonize together," he says. "As far as composing was concerned, probably I was spoilt with John as a collaborator." The New York sessions for *Ram* had made McCartney hanker for the musical closeness of the Beatles. For various reasons, he missed being in a band. "Camaraderie was one thing," he says. "Musical turn-on was another."

To this end, in June 1971, he invited Denny Seiwell and New York guitarist Hugh McCracken (who had filled the boots of the increasingly errant David Spinozza as the making of *Ram* progressed) to Scotland for a part-holiday, part potential-band sound-out. Perhaps harboring overly romantic ideas about Scotland, the Americans—Seiwell and McCracken and their respective wives, Monique and Holly—found themselves living in basic, unglamorous rooms at the Argyll Arms in Campbeltown. Neither did they take to the nation's famously stodgy, greasy food.

On the day they arrived, the party drove over to the McCartneys' farm for drinks. As they were leaving, though, the men were pulled aside by Linda and asked not to bring their wives the following day, since the plan was for the band, including Mrs. McCartney, of course, to work. This did not go down well with the women, for whom the trip wasn't turning out to be much of a holiday.

Within days the McCrackens returned to New York. Paul judged that Hugh was clearly not at one with the farm-centered or hippiefied existence and "didn't want to go that far out with his life." Seiwell, however, apparently did. Although he and Monique initially followed the McCrackens back to the States, two months later, in August 1971, the drummer returned.

Denny Laine first hooked up with Denny Seiwell at Glasgow Airport, where the two met to take the forty-minute flight across the Firth of Clyde and over the Isle of Arran, down to Campbeltown. Once they made their way to High Park, the evening was spent drinking and, for Paul and Denny Laine, reminiscing, while sketching the plans for the new band.

Laine was impressed that Paul was apparently now "just a farmer who plays guitar . . . out on his tractor, growing vegetables. . . . He's not a Beatle anymore." Paul would joke that, in green-fingered terms, whether digging the vegetable patch or tinkering around in their recently assembled greenhouse, he remained second to Linda. "She's the lead gardener," he quipped. "I'm the rhythm gardener."

But as the band started to rehearse, Linda struggled to keep up. Initially there hadn't even been any mention of her being part of the band, says Laine. "She was taking pictures and Paul would just say, 'Linda, can you just try and play that note or sing that line there?' They were seeing whether it would work."

Privately, Laine thought that the outfit would get tighter far quicker with a professional keyboard player, while slightly resenting having to coach an amateur. However, both the drummer and the guitarist understood that Linda's influence on the group, through her love of design and photography, would be great and that, crucially, she provided unconditional support and stability for Paul.

"She was his security blanket, his inspiration, his wife and mother of his kids," Seiwell says. "She was the one who got Paul off his ass when he was having to sue the other Beatles. His heart was broken. He would've sat up there in Scotland and just become a drunk. If she hadn't got on his case, none of it would have ever happened." At the same time, the drummer acknowledges that Linda wasn't an important addition to the lineup on a musical level. "Not musically. But she was more than an important element—she was a necessity."

"The thing is," says Paul, "we wanted to be together and we said, 'What right has anyone got to say we shouldn't be together in a band? Whose affair is it but ours?'"

For the musicians, life at High Park was rough and ready. With no room in the small family house for them, Seiwell and his wife rented nearby Brechie Farm, at Kilkenzie, while Laine, ever the Gypsy, pitched up in a caravan on the McCartneys' land. All visitors to the farm were expected to live the basic rural life, although some extra efforts would be made for special guests. When his father, Jim, and Jim's second wife, Angela, came to stay, Paul scrubbed the floor of the garage before laying a mattress down for them.

Seiwell and Laine were both put on a £70 weekly retainer—not exactly a fortune, but a decent working wage for the early 1970s. Paul's money remained tied up in Apple, and there was a casual understanding that there would be more to come for the musicians in the future.

Inside the small, low-ceilinged, wood-paneled musical den that was Rude Studio, the band quickly moved on from jamming rock'n'roll standards to picking their way through Paul's latest, half-finished songs. On days when the weather was fine, the musicians would move their amps and instruments outside and play alfresco.

A snapshot from the time captures the four of them rehearsing on the grass in front of the studio lean-to—all in muddy Wellies, toasting the birth of the group with glasses and cups of whiskey and Coke. Seiwell, tellingly, wears a white T-shirt printed with a green marijuana leaf, revealing the other key ingredient in their bonding. "We weren't Bob Marley and the Wailers by any means," he laughs. "We enjoyed a bit of the herb for the creative conscious, you know what I'm saying?"

The sound of the nameless band would echo freely out over the hills, but trying to confine this unbridled noise to the environment of the recording studio was to prove far harder.

Enthralled by his new group, McCartney was suddenly gripped by the notion of spontaneity. Bob Dylan had the year before recorded most of the light country breeze of *New Morning* in an impressively tight five-day period. "Coming off the back of taking a long time over records," says Paul, "it just seemed like an interesting idea to do a record quickly."

Thus inspired, McCartney blocked out a week in August at Abbey Road and the band nailed eight songs, five of them on the first take. This sense of urgency is captured right at the top of the album that was to become *Wild Life* when, in the opening seconds, McCartney can be heard excitedly shouting, "Take it, Tony" to engineer Tony Clark, asking him to roll the tape at the height of the jam that became "Mumbo."

"Paul wanted to give the world a real true look at a new band," says Seiwell. "We did not mess around with that record. It was done quickly and honestly." Still, there remained a feeling that these tracks were just being carelessly thrown down. The other engineer on the sessions, Alan Parsons, thought as much: "I was so excited to be working with Paul, but I did feel a certain lack of precision."

For all that the band appeared to be a democratic arrangement, Parsons says that when the other members pitched in their ideas, "they would occasionally be shouted down" by Paul. Meanwhile, Linda's keyboard contributions to the album were competent, and made all the more impressive by the fact that she was eight months pregnant.

Out in the wider world, it was impossible to tell whether McCartney's commercial stock was rising or falling. Within weeks of each other, "Uncle Albert/Admiral Halsey" hit No. 1 in the United States, while the far hookier "The Back Seat of My Car" struggled to No. 39 on the British singles chart—notably Paul's most miserable performance to date, whether solo or as a Beatle.

It was a sign, among others, that the last of the shine was coming off the previously untarnishable Fabs, whose post-split interpersonal relationships were further deteriorating. McCartney was invited by George Harrison to appear at Madison Square Garden, in New York, on August 1, 1971, alongside Bob Dylan, Ringo Starr, and Eric Clapton at his Concert for Bangladesh, hastily arranged as a benefit for the flood-stricken nation. Paul flatly declined. Visa problems were cited as the reason for his nonappearance when, in truth, it was due to Allen Klein's involvement and the ongoing Beatles friction.

Klein, never one to miss a media opportunity, immediately jumped on the no-show to inform the press that Paul was refusing to perform for the suffering refugees. But if he and Harrison were pushing for a Beatles reunion to crown the event, both Lennon and McCartney were less than keen. John said he couldn't be bothered rehearsing and getting into the whole "showbiz trip" that the occasion entailed. "I thought, What's the point?" Paul said. "We've just broken up and we're joining up again? It just seemed a bit crazy."

In the meantime, over the summer, Lennon had sharpened his blade for what would be regarded as his deepest and most vicious stab at

McCartney. The deceptively laid-back rocker "How Do You Sleep?," from his *Imagine* album, released in September 1971, was a swift and hateful response to what John perceived as Paul's cryptic digs at him and Yoko in "Too Many People" and "3 Legs" from *Ram,* released only four months earlier.

"How Do You Sleep?" attempted to demolish McCartney's character. The vengeful lyric accused Paul of living with "straights" buffing the ego of the king, who, with an irony surely not lost on Lennon, was utterly controlled by his wife-cum-mother figure. His music was "Muzak"; the "freaks" had been right in saying Paul was dead; his best work was far behind him, and even his doe-eyed good looks would distract the public from his shallow talent for only "a year or two." Using a sibilant echo effect on his voice, Lennon ended the choruses by mimicking the hissing sound of a snake.

It was a precision attack that hit hard at the still fragile McCartney. Cruelly, if amusingly, Lennon even poked fun at McCartney's new country life, with a postcard tucked into *Imagine*'s sleeve featuring a mocking parody of the cover of *Ram:* a photograph of John holding the ears of a snuffling pig. Harrison, who played slide guitar on "How Do You Sleep?," was silently complicit in the hazing. Starr didn't contribute to the track but was there when it was being written; he grew visibly upset as the lyrical taunts became more and more barbed, before finally saying, "That's enough, John."

Lennon was unrepentant, however. At one point, during a run-through of the song, he turned and stared into a camera documenting the proceedings for the *Imagine* film, remotely eyeballing McCartney and asking him, "How do you sleep, ya cunt?"

"The joke was," says Paul, "my answer—although I never rang him up and told him—was 'Very well.' That was the one thing: I was sleeping very well, 'cause I was in the countryside. Fresh air." He admits, nonetheless, that the track did needle him. "Oh yeah. It was a massive, massive bug. I was just really *sad,* y'know, 'cause we'd been really tight mates since about sixteen or something. So it was a very, very strange turnaround."

Upon its release, Lennon backpedaled when questioned about the savagery of "How Do You Sleep?," explaining that it was written as a bitter studio in-joke, with chipped-in contributions from Yoko and Allen Klein. He admitted, however, that he'd been blinded by fury and determined to wound McCartney. Even if Paul had only himself to blame, he argued, since he had started it.

"Listen to *Ram,* folks," Lennon instructed the public. "It's an answer to *Ram . . .* a moment's anger."

Though hurt, McCartney, as ever, plowed on. He toyed with band names ranging from the half-decent (Turpentine) to the dreadful (the Dazzlers); in the end, the trading name of the new group was to come to him in a moment of acute panic provoked by life-or-death crisis.

In mid-September, Linda went into labor and was taken to King's College Hospital in Southwark. Upon examination, it was revealed that there was a complication to the birth: she was suffering from placenta previa, a condition where tissue covers all or part of the uterine opening to the cervix, restricting delivery and causing heavy bleeding.

The doctors decided to perform an emergency cesarean section. Hurried into a waiting room, Paul, in a green surgical gown, suddenly found himself alone, "praying like mad" for his wife and unborn child. Into his racing thoughts came an image of an angel's wings, striking him with its simple, calming beauty.

The drama over, the McCartneys found themselves with a second biological daughter, Stella Nina, and a name for their new band: Wings.

For the next two months, the newly extended family disappeared in Scotland. As soon as October, however, the music press was announcing the name of the new band and reporting that they were rehearsing on the farm for upcoming live dates.

On November 7, the McCartneys came out of hiding, reportedly wasting no unnecessary costs by traveling second-class on the train from Scotland to London in preparation for the following night's launch of Wings and their debut album, *Wild Life.* Reengaging with the music industry, Paul and Linda had decided to throw a party at the Empire Ballroom in Leicester Square.

The bash was such a big deal for the McCartneys that Paul had handwritten every one of the eight hundred invitations. In some ways, though, the party served to highlight how far removed the couple now was from hip London. Along with an incongruous raffle, the assembled guests—including Elton John and members of Led Zeppelin, the Who, and the Faces—were entertained by former Cavern owner Ray McFall's jazz band and a kitsch turn by Frank and Peggy Spencer's ballroom dancing team. Then the guests were plied with food and drink as *Wild Life* pumped out of the club's speakers.

The four members of the newly minted Wings grouped together for photographs: the mustachioed Seiwell looking 1970s-suave in a gray suit and black turtleneck; Laine skinny in a retina-scorching red jacket; Linda hiding her post-pregnancy curves in a roomy dress adorned with white doves; and Paul, a touch bizarrely, in a wide-lapeled checked suit with rough white stitching. It turned out that when he had gone to pick the suit up from his tailor that morning, he'd been told that, sorry, it wasn't ready.

"Maybe not, but it's a look," Paul replied, before deciding to wear the two-piece exactly as it was. All evening, puzzled members of London's in crowd came up to him to point out that his suit wasn't finished. To this he would beamingly respond, "Yeah, I know. Great, huh?"

A reporter from *Melody Maker* asked the McCartneys why they'd chosen to launch the band on a Monday night in Leicester Square.

"Why not?" Paul responded, with typical elusive cheerfulness.

"We thought it would be a nice idea," said Linda, making it sound like an office affair, "to invite a whole lot of our friends to a big party where they could bring their wives."

"EMI are paying for it," Paul pointed out, unwittingly revealing that under no circumstances would he have shelled out from his own pocket for this kind of shindig.

The party did the trick, though, in heralding the arrival of the new band. Five days later, the first shot of the quartet appeared on the cover of *Melody Maker,* along with the words "Wings Fly!" Inside, under the provocative headline "Why Lennon Is Uncool," McCartney attempted to dispassionately respond to the public abuse hurled at him by his former friend, which, as suspected, had stung him far more than anything he could throw back at John. Touching on "How Do You Sleep?," he said, "I think it's silly. So what if I live with straights? I like straights."

It was perhaps with this comment alone that, in the eyes of the excruciatingly cool rock elite, McCartney indelibly cast himself as "straight," sounding more like a bowler-hatted banker who commuted into the city every morning on the 8:12 from Cheam than an eccentric millionaire rocker living in remote Scotland in a run-down two-bedroom farmhouse and subsisting on joint after joint.

"He says the only thing I did was 'Yesterday,'" Paul added, sounding a touch more bruised. "He knows that's wrong."

Further riled, having read the interview, Lennon fired off a blistering letter that appeared in the next edition of the music newspaper. It ended: "If we're not cool, what does that make you?"

Wild Life was met with a colossal wave of disappointment. As a Dylan-inspired attempt to bottle the lightning of live recording, it was lacking in thrills. Paul's second album in seven months, it sank faster than even the poorly received but creatively buoyant *Ram.* The record-buying public seemed baffled by how this formerly perfectionist creator of so many peerless Beatles classics could turn out such half-finished scraps. For those weaned on the mini-symphonies of *Sgt. Pepper* and *Abbey Road,* this really wasn't good enough.

The truth seemed to be that McCartney, high and happy, was simply indulging himself, without anyone to tell him no, or to edit or jettison his weaker ideas. Worse, with the gibberish words of Side 1 leading tracks "Mumbo" and "Bip Bop," he apparently couldn't even be bothered writing lyrics anymore. Later, when listening to the latter, Paul would cringe. "When you allow yourself to be playful," he says, "the morning after or the month after or the year after, you can just think, Oh, maybe that was a bit *too* playful."

The best moments in *Wild Life* were to be found further down the track list: the early stirrings of the McCartneys' animal-rights sympathies in the mournful rocker "Wild Life," the lovely Paul-and-Linda-do-the-Everly-Brothers cooing of "Some People Never Know." Amid the gentle waves of harmony in "Tomorrow," a follow-up song of sorts, an insecure McCartney pleaded with his lover not to let him down, as if recalling the female figure in "Yesterday" who had broken his heart by leaving.

At the end of the record, in the orchestrated piano ballad "Dear Friend," Paul addressed John directly, declaring his love for him and, in a highly sentimental tone, sadly asking if this really was the "borderline," the end of their friendship. "That's much more loving," Paul says of the conciliatory song. "It's like, 'Oh come on, mate.'"

In terms of sales, by Beatle standards, the album bombed, prompting EMI to cancel the release of the proposed double A-side single "Love

Is Strange" and "I Am Your Singer." "I like the record," Paul now says of *Wild Life,* before conceding, "It wasn't perhaps as good as some of the others." At the same time, McCartney points out that validation for his records can sometimes come from the most unlikely or fleeting of encounters. Shortly after the release of *Wild Life,* he was motoring down Sunset Strip in Los Angeles when a camper van, driven by "a typical Woodstock type," pulled up beside him. Spotting McCartney, the grinning hippie waved a copy of the record out of the van's window before shouting over to tell him that he was heading up into the hills with the LP, doubtless to get high and listen to the album in much the same state as it had been created. "He said, 'Great record, man,'" remembers Paul. "To me, that was it."

Others weren't so enthusiastic. *Rolling Stone* head-scratchingly wondered whether the LP was "deliberately second-rate," theorizing that it was perhaps an exercise in creating banal music that would infuriate Lennon by outselling his apparently more meaningful records. This ridiculous notion was instantly disproved by the fact that, in a perhaps commercially hobbling move, on its initial release in the United States it didn't have any words at all on its cover. In an effort to prop up the record, Capitol hastily affixed a sticker to the remaining stock bearing the legend "Paul McCartney & Friends."

Still, the photograph that appeared on the front of *Wild Life* seemed to say it all: Paul was now just a member of a band, and one that, to his mind, needed no introduction. In the pastoral scene, foregrounded by hazy sunlit foliage, the barefoot members of Wings—positioned at the bottom of the picture, almost as an afterthought in the framing—balance on a horizontal branch a few feet above a stream.

Second from left in the lineup, McCartney stands knee-deep in the river, strumming an acoustic guitar, too distant from the camera for anyone other than the sharp-eyed—and maybe this was the entire point—to recognize him as Beatle Paul.

As Wings was splashing around in the country, the glitter-and-glue stomp of glam rock was fast becoming the soundtrack of the times, making the Beatles, and their solo efforts, seem hopelessly passé, only a year and a half after their demise.

In an effort to toughen up his new band's sound, as hard-rocktinged pop began creeping into the charts, Paul decided to expand Wings to a five-piece by drafting in a lead guitarist. Over twelve intensive days of rehearsals in January 1972 at the Scotch of St. James club, an old hangout for the Beatles and the Stones just off Piccadilly, McCartney worked up new songs with the band, inviting down, through a tip-off from a roadie, Henry McCullough.

Painted by *Melody Maker* as "an eternal drifter wandering from gig to gig," McCullough, from Portstewart in Northern Ireland, was a road-worn rocker with many touring miles to his name. Three years earlier, during Joe Cocker's star-making set at Woodstock, McCullough had been part of the backing Grease Band; they had performed a grittier version of Lennon and McCartney's "With a Little Help from My Friends."

As such, he was only slightly daunted by the prospect of working with a Beatle. "But I was a little bit," McCullough admits. "I mean, this is Paul McCartney. I grew up with the Beatles. But we had a long talk and he told me what the score was going to be and it was all very exciting. I wasn't scared. He was easy to be about if you were in the gang, y'know. After a month or two, you got used to his face."

McCullough further proved himself to be a perfect fit when he quickly settled into life on the McCartneys' farm: "It was all good fun. You could get dirty. There was nobody afraid of getting shite on their boots."

With the band now complete, Paul began itching to get out on the road. But, recognizing how difficult a high-profile reentry into touring might be, nearly six years after the Beatles had taken their last bows, at San Francisco's Candlestick Park in 1966, he began formulating a plan.

This time, he would do things differently. He hinted as much in the press. "I just want to get into a van," he said, "and do an unadvertised Saturday-night hop at Slough town hall or somewhere."

Or, as it turned out, anywhere.

4

ROAD TO ANYWHERE

You banned yourself from playing any Beatles songs live with Wings in the early days . . . that must have been tough?

Yeah, but I wanted to grow Wings from a seed. And that was what we ended up doing. However, this meant that, y'know, if you had a bad spring and you didn't get enough rain or enough sunshine . . . you were fucked.

You'd find that you'd had a pretty poor song harvest?

Yeah! And we had some pretty bad weather in the early days.

T HEY GATHERED ON THE PAVEMENT for one last photograph before leaving. Out in the road at the front of the Cavendish Avenue house they stood, a scruffy assemblage of longhairs. At its center were the McCartneys and their daughters, along with the Seiwells—Denny's wife, Monique, holding baby Stella, underlining the sense that they had now become one big family. To their right, looking like shaggy-haired escapees from the Faces or the Stones, were brother-in-law roadies Ian Horne and Trevor Jones. To their left, Henry McCullough and Denny Laine, the latter pulling a comically vacant Stan Laurel face. All wore big winter coats to keep out the February chill. All waved to the camera, except for the too-cool-for-school McCullough, who kept his hands deep in his pockets.

Behind them stood a green Transit van and an Avis rental three-ton lorry stuffed with their equipment. Given his head entirely, Paul was at last getting his wish—as expressed to the uninterested Beatles during their dying days—of embarking on a low-key, last-minute tour of small venues or civic halls. The plan for this upcoming jaunt was a similar one, if far looser, and in keeping with the laid-back mood of the times. Everyone—musicians, roadies, kids, even dogs—was to pile into the vehicles and take off up the motorway, heading for university towns in search of somewhere to play.

This tapped into McCartney's romantic notion of the vaudeville or circus troupe setting off over the horizon, en route to anywhere. Moreover, the scheme allowed him to ward off his fears about returning to live performance. He was, he confessed, "very nervous." The nightmare scenario, in his mind, was facing row after row of reporters at the front of the stage, sitting in judgment with their pads, scribbling snippy notes about how he wasn't as good as he used to be.

Instead, by not announcing shows beforehand, he could keep one step ahead of the press. In effect, he thought, he could outrun his critics.

And so, on the morning of February 8, 1972, this strange coterie of hippies, kids, and animals set off, pointing the noses of their vehicles in the direction of the M1 motorway, destination unknown. "We were," says Paul, with barely disguised pride, "a bunch of nutters on the road."

It was an emboldened Paul who faced the beginning of 1972. With Lennon's cutting accusation that McCartney created anodyne "Muzak" still ringing in his ears, he determined to push into new and, for him, uncharted territory by toughening up his sentiments and stepping into the unlikely arena of the protest song.

After trading low blows the previous year, John and Paul had reached some kind of détente. Surprisingly, given his growing reputation as a peacenik in all areas except for his more bitter personal relations, it was Lennon who first extended the hand of friendship. Trying to repair the damage, John used journalist Ray Connolly—the same writer who had faced McCartney's swift denials that he'd announced that he'd quit the Beatles in his infamous Q&A press release—as a go-between to hand-deliver a letter to Cavendish Avenue. A visiting Jim McCartney took the envelope from Connolly at the front door before unhappily warning the writer, "If I were you, son, I wouldn't get involved in all this."

On the last weekend of January, Lennon and McCartney hooked up for the first time since the ruckus began. Saturday saw Paul and Linda fly to New York and accept an invitation to visit the Lennons at the apartment they were renting, at 105 Bank Street; the couple had now taken up permanent residence in Greenwich Village. Over dinner, John and Paul chatted amicably, if still a touch guardedly, and agreed to stop slagging each other off in public, whether in the press or in song. At the same time, it seems, the fact that Lennon was living in such a febrile countercultural environment, hanging with hirsute radicals and becoming increasingly politicized, rubbed off on McCartney.

The following day, as events quickly unfolded on the other side of the Atlantic, Paul found his cause to support, his enemy to kick against, however lightly. On Sunday, January 30, in the Bogside area of Derry, Northern Ireland, a march by a civil rights organization representing the Catholic minority suddenly descended into rioting. Under attack, albeit from a group of rowdy teenagers, British soldiers fired live rounds at the protesters, resulting in twenty-six unarmed civilians being shot. Thirteen died that day, escalating the Troubles, which were to violently stain the United Kingdom for decades.

McCartney, along with much of the civilized world, was outraged. Giving an interview to U.S. radio station KHJ in the hours after the event, Paul talked little about Wings, instead railing against the British government, reportedly using "strong language" that needed much in the way of editing by the station before it could be broadcast. The next day, the McCartneys flew home, but not before booking a session at Island Studios in west London for an impromptu recording session on Tuesday, February 1, for Wings' first single, the hastily penned response "Give Ireland Back to the Irish."

Paul had always thought that Lennon was "crackers" to write overtly political material. This, however—doubtless because of McCartney's Irish heritage—felt different. "It took us aback," says Paul. It wouldn't harm his image, either, of course, to be seen making such a potent statement. "I knew what I was doing," he admits.

At the studio, a TV crew from ABC in the States filmed the band rehearsing a harder-edged version of the song than would appear on the slightly vanilla-sounding 45, with Paul lustily belting out his lyrical protest. In truth, it was fairly tame stuff: Great Britain was "tremendous," but its creation of a police state in Ireland and its imprisoning of those with a passion for "God and country" was totally unacceptable.

In the two-minute TV news segment, Paul sat with Linda, being interviewed, while periodically laughing at the continual interruptions of one of their dogs howling in the background. No, said Paul, he wasn't worried about being an entertainer making a political statement. In fact, from his impassioned demeanor, it was clear that he enjoyed having an agenda.

"I don't now plan to do everything as a political thing," he told the unseen reporter, before repeatedly stabbing the air with his finger to emphasize his point. "But just on this one occasion I think the British government overstepped the mark and showed themselves to be more of a sort of repressive regime than I ever believed them to be."

EMI chairman Sir Joseph Lockwood, more used to having to deal with the controversies stirred up by Lennon than McCartney, tried to talk Paul out of releasing the single. "He rang me up and said, 'Woo, y'know, don't do this.' I said, 'Hey, man, y'know, although I'm not a protest songwriter normally, this time there's no stopping it. I've gotta do this. It's gotta happen.'"

For his part, as a young Northern Irishman recruited into a band that was overnight making such a pointed comment about the divisions in his homeland, Henry McCullough felt strangely ambivalent about the whole affair. "I never thought about it once, and that's the God's truth," he says. A traveling musician, the guitarist had been out of the country and on the road when the Troubles had begun to intensify in Ireland, in the late 1960s. "I don't think it was a bad thing to miss that tragic period," he points out.

Not that his involvement in the record was to go unnoticed, however. Amid the fuss to come with the subsequent release of the single, the guitarist's brother was thumped in a pub in the Irish expatriate stronghold of Kilburn, in North London: "It was, like, 'Are you Samuel McCullough?' 'Yeah.' 'Is your brother Henry that played on "Give Ireland Back to the Irish"?' 'Yeah.' *Bang.*"

For a lineup of individuals who might as well have bumped into one another while queuing for a bus, the five members of Wings quickly bonded in rehearsals. Though the group was as manufactured in some ways as any toothsome teen-scream pop band, all of its members— except Linda, of course—were nothing if not professionals who could adapt to any musical scenario.

Mirroring the segment in *Let It Be* where the four Beatles are each shown separately arriving at Apple Studios in Savile Row, the members of Wings were filmed coolly rolling up one by one to the Institute of Contemporary Arts on the Mall, the location for their first intensive batch of rehearsals. Inside, on the stage, the quintet was filmed rattling through old rock'n'roll standards such as "Lucille" before working their way through a raw live take of "Wild Life," along with the stomping "The Mess," which (with its line "The mess I'm in") owed much to the Band's "The Shape I'm In," released two years earlier.

More and more, Linda appeared to be comfortable and confident behind her keyboard setup. In truth, however, there were already murmurs of dissent within the ranks over her role in the band. The forthright Henry McCullough even brazenly suggested to Paul that the band get a "proper" piano player. "I'm quite ashamed of it," he says now. McCartney instantly rebuffed the guitarist, firmly informing him that it was his decision alone who was in the band or out of it. "I was like, 'All right,'" says McCullough. "It was never brought up again, on my part anyway." But at certain points, it seemed Paul wasn't entirely convinced that having his wife in the band had been such a great idea. Once, in a moment of irritation, he threatened to replace her with Billy Preston, the American keyboard player who had done such a fine job augmenting the Beatles during *Let It Be*. Later, a little uncharitably, he would admit that Linda had been "absolute rubbish" when she'd started playing. Then, in a spot of double-damning, he tried to qualify this harsh assessment by saying that George Martin had dumped Ringo from the Beatles' "Love Me Do" session for exactly the same reason. His circuitous, slightly cack-handed point seemed to be: she's getting better.

"It was the weirdest thing," he says today. "There was me, having been one of the world's most famous people, a member of the Beatles, suddenly playing in this semiprofessional band kind of thing."

There was no little amount of defiance in Paul's decision to stick by Linda, not least when his contemporaries began to mock him. "We had people like Jagger saying, 'Oh, he's got his old lady in the band.' We had to take all that. I would think, Oh, fucking thanks a lot . . . tosser." Linda herself was ambivalent about the prospect of being a touring musician, telling a friend that she'd "just as soon have stayed on the farm with the horses and kids." But Paul wanted her there, and so there she was.

Ultimately, McCartney saw Wings as an experiment. Acknowledging that he couldn't replicate the Beatles, he was striking out in another direction entirely and now road-testing the band with this freewheeling, haphazard tour. "We didn't even have hotels," he points out, almost incredulously. "Anyone else at least would've booked a hotel."

Once they'd hit the road, the Wings touring party motored northward and began scanning signs for a likely place to stop. Taken with the exotically named Ashby-de-la-Zouch in Leicestershire, they exited the M1 and headed for the small market town. Passing through its center, Paul and Linda spotted a pony tied to a lamppost and, prone to impulsive equine purchases, tried to find the owner and make him an offer for it, to no avail. Getting back to the matter in hand, the group discovered that, of course, there was no university in tiny Ashby-de-la-Zouch. Undeterred, they headed back to the motorway.

A safer bet, they decided, was to aim for Nottingham, a city where they reckoned they'd be guaranteed a gig. Arriving on the university campus around five o'clock, they sent roadie Trevor Jones ahead into the building to scout the location. Jones asked around for the social secretary and was directed to the bar, where he found student Elaine Woodhams. He told her that he was with Paul McCartney's new band and they were looking for somewhere to play a spontaneous gig. In fact, he said, Paul was already waiting outside.

Initially skeptical and suspecting a practical joke, Woodhams was led by the roadie out to the van. The door slid open to reveal McCartney, turning the social secretary's expression into a goldfish gape. A gig was duly arranged for the following afternoon and announced in a scrawl on the blackboard in the bar: *Entrance—50p*. The word that the ex-Beatle was to break his concert silence here, of all places, quickly filtered through the campus. "It was a big deal for them," says McCullough. "But it was a bigger deal for us. It was like, 'This is it, the first fucking gig . . . let's see what happens.'"

The following lunchtime, in the dining hall–cum–ballroom, Wings publicly took to the stage for the first time—Paul wearing a red-and-white-striped shirt with a pair of dungarees—before a crowd of eight hundred, their number constrained by the fire safety limit. The band sounded lively, if a touch scrappy. Proudly displaying his rock'n'roll roots, Paul launched into "Lucille" as an opener, then led into the first airing of "Give Ireland Back to the Irish." The rest of the set was largely composed of songs from *Wild Life* ("Bip Bop," "Some People Never Know"), one from *Ram* ("Smile Away"), and a filler blues jam fronted by McCullough ("Henry's Blues"). Running out of material, since McCartney had a self-imposed rule not to perform Beatles songs, they played "Give Ireland Back to the Irish" and "Lucille" again. In a moment of dopey dizziness, they slipped into "The Grand Old Duke of York." Paul admits that not allowing himself to play any of his most famous tunes was "a killer. . . . We had to do an hour of other material, and we didn't have it."

Strangely, perhaps, one of the most satisfying elements for Paul in all of this was being handed the band's agreed half-share of the door profits at the end of the gig, a bag of fifty-pence coins, which he then evenly distributed among the musicians. Given the fact that, after signing with Brian Epstein's NEMS management company in January 1962, the Beatles had never handled actual money earned from their performances, this was something of an unanticipated thrill. It was the first time in ten years that Paul had seen any cash after a show, and he enjoyed the working musician's dignity-of-labor aspect of it, feeling like "Duke Ellington divvying out the money" to his band. "Two for you and two for you," says Henry McCullough. "We were like children. But it was all fifty pees. You walked out of the university and your trousers were tripping you."

By day two, the press was already gaining on them, and Wings felt they were losing the chase. Exiting the van at Leeds University, the band was accosted by a gaggle of reporters and TV crews. As their hunted leader, Paul immediately made the call: the gig's off, everyone back in the van. Instead they headed for York, where a show was arranged at York University's Goodricke College, only six hours before stage time. Too late to book the union's theater, they again used the refectory for the performance, with 550 students crammed into the space and another 400 stuck outside.

But Paul hadn't quite managed to shake the reporters tailing him. A stringer from the *Guardian* was in the audience at York, noting that Wings seemed slightly old-fashioned when faced with a crowd that, in hippie fashion, sat on the floor for most of the duration. McCartney was "seemingly oblivious of the passage of time," since the highlights of the set were "old dancing numbers." By the end, though, the students were on their feet. The band played "Give Ireland Back to the Irish" twice, with Paul quipping that they needed "to get some practice."

The still-unreleased single was already drawing some heat. On the day of the York gig, the BBC banned it on the grounds that it was politically biased and didn't account for the suffering caused to many on the other side of the divide. Asked by the *Guardian* whether the gigs were actually secret fund-raisers for the IRA, Paul "refused to be drawn." The fact that his reply was noncommittal shows the strength of feeling in the wake of Bloody Sunday: the idea of passing around the collection hat for the IRA—which only months later intensified its terrorist bombing campaign—was not yet considered taboo. "We're simply playing for the people," Paul said.

Literally escaping the controversy, one night Wings was forced to drive through a mob of protesters. While the band was trying to exit through the campus gates in their van, students menacingly crowded around the vehicle, frightening everyone inside. Denny Laine, who was behind the wheel that night, says, "I put my toe down and they all jumped out the way. They were pretty threatening."

For the most part, though, McCartney successfully managed to give both the media and his detractors the slip. Back in London, his assistant Shelley Turner playfully fielded calls from journalists fishing for information about the next destination of the tour. "They have taken a lot of sandwiches with them," she offered coyly. "They could turn up anywhere." Countering growing rumors that EMI, in the wake of the BBC ban, was refusing to issue "Give Ireland Back to the Irish," Turner said that the record company was "100 percent behind it. . . . It will probably be in the shops next week."

As the tour progressed, Wings and the crew developed something of a routine around these guerrilla gigs. Each morning they'd pick up the map and decide where to go that day. Sticking mainly to larger towns and cities, they would arrive at a university in the early afternoon; Trevor Jones would be dispatched to make the gig arrangements, and then a local B&B would be found before the roadies returned to the venue to set up the equipment.

After the gig, the bounty of fifty-pence coins was dished out and the party returned to the B&B for fish and chips or cheese sandwiches and a game of darts. Baby Stella would be placed in a makeshift cot fash-

ioned from an open drawer lined with blankets and pillows. Bottles of
wine would be uncorked, smokes sparked up, and the guitars whipped
out for a jam through old rock'n'roll numbers. One night everyone sat
around and listened to the tapes of the gigs recorded from the sound
desk by Trevor Jones on a couple of reel-to-reels borrowed from Abbey
Road. Disappointingly, they sounded rough. There was still much work
to do.

If the universities jaunt was distinctly lacking in glamour day to day,
and far removed from the luxury afforded to the Beatles during their
touring years, it was overall an enjoyable experience for everyone, pecu-
liarly British and very 1970s. Henry McCullough likens it to "a black-
and-white *Sgt. Pepper*. . . . You were staying with Mrs. McGonagall on
the promenade." The buzz for all involved was getting up in the morning and not knowing what the day was going to bring or even where they
were going to end up. "It was just as exciting traveling in a green Transit
as it was in a fucking Rolls," says the guitarist. "You probably had more
room in the van."

Before long, the touring party began to suspect that the student
organizers were preparing in advance on the off chance that Wings
would drop in. On their arrival at Hull University, the PA was already
set up in the concert hall. Driving around looking for accommodations,
the band was forced a mile out of the center of town to Pearson Park,
where they booked into what McCartney remembers as a "third-rate"
hotel, run by, in Denny Laine's opinion, an "asshole" landlord. "Some
little weird old guy," says Paul. "Got very annoyed with us because apparently one of the roadies was smoking something."

Here there was an altercation between McCartney and the landlord, though not, as Laine remembers it, because of dope smoking.
After the gig, the band returned to the bar, helping themselves to drinks
(but leaving money) and eating their fish and chips, though neglecting
to tidy up after themselves. "When the guy came down in the morning
and saw all the mess," says Laine, "he got upset."

McCartney happened to walk into the room at breakfast time as
the landlord was loudly telling off the roadies. An argument broke out
and Paul—"accidentally on purpose," according to Laine—elbowed the
proprietor in the nose. Enraged, the landlord threatened to call the police. Nine-year-old Heather ran around the band members' rooms,

knocking on the doors to rouse them. The group and entourage quickly fled before they found themselves deeper in trouble.

A week into the tour, Linda talked to *Melody Maker* about how the tour was going and, specifically, how her eldest daughter was coping with rock'n'roll road life. The McCartneys, she said, had given Heather "the choice of school or coming with us, and she chose the latter." Revealing her blasé, university-of-life attitude, Linda added, "I mean, this is an education in itself, isn't it? We're just a gang of musicians touring around."

On one key date, however, Linda's credentials as a musician were once again called into question. Having aborted the Leeds University gig because of the press attention, the band arranged a date for February 16 in the city's town hall, a larger and more imposing venue. Taking to the stage a touch intimidated, Paul sang the opening bars of "Wild Life" solo before turning to his wife and counting in her staccato piano introduction. There was silence. Linda had frozen. She mouthed to Paul, "I've forgotten the chords."

"The audience thought, This is good . . . this is a little joke they've got going," McCartney remembers.

Paul stepped over to his wife's side of the stage and placed his hands on the keyboard before realizing that he, too, couldn't remember how the song began. Nervous laughter began to rise up from the stalls. "It looked even more like a joke, like a great big setup thing," Paul says. "For a moment, there was panic." Then Linda suddenly remembered the sequence, began playing the simple, descending three-chord riff, and the band fell in behind her. "We went into the song, our hearts beating fast," says Paul.

Very quickly, the novelty of the tour began to wear off. In Manchester, Wings played in a theater in Salford where the owners worried that the band's low-end rumble might somehow damage the scenery of the venue's current production. In Birmingham, Wings visited Laine's parents and then played a very average show at the university. In Swansea, with only seventy-five minutes' notice, eight hundred fans—by now wise to Wings' modus operandi—suddenly appeared. The element of surprise was gone. The game, it seemed, was up.

On February 23, after eleven dates, the tour was over, with the plan to continue for another week abandoned. Denny Seiwell says it was proving a bore to have to find a B&B every day that had six free rooms and allowed animals. In addition, an American drummer could stomach only so many fish-and-chip suppers.

Two days later, "Give Ireland Back to the Irish" was released, a mere three weeks after it had been written and recorded. Following the BBC's lead, the Independent Television Authority and Radio Luxembourg immediately banned it. Paul's response was one of faintly comic defiance. "Up them!" he said. "I think the BBC should be highly praised, preventing the youth from hearing my opinions." Radio 1 DJ John Peel was the sole voice to speak out in defense of McCartney, saying that the ban disturbed him. "The act of banning it," he argued, "is a much stronger political act than the contents of the record itself. It's just one man's opinion."

For better or for worse, "Give Ireland Back to the Irish" marked the beginning and the end of Paul McCartney's career as a protest singer. As relatively weak a song as it was, at least it was better than Lennon's awful folk dirge "The Luck of the Irish," released later that year on his worst album, *Some Time in New York City*. In the end, the first Wings single reached No. 1 in two countries—Ireland and Spain. "Basque separatists loved it," says Paul now.

As Abbey Road was to the Beatles, Olympic Studios, in the southwest London suburb of Barnes, was the preferred recording hive of the Rolling Stones. McCartney had used the facility in the past, not least during the sessions for *Abbey Road* (only partly recorded at the famed St. John's Wood studio). Although the venue had produced a fine Beatles album, the band's experience had been troubled. As was quickly to be proved, it was not a lucky environment for Paul.

It was here that, irritating the other Beatles, Yoko Ono had been laid up in a double bed installed in the studio, recovering after the car crash that she and John had suffered in Scotland in the summer of 1969, Lennon giving her a microphone so that she could, as she now remembers, "just experiment or do something." It was here that Paul had fought against being press-ganged into signing the Allen Klein management agreement by his bandmates, a decisive moment in the disintegration of their long friendship. And now, in March 1972, it was here that he returned for the beginning of the difficult sessions for the first album to be released under the name Paul McCartney and Wings, *Red Rose Speedway*.

Having decided to employ a producer for the first time in his post-Beatles career, Paul brought in Glyn Johns, the studio name of the day thanks to his recent wave of successes with the Rolling Stones, the Who, and Led Zeppelin after his dedicated if ultimately failed attempts to create the *Get Back* album. A self-assured, headstrong character, Johns was in no way intimidated by McCartney on any level.

Wings set up in the grand, ballroom-like Studio One at Olympic and began jamming their way through Paul's new songs. Roundly unimpressed by the sounds emanating from the studio, Johns sat with his feet up in the control room, reading the paper and refusing to roll the tape. On day one, McCartney had asked the producer to consider him just the bass player in the group, in an attempt to underline his apparent desire for Wings to be a democratic and "normal" band. Of course, when the blunt Johns began to treat McCartney just as he would any old musician, the shirking bandleader, he says, grew disgruntled.

Very quickly the two began to rub each other the wrong way. Laine says that Johns wasn't willing to accommodate McCartney's more experimental ideas, like "going into funny little rooms to get weird guitar noises." The producer declared the music Wings was making to be "shite." Inevitably, this provoked a shouting match between Johns and McCartney. "Anything like that, I always stood five feet behind Paul," says McCullough. "That's his territory, that's his business. He was speaking on his own behalf, but he was letting us in on it and holding us together, like, 'Okay, boys, I'll take care of this. You don't want to get involved.'"

Four weeks in, Glyn Johns walked out of the sessions for *Red Rose Speedway*. "I think he felt we were too lackadaisical," says the guitarist. "He got quite angry about the whole thing."

Whether Paul was right or wrong in his motives and maneuvers, his next step would have almost everyone wondering if he'd entirely lost the plot. Back in January, on the farm in Scotland, mainly to entertain his middle daughter, Mary, he'd started tinkering around with a new composition that set the nursery rhyme "Mary Had a Little Lamb" to a new melody.

This lilting and inoffensive, if bizarre, track was to become, in May, the second Wings single, bamboozling a large portion of the rock-buying public, which was then enjoying glammier or harder, hairier sounds. Still, as bewildering a record as it was, touted as "a song for spring to make people happy," "Mary Had a Little Lamb" reached No. 9 on the U.K. charts, purely on novelty value. Over in America, discerning DJs simply ignored the track, flipping the single over and playing its New Orleans–flavored B-side rocker "Little Woman Love."

For Paul, this kind of children's song was part of the strain of his writing that had produced "Yellow Submarine," "When I'm Sixty-four" and "Maxwell's Silver Hammer," a bit of sing-along fun that harked back to the old days and the music halls. Public tastes had moved on, though, and such featherweight fare was considered utterly uncool. When the record was panned by critics, Paul quickly realized just how out of step he'd become, admitting, "I do things that aren't necessarily very carefully thought out." He even blamed his star sign for giving him this trait: "Geminis are supposed to be changeable. I'm crazy. I've always been crazy from the minute I was born."

Yet even while holding his hands up in defeat, McCartney tried to claw back some of his cool, claiming that the daughter of the Who's guitarist, Pete Townshend, had pestered her dad to buy the single for her. "I like to keep in with the five-year-olds," Paul remarked. Then, even more wrongheadedly, he tried to justify the song in "deeper" terms, using the hippie-hangover parlance of the times; he pointed out that the lamb follows Mary to school, but then, after having been thrown out by the teacher, hangs around like a devoted child.

"To me, that's a heavy trip, those lyrics," he mused, like the stoner who has just discovered an entire universe on his fingernail. "It's very spiritual when someone hangs around because it's loved. I'm sure no one ever thinks about those kind of things."

To spotlight the incongruity, on May 25 Wings performed the fluff-light nursery rhyme on a *Top of the Pops* bill that included Elton John offering the stirring, otherworldly ennui of "Rocket Man (I Think It's Going to Be a Long, Long Time)" and the utterly of-the-moment T. Rex thundering their way through "Metal Guru," one of the 45s that would define the era.

Capping it all, Wings' next appearance was a slot on *The Basil Brush Show*. The singers mimed their way through a performance of

"Mary Had a Little Lamb," footage of the band spliced together with cheap cartoon sequences illustrating the words, in a break from the antics of the starring fox puppet. On TV, the otherwise wine-slugging, weed-puffing band members sang along through sprayed-on grins. They all now admit they were slightly bemused by their newfound roles as children's entertainers.

"Listen, how do you think I felt?" says Henry McCullough. "I was coming off the road after three years in America with Joe Cocker and I end up playing 'Mary Had a Little Fucking Lamb.'"

"We're supposed to be a rock band," says Denny Seiwell. "I said, 'What's with all this shit?'"

Even the ever loyal Denny Laine, it seems, suffered a moment of doubt, admitting that he was privately thinking, *I didn't sign up for this, Paul.*

Looking back on "Mary Had a Little Lamb," Paul confesses that he's slightly stumped himself as to why he made this unarguably odd record. "I can't believe that now," he says. "It seemed like a good idea at the time." Perhaps it highlights the fact that McCartney always acted impulsively and instinctively, and then did the heavy thinking later.

This whimsical, semidetached part of McCartney's character was quickly understood, however, by McCullough, who says that even if Paul is generally seen as being down-to-earth, in some respects he's quite the opposite—spacey and often somewhere else. "He does what he does," says the guitarist. "We were put into his bubble, basically."

And so, by the summer of 1972, the members of Wings had every right to be confused: they didn't know whether they were supposed to be angrily shaking their fists at the British government over its actions in Ireland or singing storybook lullabies for the under-tens. They were en route to somewhere, but sometimes the musicians must have wondered where exactly Paul was taking them.

5

LIFE IN THE SLOW LANE

It was always hard for you to lock in a lineup with Wings. As a band, you always seemed to be in a state of flux.

Yeah, exactly.

What would you put that down to?

Um. Musical differences.

THE BUS WAS AN OPEN-TOPPED Bristol Commercial Vehicles double-decker whose speed maxed out at an unimpressively chugging 38 miles per hour. Yet for Paul, this was the ideal vehicle to ferry Wings around for the duration of their first European tour.

There was method in this apparent madness: if his band and family were to spend the summer months motoring around the continent, he figured they might as well make it a pleasant experience. Rather than be stuck inside a van or coach, gasping for air in the breathless heat of July and August, they could all be lazily sunning themselves on the upper deck.

The notion recalled *Magical Mystery Tour* and, more directly, Cliff Richard in *Summer Holiday*. McCartney had the bus painted in a screaming, multihued psychedelic design that might have been hip five years previously but already looked out of date. Where the bus's advertising strip had once been was now written the legend WINGS OVER EU-

ROPE, atop a cartoon mural depicting verdant, sunlit mountain peaks against a duck-egg-blue sky.

On the back of the bus, the band members' names were stenciled in a telling pecking order: Paul & Linda McCartney, Denny Laine, Henry McCullough, Denny Seiwell. On the front, backdropped against a deeper shade of blue, a pair of white wings fanned out, framing the spinning destination indicator, for which a new set of names had been printed: Châteauvallon, Juan-les-Pins, Arles, and so on, to be rolled out as the tour trundled onward.

Inside, the lower level had been carpeted and fitted with a galley kitchen at the rear. There were bunks for the kids, and four of the original seats remained behind the driver's cockpit. The upper level, meanwhile, was basically a hippie crash space—albeit one with a playpen, its floor strewn with fraying sofa cushions and enormous, puffy beanbags. "Bit of dope in the fridge," says Henry McCullough. "Magical. Like being part of a movie."

The McCartneys really had become a touring family. Wherever the band went, so went the kids. During rehearsals in London at Manticore Studios, a converted cinema in Fulham owned by the notoriously unrestrained progressive rock trio Emerson, Lake and Palmer, Wings had pounded away on the stage while the kids, clearly quite used to this kind of thing, mucked around and enjoyed a picnic on carpets and mats in the empty auditorium. Paul and Linda would sometimes have to break from rehearsals to go and change Stella's nappy.

There was never ever any question of the kids being left with nannies or sent away to boarding school or summer camp while the band was on the road.

"That's right, and we even got slagged for that," Paul says now. "I remember somebody saying, 'Oh, they're dragging their kids around the world.' And our answer for that would be to say, 'Yeah, look, the thing is, number one, we love 'em. Number two, what are we gonna do? We're gonna be in Australia, and a nanny's gonna ring up and say, "Ooh, your kid's got a fever of 105."' Shit. We would wanna be there, so that was it."

From here on in, tutors were to be employed wherever possible. "We'd get them to talk to the school first and find out what subjects they were gonna cover," he remembers. "We kind of kept up. The kids tell me now they didn't really keep up. They did inevitably sort of fall behind a bit. But we had the freedom to do what we liked with our family and we were just careful to not have it sort of damage them." When he attracted criticism for forcing his offspring to join the circus, Paul would shrug and laugh, saying, "It's a geography lesson."

"Mary's friends used to call her a hippie commune kid," he recalls. "But it was just kind of a question of mucking in. It was more like Gypsies than anything else. This family was gonna move around." This easygoing attitude wasn't always prevalent, however. If one of the kids got ill, it would cause Paul and Linda to bicker. "It would be a strain on our relationship," Paul admits. "But at least we were doing what we wanted to do. Life causes arguments, and there were plenty of reasons for that. I don't think having the kids on tour was particularly stressful. I think just people living together can be stressful. Y'know, it was a great love affair, but nobody's perfect."

The first show of the European tour was booked for a deliberately out-of-the-way location: a two-thousand-seat Roman amphitheater at Châteauvallon, high in the pine-forested hills above Toulon on the southeastern coast of France. Here, before the gig, on Sunday, July 9, 1972, Paul gave an informal press conference.

"I'm starting all over again and working my way upwards," he admitted. "You don't fight Cassius Clay on your first time out." He hinted at his recent crisis of confidence and the worry of being smothered by the weight of his reputation: "A year ago, I used to wake up in the morning and think, *I'm a myth. I'm Paul McCartney.* And it scared the hell out of me."

Presaging Lennon's later declaration that Yoko had "showed me what it was to be Elvis Beatle and to be surrounded by sycophants," Paul admitted that his time with Linda, particularly his "hermit" period in Scotland, had similarly opened his eyes. "It wasn't until she came along that I realized what was happening to me," he said. "She made me see I was surrounded by con men and leeches."

This statement underlined just how much Paul now relied on Linda and explained why she was a constant presence by his side. Not that her role as her husband's musical co-conspirator was getting any easier— a fact that she sometimes chose to hide from her partner. Before their show at Châteauvallon, the Wings band members were apparently "scared shitless," though none more so than Linda, who was so terrified that she cried on Denny Seiwell's shoulder. "She was unhappy and frightened," says the drummer. "But she had a lot of chutzpah. She wasn't much of a piano player or a singer, but, boy, she had the heart for it."

"I didn't want to let Paul down," Linda reflected. "I didn't want to let the band down. It was too much to hope that I'd be ignored, like I deserved."

In the end, she coped, and the Châteauvallon show was a success. In the wake of the chaotic university tour, Wings was becoming a more polished operation. Whereas before the band would just rock up and play, there were now some production values. Paul sported a glittery black stage suit; there were backdrop films of scenes from Argyll—crashing waves, galloping horses—and climactic explosions of confetti as the band charged around the stage and Henry McCullough fell to his knees soloing.

If Wings was now beginning to resemble a credible rock band in step with the early 1970s, there was still daftness afoot. Throughout the tour, McCartney roped the band into making sideline appearances for a planned but unreleased film called *The Bruce McMouse Show.* Intended to be a mixture of animation and live action, interspersed with Wings performances, it was to feature the titular cartoon mouse and his family, who lived under the stage on which the band was performing. The musicians were even taught a choreographed music-hall dance routine, though it was clear that their hearts weren't in it. McCullough admits that he "never quite made the grade" in this particular respect. Seiwell recalls the time he had to stand in a crowded backstage room and speak prepared lines to an imaginary mouse as agonizingly embarrassing and "one of the hardest things I ever had to do in Wings."

In other ways, in spite of their outward family image, Wings attracted much the same kind of attention as other rock bands. The European tour was the first time predatory females began turning up backstage. After the show in Zurich, the intimidating, omnivorous Anita Pallenberg made an appearance. Her considerable reputation preceded her; she already counted three members of the Rolling Stones—Brian Jones, Keith Richards, and Mick Jagger—among her conquests. Now she apparently made a beeline for Denny Laine.

In a recent development, however, the guitarist was already spoken for. In Juan-les-Pins, three dates into the tour, a strikingly pretty, almond-eyed brunette by the name of Joanne Patrie, a Boston-born model working the European catwalks, had managed to maneuver her way into the Wings dressing room. Jo Jo, as she preferred to be known, already had a rock-star-devouring past, having lost her virginity to Jimi Hendrix backstage at Woodstock, spent a "wild night" with the booze-soaked, in-decline Jim Morrison, and enjoyed a two-year off-and-on relationship with Rod Stewart.

Linda was instantly suspicious of Jo Jo, and, as it transpired, with good reason. As a seventeen-year-old Beatles fan, Patrie had written devotional fan letters to Paul, before turning up in Britain three years later with the express intention of meeting and marrying him. Following the Juan-les-Pins show, she had ended up seducing one of the Wings roadies, securing herself a place on the crew's tour bus, which drove in convoy with the band's more colorful transporter. In the days that followed she made a play for Denny Laine, engaging in flirty eye contact with the guitarist whenever the group's open-topped bus pulled level with the roadies' vehicle. Later, Laine walked in on Jo Jo taking a bath in her roadie beau's room. Within days the two were an item and inseparable. It was at this point that Jo Jo stepped into the inner circle.

The McCartneys were less than happy about this development. A week into their relationship, Denny sat Jo Jo down and told her that Paul and Linda were "very uptight about you being around." Linda, especially, was convinced that Jo Jo was simply using the guitarist to get close to Paul. Patrie began crying, having effectively suffered the rejection of her former pin-up. While the guitarist and the groupie's affair was to prove far more enduring than these flaky beginnings promised, the future Jo Jo Laine's relationship with the McCartneys was to remain painfully strained.

Meanwhile, the tour rumbled on. Sometimes, when the struggling double-decker clearly wasn't making the distance and it looked as if the musicians were going to miss their stage time, an emergency convoy of vehicles would be dispatched from the venue to collect them. This, if anything, added to the general air of hilarity and joie de vivre within the band. Paul, meanwhile, was becoming increasingly playful with reporters. At a press conference in Paris, he introduced the band members one by one before turning to his wife with the words ". . . and Yoko." Embarrassingly, though, and unthinkably for a returning Beatle making his first live appearances in France since 1965, the show in Lyon had to be canceled because of poor ticket sales.

Unperturbed, the group booked studio time at EMI's Pathé Marconi Studios in Paris, where they knocked out the Linda-fronted reggae-lite song "Seaside Woman," written as the result of a playful challenge from her husband when Associated Television first accused her of not being a capable songwriter. It would be another five years before this sweet, if slight, offering was released under the band name Suzy and the Red Stripes.

As the tour reached Sweden in the first week of August, the carefree mood began to darken. First of all, the press there began trashing the McCartneys, claiming that they'd been horrible to staff at various hotels when they'd complained about being forced to accept, as one report put it, "conventional Scandinavian single beds. . . . Their attitude seems to be, I want it, therefore it must happen."

When the band was out drinking one evening in a nightclub, things turned disturbingly nasty. A young man in a green jacket sidled up to Paul and calmly informed the ex-Beatle that he had a revolver in his pocket and planned to kill him. Having coolly revealed this threat to McCartney, the youth swaggered over to the bar and stood there staring and grinning at the singer.

McCullough and Laine arrived not long afterward. McCartney, clearly shaken, whispered to his bandmates, telling them what had just happened and gesturing toward the stranger. The guitarists, particularly the streetwise McCullough, who had begun his musical career as a showband player in the rough Northern Irish dance halls of the early 1960s, quickly took control of the situation. Pulling a knife out of his boot, and with Laine in tow, he wandered over to the bar. The pair flanked the now flustered wannabe thug, who began to protest his innocence, claiming it had all been a misunderstood joke. Laine and McCullough quickly wrestled him to the floor and searched him, producing no weapon. As soon as they let him go, the youth scrambled to his feet and took off into the night.

In McCullough's opinion, it was "one of those incidents that happens a thousand times on a Saturday night in any given city. I felt very protective of Paul because of his vulnerability. . . . He needed a strong helping hand from whoever was around him."

It was four dates into the Swedish leg, in the west coastal city of Gothenburg, when trouble really hit. On Thursday, August 10, at the Scandinavium arena, as Wings finished the last number in their set, a fiery "Long Tall Sally," the power to the PA was unceremoniously cut. A line of armed policemen then appeared in the seated upper levels of the arena. "They all came shuffling round with rifles," says Henry McCullough. "We're thinking, What's going on?"

When the band tried to make their way to the dressing room, their path was aggressively blocked. Paul, Linda, and Denny Seiwell were forcefully peeled away from the others and told that they were being arrested for possession of marijuana. The McCartneys, as it transpired, had earlier that day collected a postal package containing weed, addressed to Denny Seiwell, from their hotel—unaware that they were being watched.

The scene in the concert hall quickly descended into chaos. As the police gripped the suspects more firmly than was strictly necessary, Linda shouted to tour photographer Joe Stevens to keep on taking shots. "Just get the pictures!" she yelled. One dramatic frame caught the McCartneys amid the tumult—Paul burying his head in the bosom of a distressed Linda, who was bawling furiously at the policemen. In the event, the three suspects, along with tour secretary Rebecca Hines, were dragged off for questioning.

Throughout an intense grilling, all sorts of threats were thrown at them, not least that the police would refuse to let the McCartneys and Seiwell leave until they offered their confessions. Any denials were worthless: the Swedish police had been snooping on McCartney, a known marijuana smoker since his Beatle days, since he had arrived in the country. They'd even recorded a call Linda had placed three days earlier, from Stockholm to MPL in London, arranging for two cassette boxes of weed to be posted to the band.

"Where shall they send it?" Linda could be heard asking Paul on the recording. "Do you have a copy of the itinerary?"

"Send it to Gothenburg," Paul said, "to the hotel."

It was a system that had worked until now. Henry McCullough remembers that at the beginning of the tour they'd "set off with a small bit each, and then there was weed sent from the office." In each new country, there would be an agreed destination for the band's postal drop. As a result, Jo Jo Patrie remembered, when leaving one country for another, Paul would force everyone to jettison their remaining supplies before the party reached the border. Together, they would dejectedly perform a ritual where they chucked "big handfuls" of weed over the side of the open-topped bus, as if scattering the ashes of a dear departed one.

At the police station, in the early hours of the morning, after three hours of questioning, Seiwell and the McCartneys finally admitted that the weed was theirs. It was a hefty amount—seven ounces—which revealed how heavy their intake was, considering that this was intended to last them for only the remaining two days they were to be in Sweden. The police later claimed that the three confessed that they smoked marijuana every day and were effectively addicted to it.

Ultimately they were forced to convince the authorities that the dope was for their own personal use and not for sale—the charge of intent to supply being a far more serious one than personal possession. Of course, in the end it was not difficult to persuade the police that the ex-Beatle had not become a pot dealer to help make ends meet.

Nevertheless, tour manager John Morris, likely anticipating the unwanted effects the bust would have in terms of acquiring international visas in the future, attempted to play down the situation. "Lots of people send drugs to the band," he told reporters. "They think they are doing them some kind of a favor. Instead it causes all kinds of trouble. It was simply a case of pleading guilty, paying the fine, and getting out of the city. As far as we're concerned, the whole business is finished." The three were fined a total of $1,800 and sent on their way.

The bust made the front page of the *Daily Express* in Britain the next day, with the ambiguous if unwittingly accurate headline "McCartney Fine After Police Raid Concert." Rather than being ashamed, all involved were defiant, and quietly tickled by the thought that this kind of notoriety would lend Wings an air of outlaw cool.

The day after the bust, an unrepentant Paul and Linda gave an interview to the *Daily Mail,* published under the provocative splash "Why I Smoke Pot—by Paul."

"You can tell everyone that we're not changing our lives for anyone," he stressed. "We smoke grass and we like it, and that's why someone sent it to us in an envelope. At the end of the day, most people go home and have a whisky. Well, we play a gig and we're exhausted, and Linda and I prefer to put our kids to bed, sit down together and smoke a joint. That doesn't mean we're heavily into drugs or anything. You can't expect us to pretend we don't smoke for the sake of our fans. But now that I've been caught, I'll say, 'Yeah, it's true.'

"We're not the kind of people who can't go on without it," he added, perhaps disingenuously. "We wouldn't be on tour if we were."

In the wake of the arrest, Linda clearly now saw herself and Paul as pro-pot campaigners, publicly arguing the case for marijuana use. "Every time we appear in public and people see that we are smoking hash or pot, it'll make things just a bit easier for an ordinary person," she stated. "I'd love to be one of the reasons for people changing their minds about soft drugs. But people must lead their own lives. They must make up their own minds. And I know that Paul and I like weed. To us, it's just like nothing, and when other people share that point of view, I'll be happy."

Paul, however, ended the interview on a slightly resigned and unhappy note. "We're just easy people who like to smoke if we can," he offered. "But now that's out of the question, and I'm sorry."

In reality, as Denny Seiwell recalls, despite the McCartneys' professed contrition, the band's dope supplies were quietly replenished by a local source in Lund. This, more than anything, spotlights Paul and Linda's outlook at the time on marijuana and the laws that prevented them from smoking it. By scoring more weed the very day after they'd been so publicly busted, the couple clearly showed that they were unrepentant.

If there was a trace of arrogance to be detected in all of this, it was surely rooted in the fact that the Beatles had enjoyed almost diplomatic immunity when crossing international borders. Now that the untouchable Fabs were over, though, gone too were those privileges. And so this carefree (and careless) way of dealing with their fondness for dope was, as the decade progressed, to cause the McCartneys problems time and time again.

Five weeks later, in Argyll, Norman McPhee, a police constable from Campbeltown, fresh from a drug identification course among the bright lights of Glasgow, decided to have a nose around the vacant High Park Farm. Following the publicity that surrounded the Swedish bust, he was looking for anything suspicious, on the premise that he was checking the security of the property. Peering through the glass of the McCart-neys' greenhouse, among the tomato plants, he spied cultivations of an altogether more exotic nature, bearing the distinctive serrated leaves he had recently been taught to recognize.

He left, taking with him a couple of the plants to have them checked out back at the police station in the town. When they were positively identified as marijuana, McPhee returned to the farm with seven col-leagues, and they found more plants at the Low Ranachan property. Once the search was completed, the police had collected five tiny plants, the product of which would have amounted to very little weed.

It was beginning to look like open season on the apparently lawless McCartneys, who were back in London at Cavendish Avenue when they were given the news. Worse, Paul's lawyer in Scotland, Len Murray, had heard that the raid had been prompted by a local tip-off. Three days after this second bust, on September 20, McCartney was charged in ab-sentia on three counts—two of possessing marijuana and a third of growing it.

Paul was now viewed as a notoriously open dope smoker. From 1965 on, the Beatles had used the drug to spark their imaginations, but McCartney admits that, in creative terms, by the early 1970s, it had begun to have the opposite effect at times, leaving him lost in clouds of indecision. "In songwriting," he says, "the amount of times I have got stuck on a word that really didn't matter. . . . It was absolutely inconse-quential what the word was—it could've been 'boot' or 'chump.' It did not matter, y'know. And you just totally come to a grinding halt, so the song never gets finished. I had a lot of that through substance misuse."

There remained flashes of real inspiration in McCartney's song-writing, however. One day, talking to former Apple Records head Ron Kass, Paul mentioned his previously unspoken ambition to write the theme for a James Bond film. Kass said that he knew the Bond produc-ers, Harry Saltzman and Albert "Cubby" Broccoli, and that he was sure they would love the idea of the former Beatle penning the title song for the next movie. The connection duly made, and with the producers more than agreeable to the idea, McCartney was given a copy of the book *Live and Let Die,* which he read one Saturday in October 1972 before starting and finishing the song the following day.

Paul says he relished the idea of being commissioned to write to order. "As a writer who thinks of himself as part craftsman," he says, "the idea is akin to being asked to make a bit of furniture for the national collection or something. Y'know, there's a prestige thing. There was for me, anyway." Working the title into the lyrics was the trickiest part of the process for him. "I thought, live and let die . . . okay, really what they mean is live and let live, and there's the switch. So I came at it from the very obvious angle. I just thought, When you were younger you used to say that, but now you say this. So it just found its way easily into a song, really."

The gorgeously atmospheric ballad, mined with explosive uptempo instrumental passages, was to prove one of McCartney's most enduring creations, revealing that he worked best perhaps when given a directive or challenge or, as in his partnership with Lennon, a spot of friendly rivalry. The song was quickly recorded with Wings at Morgan Studios in Willesden the next week, with its dynamic orchestration added later by George Martin at his studio, AIR Studios, in Oxford Circus.

Once the work was completed, Martin flew to Jamaica with an acetate of "Live and Let Die" to play for Saltzman. The film producer was impressed but, mistaking the recording for a demo, casually wondered aloud who Martin and McCartney were planning on asking to sing on the master. It was down to the diplomatic Martin to point out that this was indeed the final version. "I think they were looking for Shirley Bassey," laughs Paul. "Burly Chassis."

The same week they recorded "Live and Let Die" at Morgan, Wings laid down their next single, "Hi Hi Hi," a shuffling rocker and seemingly blatant paean to the wonders of smoking dope. Paul felt that the lyrics invited interpretation, in much the same mischievously playful way as the "everybody must get stoned" double entendre of Bob Dylan's "Rainy Day Women Nos. 12 & 35." "It was like, 'Ooh, what does Dylan mean?'" says McCartney. "'Does he mean you get high? Or does he mean getting stoned, like getting drunk?' So there was the ambiguity, and I assumed the same would apply to me."

He was soon to learn that it didn't. Upon its release in the first week of December 1972, "Hi Hi Hi" was instantly banned by both Radio 1 and Radio 2. Ironically, however, it wasn't the apparent drug reference that got it blacklisted but an innocent line sexually misconstrued. The song's publisher, Northern Songs, had sent a wrongly typed lyric sheet to the radio stations, someone having misheard the abstract innuendo of the line "Get ready for my polygon" as "Get ready for my body gun."

That month, Paul's trial for the High Park Farm bust was set for March of the following year. And so, for McCartney, 1972 was characterized by two drug busts and two banned singles. Interviewed at the close of the year, Denny Laine looked ahead to the upcoming twelve months with a quote that, in retrospect, would seem loaded with unintended portent.

"The next year is really going to be exciting for Wings," he frothed. "A lot of amazing stuff is bound to happen."

La Mamounia—its name means "safe haven" in Arabic—is one of the most exclusive hotels in Marrakech. Once described by Winston Churchill, who regularly spent his winters there, as "the most lovely spot in the world," it was a destination of choice for Charlie Chaplin, Charlton Heston, and Alfred Hitchcock, who in 1956 used it as a central location for his James Stewart and Doris Day film *The Man Who Knew Too Much*.

Bucking his reputation for extreme thriftiness, it was to La Mamounia in February 1973 that Paul McCartney took his Wings bandmates, treating them to a two-week Moroccan holiday. The musicians swam or loafed around the pool, strummed acoustic guitars, meandered through the hotel's twenty acres of citrus trees and olive groves, and went on long camel treks in the deserts outside the city.

Ever productive, Paul spent the time writing songs for the next Wings album. "Then it would be 'Wait till you hear this, lads,'" Henry recalls. "It was a lovely place to be. It was also another bonding period. It was as much a holiday as Wings Over Europe was."

Paul returned to face his trial at Campbeltown Sheriff Court. Clearly keen to waste no more time than was necessary on this jaunt north, the McCartneys hired a private plane to fly them to RAF Machrihanish. When they emerged from the plane, their lawyer, John McCluskey, immediately noticed that Linda appeared "stoned out of her mind." Arriving at the court, Paul seemed keen to treat the proceedings with something approaching respect, while his wife clearly saw it all as a bit of a laugh.

Once the trial got under way, McCluskey presented McCartney's flimsy defense: he had received the seeds in the post from a fan and, curious, had naïvely planted them. The attorney told the court that McCartney's innocence could be proven by the fact that no attempt whatsoever had been made to conceal the plants. This argument seemed to sway the judge, Sheriff Donald McDiarmid, who gave McCartney a £100 fine and allowed him fourteen days to pay it, prompting an outburst of open laughter in the courtroom. Speaking to a reporter in an anteroom immediately afterward, Paul said that, if jailed, he had planned to pass his prison time writing songs. Typically ebullient, and a touch relieved, he described the judge as "a great guy."

Stepping out of the court building, the McCartneys were interviewed by a Scottish television reporter. Paul, in gray suit with a white scarf swept rakishly over his left shoulder, his haircut now a proto-mullet, was faux-sincere, peppering his statements with knowing smiles. Linda, wearing a bowler hat pinched from McCluskey, and looking like a toddler emerging triumphant from the dressing-up box, giggled by his side.

"It was said that those seeds had been sent to you," noted the reporter. "How did you come to grow them?"

"Yeah, well, we got a load of seeds, y'know," Paul replied, fixing the reporter with his doe eyes, playing the innocent wee laddie. "Kind of in the post. And we didn't know what they were, y'know. And we kind of planted them all and five of them came up, like . . ." He paused, trying not to laugh, smiling impishly. "Five of them came up illegal."

"Now, of course, this conviction," the reporter went on, "it might affect your entry to the States, where you have considerable business interests. How do you feel about that?"

"Well, y'know, I understand that I might not get stopped from going into the States," Paul went on, looking entirely unruffled. "I hope not, anyway."

Around the same time, a different legal pothole was finally smoothed over. In February, Lew Grade of Associated Television had tracked Paul down in Morocco and sent over an emissary with an unusual offer to settle their legal tussle over his post-Beatles songwriting partnership with Linda. If McCartney would make an hour-long television special for the company, the $1 million lawsuit would be dropped. Paul immediately agreed to the deal. The resulting program, titled *James Paul*

McCartney, was an ambitious affair, the first time since the misunderstood and derided *Magical Mystery Tour* that a major pop act had attempted a prime-time TV special.

Still, when filming began, it seemed as if the grand concepts dreamed up for the show might be upended by hubris. On March 10, 1973, shooting on location on Hampstead Heath, in North London, the band mimed to the perhaps better buried "Mary Had a Little Lamb." It was a bizarre performance, with the band dressed all in white—save for Denny Seiwell in unsportingly beige trousers—and looking like piously virginal New England pioneers. The musicians arranged themselves under a weeping willow as Paul sat pawing away at an electric piano among a flock of actual sheep. Linda, done up like a crinoline-skirted Royal Doulton milkmaid figurine come to life, swung back and forth on a tree swing over a pond, singing and bashing a tambourine. Later, the group marched the sheep over a bridge, then juggled themselves into a rowboat for a leisurely bob on the water.

All the members of Wings appeared entirely at ease with this scenario, except for Henry McCullough, who looked mortified. "I had to stand playing a mandolin, dressed in white trousers and a white shirt," he says, cringing. "The shepherd had the sheep running round our feet. It was just a bit strange."

There was worse to come. In the tradition of "Your Mother Should Know" from *Magical Mystery Tour,* Paul further indulged his song-and-dance-man fantasies in a Busby Berkeley–flavored routine called "Gotta Sing—Gotta Dance," in which dozens of dancers appeared in vertically divided half-male, half-female costumes: part slick-haired 1930s gent, part blond-locked showgirl. An oily-mulleted and fake-mustachioed Paul fronted the routine, tap-dancing in glittery golden shoes and a pink suit with tails. As daft and camp as it was intended to be, the result looked hopelessly out of step with the shaggy, bell-bottomed fashions of 1973.

But it turned out that McCartney had shied away from an even grander transformation: "At one point I was gonna be in drag and do a full-blown impersonation of Diana Ross. But as the moment grew nearer and wardrobe started to measure me for the frock and get all serious with the wig and stuff, I started to bottle out." When the show's U.S. sponsors got wind of the fact that the singer was planning to go tranny for TV, they warned him to back down. "Luckily this telegram came from the conservative Chevrolet people, who said, 'Under no account must McCartney do drag impression of Diana Ross. We'll pull funding if he does.' "

The special wasn't all bad. It opened with Wings performing "Big Barn Bed"—the throwaway if grooving opening track from *Red Rose Speedway,* which would be released under the more commercially viable name Paul McCartney and Wings in May—in front of a futuristic bank of televisions. Later in the show, an impressively atmospheric, surreal clip for "Uncle Albert" started with a long shot of Paul scribbling solutions into a newspaper crossword and Linda making tea, as distortedly filmed through a fish-eye lens. The picture melted into forks of lightning and dark, thunderous clouds before fading into rows of *Stepford Wives*–like female typists working in a bureau. The camera passed through a throng of old men, all talking into curly-corded brown telephone receivers, before a "straight" bespectacled and besuited McCartney appeared, sitting behind a typewriter, sadly replacing a phone on its cradle as the song ended. It was evocative stuff and richly redolent of the Beatles.

Elsewhere, there was a live recording of "Live and Let Die," filmed at Elstree Studios in Hertfordshire, along with the other full-band "concert" segments shot before an audience. This performance of the Bond theme proved more explosive than intended, however, when pyrotechnics stuffed inside a dummy balsa-wood piano turned out to be far more powerful than anticipated. When the detonation occurred, at the end of the song, it threw McCartney back on his piano stool, lifted Henry McCullough clean off his feet, and sent chunks of burning wood flying into the air and raining down on the shocked orchestra members.

The most misguided section of the program, however, came with the footage filmed in a dockside pub, the Chelsea Reach, in Wallasey, Merseyside, where Paul's extended family and friends had been invited for a boozy party for the benefit of the cameras. The idea was clearly for Paul to show off his working-class roots. But Linda, for one, wasn't keen on her husband presenting himself as a booze-chugging man of the people. "She had such a go at Paul over that," says Robert Ellis, who had become Wings' official photographer. He remembers Paul arguing long and hard about wanting to shoot this sequence. "In the end, they filmed it, and everybody in that thing is just cringing."

It did make for uncomfortable viewing in its painful staged encounters with Paul's relatives, including his father, Jim, and aunt Gin. "I'm the only one paying for drinks here this evening," Paul stiffly jokes, sipping a whiskey and Coke and puffing on a Senior Service before tapping his dad for a fiver. "Isn't it terrible?" he said later. "I'd come without me money." As the drink flows, the packed partygoers, and even Paul, visibly unwind and break into spirited sing-alongs of "April Showers" and "Pack Up Your Troubles in Your Old Kit-Bag."

The members of Wings mingle with the crowd, sipping nutty brown ales from dimpled pint glasses—though, in Henry McCullough's case, worryingly overdoing it. The guitarist vaguely remembers that Paul, possibly now seeing his bandmate as something of a liability because of his increased drinking, had McCullough stay with one of the McCartney relatives.

"Get Henry out of the fucking way," says McCullough. "Maybe it was the right place for me at the time." The evening ended with the guitarist having a shouting match with his wife, then somehow losing his shoes and wandering, in a fancy rhinestone-studded coat, lost and confused, through the streets of nearby Liverpool. "I plodded in my bare feet with this jacket that was flashing all over the place," he dimly recalls. "I was crawling to get home."

When *James Paul McCartney* aired in the United States, on Monday, April 16, 1973—it premiered in the United Kingdom on ITV nearly a month later—John Lennon was watching at home in New York. He later commented, with notable warmth and tact, "I liked parts of Paul's TV special, especially the intro. The bit filmed in Liverpool made me squirm a bit. But Paul's a pro. He always has been."

The critics were brutal, however. *Melody Maker* denounced the program as "overblown and silly." Linda's former friend Lillian Roxon, reviewing it in the New York *Daily News,* comprehensively savaged it and its participants, slagging Mrs. McCartney's various hairdos, calling Paul "sweaty, pudgy, slack-mouthed," and loftily, if perhaps revealingly, announcing, "I can tell you right now, she didn't marry a millionaire Beatle to end up in a Liverpool saloon singing with middle-aged women called Mildred."

In interviews from the time, Paul stuck up for himself and the TV special, saying he'd received a wave of fan letters posted from remote locations in America after it was shown, the subtext being that it had touched the kind of ordinary people that snooty critics would never understand. "The funny thing was, only the hip people didn't like it," he pointed out. "But we got millions of letters from mid-America saying they loved the show."

More illuminatingly, he confessed to occasionally feeling burdened. "Sometimes I feel as if I have a ten-ton weight on my shoulders," he said, before shrugging off this statement with characteristic good cheer. "There's many a person has committed suicide over the fact that his special wasn't so good," he added. "But I wouldn't give a crap."

Still, even Linda felt it was "a terribly unsure period." Paul himself admitted that sometimes he'd come home from Wings rehearsals with the nagging feeling that "it's not right, we could do much more." He was, he allowed, "a born worrier." Linda described *Red Rose Speedway*, which had been recorded in protracted sessions throughout the previous year, as "such a non-confident record."

"I don't remember a lot about it, actually," Paul now says of *Red Rose Speedway*. "I think the fact that I don't remember it too well bears that out."

The album certainly had its moments—the strident rocker "Get on the Right Thing"; the rolling Pink Floyd–echoing instrumental "Loup (1st Indian on the Moon)"; the dreamily strummed ballad "Little Lamb Dragonfly," inspired by a neighboring farmer at High Park bringing a near-frozen lamb to the McCartneys for them to nurse. "He knew we were softhearted," says Paul. "He wasn't sure it was gonna survive, so we took it in and warmed it up and fed it and it did survive."

To close the record, McCartney attempted to repeat the trick the Beatles had so successfully pulled off on the second side of *Abbey Road*, knitting fragments of incomplete songs into a seamless medley. Only this time, it didn't work. The song cycle—"Hold Me Tight," "Lazy Dynamite," "Hands of Love," and "Power Cut"—was entirely forgettable, even to its creator. "I don't remember it," he confesses.

The fact that *Red Rose Speedway* was slimmed down to a single album from a planned double spoke volumes. "Double albums are notoriously hard to pull off," McCartney remarks. "If you've just got loads and loads of top, top material, then that's the way to go. And I think you can see that by pulling the songs into a medley at the end, maybe I didn't think I had loads and loads of top material."

There was, however, one unarguable standout on *Red Rose Speedway*. "My Love" was a magnificent McCartney ballad in the vein of "The Long and Winding Road" and "Let It Be," confidently recorded live with an orchestra at Abbey Road. It was also notable for a last-minute musical mutiny from Henry McCullough that produced the song's beautifully liquid, entirely improvised guitar solo.

"I was ready to put on a guitar solo along with the orchestra," says McCullough, "and whatever it was that was suggested to me to play, I wouldn't play it. I just said to Paul, 'Look, y'know, I'm changing the solo.' And he says, 'Well, what are you going to play?' I said, 'I have no idea.'"

"I had to make a decision," says McCartney. "Either it was like, 'No, stick to the script.' Or, it was 'Do I believe in this guy?' Yeah. And he played the solo, which had come right out of the blue. I'd never heard it before. And I just thought, Fucking great."

"The orchestra started and I hit a lick and that was it," says Henry. "I put my guitar down and I went into the control room and I knew that I'd either hit the jackpot or else it was shite. But if that had've been the case, then I would've withdrawn my horns. Anyway, I got lucky. To capture a solo like that in one take in a studio . . . it was just a stroke of luck, a gift from God really, and you get that in music."

The increased respect Henry had earned from Paul with this spontaneous move was soon to be destroyed, however. Filming a performance of "My Love" for *Top of the Pops,* the guitarist, suffering the ill effects of his imbibing, threw up onstage, sickening and embarrassing Paul.

Nevertheless, in May, Wings headed off around the country on their debut theater tour of the United Kingdom, the first scheduled jaunt in Britain by any of the Beatles since 1966. Further underlining the idea that Paul felt like a variety-show turn, the bill included a hoop-throwing juggler. Interviewed backstage in Newcastle, McCartney enthused about the wonders of modern touring—better planning, improved sound systems—and indicated that he wanted to do a lot more of it. "It hasn't ground me into the ground, anyway," he said.

The McCartneys were now almost becoming part of the showbiz establishment. After a sold-out three-night run at the Hammersmith Odeon, they threw a party in the reception hall of the Café Royal, where Paul starrily duetted with Elton John, and they attended the premiere of *Live and Let Die,* Paul wearing a tuxedo and bow tie but, wackily, no shirt.

Wings, finally, appeared to be stabilizing. One of the comments around this time, from the increasingly dissatisfied Henry McCullough, told an entirely different story, though.

"I don't suppose we'll be together forever," he mused dolefully. "I'm sure Paul's got more of a tie to the Beatles. Wings has all the makings of a great group, but our battle is to not let it fall apart, as it could so easily do."

6

PANIC IN LAGOS

You put together a really strong set of songs for the Band on the Run *album. Did you feel that yourself?*

Yeah, I thought they were a pretty strong set of songs. I think at this point I was getting it a bit more together. I'd been through the sort of raw stages of Wings. I was now settling with the idea of it.

As THE NOSE OF THE JET DIPPED on its approach into Lagos, Paul began to get the jitters. Invited into the cockpit to witness the landing, he heard an unsettling exchange between the pilots. Flying low over a thick, misty carpet of jungle, the captain began searching in vain for the airport, turning to his copilot and wondering aloud, "Is that it down there?" McCartney was thinking, Oh my God, *they* must know.

There was already much on Paul's mind. The night before, in London, he had received a phone call giving him news he really didn't want to hear: Denny Seiwell was quitting the band and wouldn't be coming on the planned recording expedition to Nigeria the following day. Compounding the agony, two weeks earlier, Wings had suffered the first split in its ranks, when Henry McCullough had angrily walked out on the band. Virtually overnight, Wings had gone from being a sturdy quintet to an apparently shaky trio composed of Paul, Linda, and Denny Laine.

———

Behind their happy hippie-family façade, the discontent within Wings had been stewing for some time. For all McCartney's protestations and gestures to the contrary, the supposedly democratic band was in reality little more than an autocracy. Even the compliant Denny Laine would get irked anytime one of his friends asked after the guitarist's "boss." "He wasn't really my boss," he now insists. "He was just a mate I knew for many years before I even joined Wings. But I allowed him to be the boss. That was fine by me."

Henry McCullough, meanwhile, had become increasingly disgruntled. After he'd appeared unannounced with jazz singer Carol Grimes at the Roundhouse in London, a newspaper review the next day mentioned that the guitarist had played on a few songs at the gig. When McCartney found out about this, he took McCullough to one side and pointed out that he was on a retainer with Wings. "Paul said, 'Look, Henry, I'm paying the wages. And when I pay the wages, you don't play for anybody else.'"

Then one week Henry received his pay slip and noticed that his £70 retainer had been docked £40 for the rental of an amp. "That's not just tight," he laughs. "That's *welded*, that is. I had to pay for the hire of an amp to fucking play alongside Paul McCartney."

The guitarist had grown tired of McCartney forcing him to play the same parts over and over, and felt creatively shackled. "It's like being in a show band," McCullough moaned. Denny Laine had long seen the rift coming, noting that Henry essentially wanted to get stoned and rip through lengthy blues solos—which, given Paul's inherent pop sensibilities, was always going to make for an awkward fit. "He had some musical differences with Henry," says Denny Seiwell. "Henry was at a tough point in his life. It probably was the beginning of the demise."

On the upside, the songs Paul had written for the third Wings album were clearly shaping up to be the best of his post-Beatles career. Keen to hole up far from the London music business, he, Linda, and the band once again escaped to High Park. Running a generator in the unheated barn at Low Ranachan, over the hill, the band set up a makeshift practice space, with Paul and Linda, in rural-hippie style, arriving at rehearsals every day on horseback.

McCullough, though, was beginning to air his frustrations through his playing. The guitarist would dutifully ape the riffs written by McCartney, then continually change them from one run-through to another, frustrating the bandleader. While Paul, missing the camaraderie of the Beatles, was eager on some levels to mold Wings in their image—with intraband banter and jokey jams and all hands on the mixing desk in the studio—he clearly still reserved the power of veto over the ultimate musical decisions.

"Let's be honest—he wanted to be in a band in a *sense*," Laine says. "But he would still have the final call."

"The thing is, if you come out of the Beatles and you go into another group, you're not just anyone," Paul argues. "You're the guy out of the Beatles. It was just natural for me to try and run the band in the way that I saw fit. I'm not trying to avoid the fact that I was the boss."

Tensions between Paul and Henry escalated. "He didn't really like the music that much," says Laine of the latter. "He was rebelling a lot and also drinking a lot, too." During one afternoon's rehearsal, McCartney recalls, he asked McCullough "to play something he didn't really fancy playing." Henry argued that the part "couldn't be played." Paul became rattled. "I knew that it *could* be played," he says. "Rather than let it pass, I decided to confront him with it."

Once the session was over, Laine and the defiant guitarist disappeared to a pub in Campbeltown and downed a few pints, the effects of which further emboldened McCullough to stand up to his boss. He returned, lightly refreshed, to the rehearsal barn. "I'd had a couple of drinks," says Henry. "I wasn't falling down. But I was angry because I had drink in me."

An argument broke out between the two that ended with each shouting "Fuck you!" at the other. Face-to-face with the incensed Irishman, Paul became a "bit choked," stormed out of the rehearsal room, and huffed his way back to High Park. Henry sat alone in the barn, raging. "Something had been cut," he says. "Or was just about to be cut. I think he left it to me to make up my mind, and that's what I did." McCullough dumped his guitar and amp in the back of his car and angrily revved away, never to return. "If I hadn't got out then, I think I would have been sacked," he says. "It was the most unprofessional thing I've ever done in my life. I was driving off the edge of a cliff."

Now, two weeks later, Denny Seiwell had followed. In his tense phone call to McCartney, the drummer told Paul that he felt that the band wasn't ready to record after McCullough's departure. What's more, even though he accepted that McCartney's finances were tied up in the ongoing dispute with the other Beatles over the fate of Apple Records, he couldn't exist any longer on the retainer he was receiving from Wings. "We worked for seventy pounds a week," Seiwell says. "But I was making two thousand a week in New York as a session guy."

For the drummer, money had been a constant bugbear. While on tour, the band members were forced to pay their own expenses, meaning they'd often return home broke. During Wings' downtime, Seiwell was sometimes forced to fly to New York to play a few top-up studio sessions just so he could settle his American Express bill. The drummer reckons that, having been fiscally cosseted during his Beatle years, McCartney wasn't in touch with the realities of financing a band.

"It wasn't just being stingy," he says. "Y'know, the Beatles made fifty pounds a week in their pay packet. But if they wanted a house or a car, they went and they signed for it and Apple picked it up. But cash money in your pocket? You got fifty quid a week.

"And this was only a couple of years later, so we got a raise," he laughs. "But we couldn't sign for a house or a car. I had to go to Barclays bank and borrow three thousand pounds to buy an old, beat-up Mercedes to run around London."

Gallingly, perhaps, in May Paul bought himself a Lamborghini and went on holiday to Jamaica. The loyal Denny Laine was happier with his lot: he was playing guitar with a Beatle, and he had a one-bedroom flat in London now, whereas only two years earlier he'd been crashing in his manager's office. During the rehearsals in Scotland, Paul, rewarding Laine's loyalty, pulled him tighter into the firm. The pair had climbed a hillside to smoke a joint at sunset when McCartney offered to share the royalties with him on the next album, telling him, according to Jo Jo Patrie, "Just think, man, you'll get, like, quarter of a million." It was no coincidence, either, that this was the same month the band was due to leave for Lagos and that Jo Jo had given birth to the couple's first son, Laine Hines, at Campbeltown Hospital.

Seiwell, for his part, was getting sick of being broke and at the beck and call of the McCartneys. "I should've sat down with him and said, 'Look, I need some sort of a document, a written agreement on paper as to what my share of this band is.' You're playing with a Beatle, for fuck's sake. And you're one of the top bands in the world. You're on call twenty-four hours a day. Whatever needs doing, whether it's photo

shoots or press interviews or rehearsals or recording or special appearances at TV shows. It just wasn't right."

When Seiwell told Paul he'd had enough and that he wasn't coming
to Africa the following day, McCartney was initially stunned. Then he
boiled over into rage.

"I got off the phone," he fumes, "and I just thought, Well, thanks,
nice. Thanks for letting me know in plenty of time. Then I just thought,
Right, we'll show you."

Having been ensconced within Abbey Road Studios during his time
in the Beatles, Paul was increasingly drawn to the idea of recording on
location. Knowing that EMI, whose slogan boasted that it was "the
greatest recording organisation in the world," had studio facilities dotted around the globe, he had staff at the label draw him up a list of their
locations. For a time he mulled over whether the band should decamp to
Bombay, Beijing, or Rio de Janeiro. But, given his burgeoning interest in
African rhythms—and a vague notion that the trip could in essence become an intensely creative working holiday—he settled on Lagos.

"We thought, Great . . . lie on the beach all day, doing nothing," he
says. "Breeze into the studios and record. It didn't turn out like that."

Once their plane had safely touched down in Lagos, on August 30, 1973,
the Wings party—Paul and Linda and the kids, Denny Laine and engineer Geoff Emerick—suffered severe culture shock. It was the monsoon
season in Nigeria, characterized by heavy storms and oppressive heat.
Given the McCartneys' freewheeling ways, no one had thought to check
the weather forecast.

A forbidding military presence greeted them at Ikeja's airport. Machine gun–toting soldiers, under the rule of General Yakubu Gowon,
who had violently seized power seven years earlier, in 1966, stone-
facedly stalked the terminal. In the summer of 1973, Nigeria remained
a hazardous, volatile location. Only three years before, the country had
been riven by civil war, which had led to almost three million casualties,
whether through the direct effects of the conflict or its grim, lasting
hangover of disease and starvation.

It quickly became apparent to the group that Lagos was in chaos.
Hurtling to the studio through the alarming traffic, Laine was shocked

when he saw a man knocked off his moped and apparently killed, with no one batting an eyelid. "Life don't mean shit over here," he noted. Moreover, shit was literally floating through the streets, in open sewers. Emerick kept seeing figures wrapped in sheets and bandages. His driver calmly informed him that they were lepers.

Then the group was met with the sobering vision of the studio itself: essentially a sizable shed set two streets back from Lagos Lagoon on Wharf Road, in the port of Apapa. The studio manager and the tape operator, who Paul was utterly charmed to discover were respectively named Odion and Monday, welcomed the party.

Although the studio boasted top-grade cast-off equipment from other EMI facilities around the world, it was in a woeful state. A subsequent search eventually located the microphone collection, stuffed into an old cardboard box. When no sonic screens to isolate the musicians' equipment could be found, they were quickly built to order. Under McCartney's direction, Odion and Monday were sent out to find wood and Perspex. On their return, Paul picked up a saw to give the pair a quick lesson in studio carpentry.

Even more surprisingly, through a soundproofed door at the back of the control room was a noisy pressing plant, housed in a lean-to shack, where Nigerian EMI employees stood ankle-deep in rainwater leaking through a corrugated roof as the smell of plastic filled the air.

Rather than stay in a hotel, the group had booked into a villa complex in Ikeja, on the edge of Lagos and an hour's drive from the studio, with the McCartneys and their three daughters in one cabin and Laine and Emerick in another. The guitarist was amazed when, the morning after their arrival, he drew open the blinds to discover that a traveling African market had set up on their front lawn, selling camels and other native livestock.

The prankster in Laine enjoyed teasing the arachnophobic Emerick by leaving choice selections from the house's dead spider display in the engineer's bed. Sufficiently tormented, the producer decamped to a cheap hotel, where he slept in a room overrun by cockroaches. Back at the villa, the McCartney daughters would chase translucent lizards around the exotic gardens in fits of giggles, catching them and collecting them in a large cage they proudly displayed to everyone.

The band and crew soon settled into these alien surroundings. Keen to start every working day with a swim, Paul was given temporary membership at a local country club in return for signing a photo of the Beatles hanging on its bar wall. McCartney's international celebrity soon began to attract invitations: to a moonlit party on a nearby island where everyone was offered a buffet of local delicacies that included slices of oversized African snail; to dinner at the house of Chief Moshood Abiola, future president-elect and then chief executive of the ITT Corporation, which was in charge of developing the country's sanitation systems.

Only days into the trip, however, the McCartneys were given a rude reminder of the volatile environment in which they had placed themselves.

Wandering through the supposedly security-patrolled complex back to their own villa from Laine's after a post-studio listening party, they were surprised to see a car draw up beside them. The driver rolled down his window and offered the McCartneys a lift. Paul smiled and told the driver no thanks, they were happy to walk. The vehicle then motored twenty yards up the road and stopped, whereupon its doors flew open and its five passengers jumped out and walked quickly toward Paul and Linda. One—a short, stocky Nigerian, Paul remembers—produced a knife, which he pointed at the singer's throat.

A horrified Linda screamed, "Don't kill him, he's a musician!" Her husband, sensibly, handed over his wallet, camera, and bag—containing cassettes of his new songs—to the robbers.

"We'd been told not to walk around," says Paul. "But we were just slightly hippie. Hey, don't worry, feel good and it's all right. So we got mugged. Crazy. All my recordings went and those were all the songs I'd written. The joke is, I'm sure the fellas who took it wouldn't know what it was. They probably recorded over it all."

As the car sped off, the McCartneys were left stunned. Only when they made it back to their villa did the full realization of the horror of the incident begin to sink in. Their shock intensified when the villa was suddenly plunged into darkness. The pair, shaken and paranoid, believed the thugs had followed them home and tampered with the lights, when in reality it was only one of the city's regular power outages. The couple retreated to bed, pulled the covers over their heads, and hoped they would wake in the morning.

The next day, in the studio, the McCartneys were informed by the locals that the situation had in fact been even more dangerous than they'd imagined. A local hood called Crazy Joe, whose story had made it into the pages of *Life* magazine, had recently been publicly executed by the Nigerian police. If they had been black, Paul and Linda were told, they would almost certainly have been killed, since it was now a practice of Nigerian muggers to murder their victims, rather than leaving them alive as potential witnesses. It was only because of the color of their skins that their lives had been spared, apparently, since most robbers believed that white people found it impossible to distinguish between or accurately describe the features of black criminals.

"Really," Laine says, "that's the only reason they didn't kill them."

Having lost the tapes, McCartney frantically tried to remember the songs he'd written, relying on what he called his "Beatle training" from the days when he and Lennon, with no access to portable recorders, would have to commit a song to memory. The storming "Jet," the sing-along "Mrs. Vandebilt" and the mantra-like "Mamunia" all sprang readily to mind, but many of the others had to be reconstructed, as Emerick put it, "on the fly." Some verses of "Band on the Run," for instance, were tweaked to reflect the group's current circumstances, stuck inside the four walls of the small, cell-like studio, faced with grim uncertainty.

True to his upbeat nature, though, McCartney threw himself into the recording process, moving from drums to bass to guitar to the microphone with ease. And Linda's contributions to the music—even if only simple keyboard parts and the gentle harmonies that she, Denny, and Paul used to color the arrangements—showed vast improvement from her tentative early days working with her husband. Paul had grown to live with the criticisms of his wife's performances, although they still rankled. "It was like *oil* off a duck's back," he says. "Bit harder to shift."

If outwardly Paul was projecting utter confidence, there were other signs that inside he remained troubled.

One Friday afternoon, a fortnight into the sessions, while enthusiastically laying down a vocal, he suddenly turned white and started gasping for breath. He stumbled outside to find some air.

At the studio door, in the brutal heat, McCartney collapsed. For the second time in as many weeks, Linda was faced with the terrifying prospect of her husband's life being in danger. "I laid him on the ground," she said. "His eyes were closed and I thought he was dead."

Geoff Emerick shouted to the studio manager to call an ambulance. Given the parlous state of the Nigerian emergency services, however, it was swiftly decided that it would make more sense to take McCartney to the hospital in the manager's car. The star was unceremoniously bundled into the backseat and driven away. Back at the studio, Emerick and Laine halfheartedly continued work, nervously waiting for news.

Later that afternoon, Linda called the studio from the hospital to tell the others that Paul was recovering. For his part, McCartney remembers his return to consciousness as "floaty" and strangely pleasant. The diagnosis was that the singer had suffered a bronchial spasm caused by excessive smoking. Viewed from another angle, the incident also bore all the hallmarks of a weed-induced panic attack.

In the circumstances, it would be understandable if strong Nigerian weed had heightened the singer's paranoia. On one key night out, it undoubtedly had that effect.

As much as the band could try to block out their disquietingly exotic environment during their studio hours, any attempt to cut loose during their downtime only served to remind them of just how far they were from home.

One evening the party decided to visit the Shrine, the open-air club on the outskirts of town owned by Fela Kuti, the self-styled tribal leader of the Nigerian music scene. Only three years before, Kuti had returned to Nigeria from a U.S. tour, freshly politicized, having been inspired by the burgeoning Black Power movement in California and a reading of *The Autobiography of Malcolm X.* Renaming his Koola Lobitos band Africa '70, he had formed the Kalakuta Republic, a communal compound–cum–recording studio where he could hang out and get high with his entourage while practicing polygamy with an expanding collection of wives.

The musician was already gaining a reputation as something of a folk hero through his championing of Lagos's underclass, not least with his free health clinic set up at the Kalakuta Republic. At the same time, his brazen spouting of anti-government views in his music and his provocative newspaper advertising columns had caused the authorities to single him out as a dangerous radical.

Into this charged atmosphere stepped the McCartneys. At the Shrine, potent spliffs began doing the rounds at their table. Paul suddenly felt adrift in this unfamiliar environment: "We were a bit over-wasted, and I got the screaming paranoias, being in this place on the outskirts of Lagos with absolutely no one we knew."

Some of Kuti's musicians joined the McCartneys at their table, and the mood turned nasty. The ex-Beatle, already uneasy in his altered state, soon found himself being interrogated as to exactly why he'd come to Nigeria to record, the insinuation being that he was there to plunder African sounds. "It was very heavy," says Paul. Later Kuti and Africa '70 took to the stage with the bandleader in a grass skirt, surrounded by a host of his similarly attired, similarly topless wives. After a lengthy buildup, the group launched into their set of stirring Afrobeat and McCartney's anxiety melted away. In a rush of relief from the "stress and craziness" of his Lagos escapade, Paul burst into tears.

In the days following the visit to the Shrine, however, Kuti tried to provoke some sense of controversy over the group's presence in Lagos, announcing on a local radio station that McCartney was here only to exploit the Afrobeat sound. A summit between the two musicians was hastily arranged.

Kuti arrived at the EMI studio, glowering bodyguards in tow, and took up a position at the back of the control room. After solemnly listening, arms folded, to some of the new work-in-progress Wings songs, he was satisfied that, the odd conga part aside, they bore no traces of Nigerian influences, and he left reassured.

"I said," Paul recalls, " 'Do us a favor, we do okay as it is, we're not pinching your music.' "

"He was trying to get money out of Paul, I suppose," reasons Denny Laine. "He wanted a piece of the action."

Kuti wasn't the only musician to be put out by Paul's visit, either. Firebrand former Cream drummer Ginger Baker, a friend of Kuti's, had one foot in the Nigerian music scene, having spent two years there building a state-of-the-art studio, ARC, near Ikeja's airport; the studio had been completed and opened only seven months earlier. On learning that the McCartneys planned to use EMI's altogether inferior facility to record rather than his own, Baker felt snubbed. "I don't know why Ginger would think we were going there to work in his studio," Laine muses. "I mean, maybe he thought he could talk us into it or something."

In the end, ever the diplomat, McCartney agreed to record one song at Baker's studio. "Just to give him a little bit of a handout," says Laine. The track, "Picasso's Last Words (Drink to Me)," had been written earlier in the year, in Jamaica, at a dinner party thrown by the McCartneys at their rented house in Montego Bay. In attendance was Dustin Hoffman, who was on the island filming the 1930s-era penal-colony escape epic *Papillon*. After the meal, throwing down a challenge, Hoffman asked McCartney if he could write a song on the spot. The actor produced a magazine with an article about the recent death of Pablo Picasso, whose last words were apparently "Drink to me, drink to my health, you know I can't drink anymore." Paul picked up a guitar and immediately began fitting a melody to the quote, thrilling Hoffman and his wife.

During the recording at ARC, to show that there were no ill feelings, Ginger Baker joined in, shaking a coffee can filled with gravel as a percussive accompaniment. Denny Laine, for one, believes that the furor stirred up by Kuti and Baker ultimately served to raise the African musician's profile in the West. "After that, he came to London with Ginger and they did all sorts of stuff," he points out. "At the end of the day, it gave him a lot of publicity. Fela Kuti would never have been as popular as he was if we hadn't gone there and done that album."

Some hostilities lingered, however, even at the party thrown by the McCartneys to mark the end of their eventful seven-week Nigerian sojourn. During the high-spirited proceedings, EMI's overseas manager casually walked over to Baker and informed him that he was set to fail in his desire to lure artists away from the company's recording setup. "We're going to screw you," he whispered ominously. "This is EMI territory."

And so the McCartneys flew back to London, triumphant and ultimately unscathed by their African adventure. As a footnote to the tale, however, Paul was unsettled upon his return to Cavendish Avenue to discover a letter from Len Wood, group director at EMI, urging him to cancel his trip to Nigeria due to an outbreak of cholera in the region.

"I wonder," says Paul, "whether I even would've taken my kids there had I known. It was quite a sort of heavy episode, really."

Four weeks later, on a cold Sunday evening in the last weekend of October 1973, Paul, Linda, and Denny stood in dark, prisoner-like garb, frozen in the glare of a searching spotlight, against a wall in Osterley Park, west London. Gathered around them, pretending to be clinging together for safety, were chummy northern chat-show host Michael Parkinson, film stars Christopher Lee and James Coburn, light entertainer Kenny Lynch, boxer John Conteh, and the hangdog, deadpan writer and TV wit Clement Freud. "It was a very odd mix," says Parkinson. "God knows how Paul chose those people."

For the cover of the Lagos album, now entitled *Band on the Run,* the McCartneys—lying one night in bed, where much of their important thinking seemed to get done—had come up with a grand *Sgt. Pepper*–like concept. In passing reference to their drug busts and the fact that they sometimes felt like renegades, they had decided to stage a mock prison break, featuring famous faces of the period. Once the calls had been placed and everyone had agreed on a date, this unlikely mob met at an Italian restaurant in Knightsbridge, where they enjoyed a long, boozy lunch.

In a room at the mansion house at Osterley Park, while everyone was getting changed for the shoot, strong joints were passed around among those partial to a puff of grass. Outside, photographer Clive Arrowsmith arranged the company in their positions and shouted instructions to them from high on a ladder, the spotlight pointing at the subjects mounted on top of a borrowed post office van. "Not knowing much about photography at the time, technically," admits Arrowsmith, "I shot it on daylight film, and it was a tungsten source, so everything goes yellow."

Even this happy accident lent something to the iconic image, which was to become almost as famous as the Beatles album cover that inspired it. Released five weeks later, *Band on the Run* was initially slow out of the traps, in commercial terms. Once it had gathered momentum, though, it was to prove unstoppable, becoming the most successful solo album by any of the ex-Beatles, making the U.S. No. 1 spot three times.

Whether intentional or not, the themes in the polished, confident-sounding *Band on the Run* were flight and freedom. In "Bluebird," winged creatures flew to desert islands and coasted on the breeze. In "Helen Wheels," which appeared only on the U.S. version of the album, the carefree McCartneys cruised the length of the British Isles. "Mamunia" lifted its misspelled title from the "safe haven" of the Moroccan hotel where Wings had spent a blissful fortnight. Even the playful nonsense lyric of "Jet" offered an invitation to soar up and away into the sky.

But it was the episodic title track that best gave an insight into Paul's frame of mind. At the beginning of "Band on the Run," the mood is one of claustrophobia, of people trapped. Then, once the breakout occurs and the chiming acoustic guitar kicks in, the fugitives sprint into the sunlight, never to return. Maybe, just maybe, Paul had finally managed to escape the long shadow cast by his former group.

7

IN LA-LA LAND

Your post-Beatles feud with John was staged very publicly . . .

Yeah. But it's not like nobody else ever goes through that. We went through what everyone else did, y'know. Most people just argue with their family members, and ours was done publicly. But I don't really feel it was huge anger. It was more frustration than anger.

T HE RUMORS FIRST STARTED SWIRLING AROUND in the last days of February 1974. Ringo and Harry Nilsson—nicknamed "the Beatle across the water" by the others—were spotted hanging out together at Capricorn Recording Studio, the epicenter of bearded southern boogie, in Macon, Georgia. It was exactly the sort of out-of-the-way location where you might successfully orchestrate a secret recording session. Soon the chatter turned to overwhelming noise: John, Paul, and George were planning to fly out there to join them. The Beatles reunion was on.

It wasn't the first time this kind of tattle had circulated in the four years since the split. Eleven months earlier, a rumor had spread around Los Angeles that Klaus Voormann—Beatle pal since Hamburg, *Revolver* cover artist, bassist with the Plastic Ono Band—was to replace Paul in the re-forming group. In truth, the three ex-Beatles plus Voormann were together in the studio hammering out the Lennon-penned "I'm the Greatest," sung by Ringo on his third and eponymous album, and so the story hadn't been too wide of the mark. John later ruminated that "Paul would most probably have joined in if he was around, but he wasn't."

More promisingly, in setting the scene for a reuniting of the Beatles, Allen Klein was now out of the picture. Unsurprisingly, perhaps, his good relations with Lennon, Harrison, and Starr had by now been lost in black clouds of bad advice and incrimination. When their management contract with him lapsed, on March 31, 1973, Klein, knowing his time was up, announced that he no longer wished to represent them. Then, like a clamp-jawed terrier refusing to drop the bone, he attempted to launch a legal action against all four of the former band members.

Walking into a London radio station to do an interview in December 1973, Paul was approached by a stranger and served a writ informing him that ABKCO was suing him and the other former Beatles for the seemingly arbitrary sum of $20 million. It didn't overly trouble McCartney; he'd never signed the management agreement in the first place.

The buzz surrounding the apparent Macon summit two months later, though entirely misplaced, was lent further credence, however, by the fact that, for a fortnight in New York at the beginning of February, lawyers for both parties had begun examining the details of the dispute between Apple and ABKCO. Frustratingly, any attempts at a settlement broke down, but both Lennon and McCartney individually appeared at the meetings, sparking gossip that they were trying to work out a deal for the future of the Beatles. In Britain, *Melody Maker* went big on the speculation, trumpeting, on its cover, "Beatles Get Together!" Teasingly, none of the band's individual publicists or Apple's PR would confirm or deny the story.

Then, on February 25, Paul put out a tantalizing press release that appeared to confirm that the group was set to carry on. "As soon as things are sorted out, we can all get together again and do something," it stated. "We've talked about it, but we haven't been able to do anything because this has been going on and on." Deflatingly, within a fortnight, in an interview with U.S. TV channel ABC conducted at the London offices of MPL, he was talking the reunion down. "I don't think we'll get together as a band again," he said. "I just don't think it'll work actually. It might not be as good."

That was a real concern. The idea that the Beatles could get back together and just magically pick up where they'd left off was a naïve one, particularly after the troubled births of both *Let It Be* and *Abbey*

Road. "It wouldn't necessarily have been a great thing," Paul says. "What we did with the Beatles was so cool that if we'd started to try and reheat a soufflé . . . that would've spoiled the whole reputation. What would we do? Do some new songs and add a new addendum, a new chapter to the end of the Beatles story? And how long would that go for? And would that get a bit pathetic? And it'd be like, 'Why, boys?'"

Still, a private Beatles reunion of sorts was imminent. In March the McCartneys landed in Los Angeles, a city where in 1974 the weed-refracted hippie idealism of the previous decade had given way to cocaine-shoveling egotism and creative self-indulgence. Its recording studios, clubs, and secluded Hollywood hillside properties were riddled with the solipsistic and the drug-damaged. And it was this edgy, unstable environment that greeted Paul. The arch-irony was that for the first few weeks of the nearly two-month-long holiday in California, he wasn't sure how long he would be allowed to stay in the country, until the legal wrangling over his U.S. visa following the 1973 busts was finally resolved, in April.

Paul, according to gossiping music-industry tongues, was in town to meet up with John and talk about getting the band back together. This story gained more credibility when Lennon and McCartney were spotted together, chatting and laughing backstage, at the 16th Annual Grammy Awards at the Hollywood Palladium, where Stevie Wonder scooped Best Album for his peerless *Innervisions* and Roberta Flack walked away with Record of the Year for "Killing Me Softly with His Song." John, tempering his hardline attitude toward Paul, said he considered *Band on the Run* "a great song and a great album."

In 1974, Lennon, however, was a mess. Behind him, in New York, his marriage to Yoko Ono lay in ruins, the trigger being his drunken infidelity with a girl at a party on the night of Richard Nixon's reelection, November 7, 1972. Added to this, his career was in free fall. Badly shaken by the brutal reviews for his shoddy, poorly selling 1972 political album *Some Time in New York City,* he'd already dismissed its similarly patchy follow-up, *Mind Games,* as "just an album . . . rock'n'roll at different speeds." Also hanging over his head was a plagiarism lawsuit from music publisher Morris Levy, who had, rightly, accused him of cribbing the melody and opening lyric for "Come Together" from Chuck Berry's "You Can't Catch Me."

Further weighing on his mind was the reality that he was living under the day-to-day threat of expulsion from the States by the Nixon administration, which was secretly listening to his phone calls and tailing his cars, and attempting to use a 1968 marijuana drug charge in London as an excuse to turf this worryingly influential peacenik out of the country. The agonies were piling up, and it was clear that Lennon was on the brink.

"I just couldn't function," he later admitted. "I was so paranoid from them tapping the phone and following me. I was under emotional stress. A manic depression, I would call it."

His companion in Los Angeles was the Lennons' twenty-two-year-old personal assistant, May Pang. In an effort to control John's extra-marital behavior, Yoko had approached the wide-eyed Pang with a view to her becoming John's mistress. Pang succumbed when John made a pass at her in a lift. As much in lust as in love with this new girlfriend—eyewitnesses reported that he could barely keep his hands off her—John had effectively replaced Yoko with a model seventeen years her junior.

By this point, Lennon had been in California for seven months and was in the throes of the wildest period of his life since his days in Hamburg with the Beatles. Two unhinged characters were aiding him in his madness: the demented dervish that was Phil Spector and the spirits-guzzling, drug-ravenous Harry Nilsson. "We had some moments," Lennon said of the period in his life that became known as the Lost Weekend. "But it got a little near the knuckle."

John Lennon had moved to Los Angeles to escape the pressures of being John Lennon. The sprawling city had always been a favorite destination for the singer during Beatles tours, and he believed his problems might evaporate in the California sunshine. But his troubles were clearly not behind him. For a start, he was virtually broke, given the tangled mess that was Apple. Staying at his lawyer Harold Seider's small duplex in West Hollywood, he and Pang were living hand to mouth until Capitol Records advanced the singer $10,000 against future royalties.

In all this confusion and uncertainty, Lennon hatched a plan to get

Morris Levy off his back and, at the same time, revive his own career. Settling out of court with the publisher, he agreed to record three songs from the catalog of Levy's Big Seven Music on his next album, proposed to be a set of rock'n'roll standards produced, in typically grandiose fashion, by Spector, the architect of his first three solo albums.

Notoriously temperamental and unpredictable in the studio, Spector owed much of his recent success to Lennon and the Beatles. He was one of the few individuals to inspire awe in Lennon, and their relationship was built upon a foundation of mutual admiration. But the producer was at this point going through an acutely strange and manic phase in his life, having recently split from his wife, former Ronettes singer Ronnie Spector, after she claimed he had kept her a virtual prisoner inside their fortress-like L.A. home.

The uproarious tone of the sessions for the *Rock'n'Roll* album was set on day one, October 17, 1973, at A&M Studios, when Spector—who had packed the live room with twenty-eight musicians, including drummer Jim Keltner, Stones sax player Bobby Keys, and guitarist Jesse Ed Davis—turned up late and spent hours painstakingly miking the instruments.

Bored to tears, Lennon and the band broke the seal on a gallon bottle of Smirnoff vodka.

By day two the scene was one of surreal disorder. Spector again arrived at A&M late, having for no particular reason decided to dress as a doctor, with stethoscope and white lab coat, under which he was surreptitiously packing a pistol. His kick at the time was amyl nitrate, the chief effect of which is a disorientating rush of blood to the head. He would constantly break open and inhale ampoules of it as he directed the musicians. "John didn't take that," Pang claims. "But Phil would come around and put it under your nose anyway."

Roy Cicala, the owner of Lennon's favorite New York studio, the Record Plant, had flown in to be chief engineer on the *Rock'n'Roll* sessions. "There was a lot of speed, cocaine, everything going on," he says. "Everybody was obnoxious."

The studio banter between Spector and Lennon became increasingly bizarre and worryingly intense. The producer barked loud, distorted remarks through the musicians' headphones, at one point yelling, "What's with these fucking horns and birds and seagulls and shit?" Lennon lost his temper and cracked up, shouting, "Shut up! You fucking . . ." These shenanigans, added to the various other pressures in his life, further affected Lennon's sanity. "I was trying to hide what I felt in the bottle," he said. "I was just insane."

Matters came to a head one night when a particularly drunken Lennon started freaking out in Cicala's car after being separated from Pang by Spector in the convoy of vehicles taking them home to the Bel Air house Lennon had borrowed from record producer Lou Adler. Wild and disorientated, the singer went berserk, kicking at the windows, screaming for Pang and, perhaps tellingly, Yoko. When they arrived at the house, Spector's bodyguard grabbed Lennon and dragged him to a bedroom, where he and the producer tried to restrain the singer by tying him down, further enraging him, because he thought he was about to be abused in a weird sex game.

"He got wild because they took his glasses away," Pang reasons. "He was as blind as a bat." Spector and his bodyguard tied him up with neckties. "He started freaking out," says Pang, "because he didn't know what was going on."

From here on in, the recording sessions became even more warped. Having been thrown out of A&M Studios after a bottle of booze was tipped into the mixing desk, the party continued at Record Plant West. One day, a loud bang was heard from the control room. Everyone ducked. In the center of the room stood Spector with a gun in his hand, pointed at the studio ceiling. Pang says, "John had his fingers in his ears, going, 'Phil, if you're gonna shoot me, shoot me. But don't fuck with me ears, man, I need them.'" It transpired that Spector had got into an argument with former Beatles roadie Mal Evans and fired a live bullet into the roof. "It frightened the hell out of us," says Pang.

In the aftermath, Spector stole the album's tapes and locked them in the basement of his house, claiming to everyone—although it was patently untrue—that they'd been destroyed in a fire at the studio. Only six weeks after they'd begun, the *Rock'n'Roll* sessions collapsed.

Then into the wreckage stepped Harry Nilsson. A former bank computer operator turned songwriter for the Monkees, Nilsson had been friends with Lennon since he'd impressed the Beatles with a cover of their "You Can't Do That" on his 1967 album *Pandemonium Shadow Show,* which cleverly incorporated elements of more than a dozen of the Fab Four's songs. On its release, Lennon reportedly listened to the album nonstop for thirty-six hours. During the New York press conference announcing Apple Records in 1968, both he and McCartney named Nilsson as their favorite new artist. Instantly, Harry was made.

A brilliant if erratic songwriter whose pinballing humor found him writing lyrics about gang bangs ("Cuddly Toy") and, incredibly, even his writing desk ("Good Old Desk"), Nilsson enjoyed his greatest successes with his covers of Fred Neil's "Everybody's Talkin'," from the soundtrack to *Midnight Cowboy*, and Badfinger's "Without You," a transatlantic No. 1 hit in 1972.

Sharing a twisted sense of humor and a penchant for mischief, Nilsson and Lennon were natural buddies. It was perhaps inevitable that the L.A.-dwelling singer would gravitate toward Lennon. Lennon clearly appreciated Nilsson's edginess and was very likely looking for a male soul mate to fill the hole left by McCartney. For his part, Nilsson's feelings for Lennon ran even deeper: "I really fell in love with him. He was all those things you wanted somebody to be."

A visitor to the studio during the frenzied latter stages of the *Rock'n'Roll* sessions, Nilsson claimed to have had a calming influence on Lennon and Spector, in spite of his own reputation as a prodigious drinker and druggie. "Suddenly I was the maypole of stability, if you can believe that," he laughed. "They were at war . . . and I was a nice little centerpiece they could both dance around for a moment."

But Roy Cicala, for one, felt that Nilsson was basking in the reflected glory of having a Beatle for a friend. "Some days I would think that somebody's taking advantage of somebody," he says. "The next day I would think, Wow, John is really enjoying it."

The pair's notoriety was cemented on the evening of Tuesday, March 12, 1974, when, with May Pang, they visited the Troubadour club on Santa Monica Boulevard to watch a performance by New York's folk-tinged, mock-bickering musical comedy duo the Smothers Brothers. The intimate venue was fast becoming Lennon's favorite place in Los Angeles to hang out and get wasted. Only weeks before, he'd attended a show by soul singer Ann Peebles, pie-eyed and with a sanitary pad stuck to his forehead.

He'd asked a scornful waitress, "Do you know who I am?"

"Yeah," she'd snapped back. "An asshole with a Kotex on his head."

Both Lennon and Nilsson were heavily oiled on their arrival at the Smothers Brothers' show. The pair, along with the teetotaler Pang, parked themselves at a table in the VIP area, alongside the likes of actor

Paul Newman and *Deep Throat* porn star Linda Lovelace. They began downing brandy Alexanders (an often sickly sweet cocktail of brandy and cream) and proceeded to loudly heckle the performers, much to everyone's horror.

"Hey, Smothers Brothers!" yelled Lennon at one point. "Fuck a cow!"

Pang was humiliated. "The crowd loves it," Nilsson told her.

"No, they don't," she replied. "Do me a favor."

Then the Troubadour's manager came over and grabbed Lennon. "And you just don't grab John," says Pang. "It brought him back to the old days. All of a sudden, the tables went flying."

Swinging punches at the bouncers as they were dragged out of the club and onto the sidewalk, Nilsson and Lennon were photographed by a camera-ready fan; the shots showed them looking wild-eyed and out of it. "The next day John was mortified," says Pang. "He sent flowers to everyone."

Effectively homeless and living off favors, Lennon and Pang moved into a Santa Monica beachside property rented for Nilsson by his label, RCA. The house had been built by Louis B. Mayer and owned in the early 1960s by British film actor Peter Lawford, who lent it to President John F. Kennedy for his trysts with Marilyn Monroe. When Nilsson took Lennon and Pang to the house to show them around, he opened the door of the master bedroom, which the couple would be sharing, and said, "So this is where they did it, Kennedy and Marilyn."

The house quickly became the go-to place for overimbibing thirty-something rock musicians. Alongside Lennon and Nilsson, Ringo and Keith Moon moved in. Given the lifestyles of the cohabitants, the scene soon resembled one long stag night.

"We lived a normal, reasonable life," Nilsson later argued. "We'd wake up in the morning—well, about one o'clock. At first we were very polite. Then, after a while, it was, 'Keith, get your nose out of the amyl.'"

Ominously, then, with *Rock'n'Roll* on hold, Lennon announced that he was to produce an album for Nilsson. Its title, *Pussy Cats,* was a jokey swipe at their unruly reputation. "We called it that to show we were nice guys," Nilsson said. "Everyone thinks we're rough-house ass-holes."

Quickly the *Pussy Cats* sessions took a turn for the disastrous when it became clear to all that Nilsson's hard living had reduced his formerly flutelike, three-and-a-half-octave voice to a ravaged croak. In truth, Nilsson had ruptured his vocal cords and would frequently disappear from the recordings to lock himself away in the bathroom, where, instead of warming up his voice or practicing his scales as other singers might do, he was coughing up blood.

At the end of the first day's recording on *Pussy Cats,* at Burbank Studios on Thursday, March 28, 1974, a surprise visitor arrived in the shape of McCartney. The devastation that met his eyes shocked Paul. "That time in John's life was very wild," he says.

With the booze flowing, the musicians at the studio complex fell into a jam session. That night, for the first time since the tense sessions for *Abbey Road,* Paul and John played and sang together. "I'm afraid it was a rather *heady* session, shall we say," admits Paul. "I ended up getting on drums for some unknown reason. Then we just jammed. But I don't think it was very good."

It was terrible, as bootlegged tapes, later leaked under the name *A Toot and a Snore in '74,* were to attest. The gathered musicians—Stevie Wonder, who had wandered in from a neighboring studio, on electric piano, Jesse Ed Davis on guitar, Bobby Keys on sax, Nilsson on vocals, Linda on tentative organ, and Pang on token tambourine—sounded woozy and unfocused at their best and utterly lost at their worst.

Lennon didn't sound particularly drunk—apart from a slurred reference to past "jam *sheshions*"—but was freestyling wildly. "I fell upon my arse," he trilled tunelessly. "And no one seemed to notice. I was wearing my mother's bra. So I say never trust a bugger with your mother." There was much musical twiddling going on, but nobody seemed to be able to settle on a song.

"Ah, gee, it's been such a long time," John said, addressing Paul, before bizarrely adding, "When I look at Jack Lemmon, I'm in love again. I feel him coming all over me."

Meanwhile, the disconnected riffing and soloing staggered on. The musicians were barely even listening to one another. "If somebody knows a song that we all know, then please take over," Lennon bellowed over the racket. "I've been screaming here for hours. It's gotta be something done round about the '50s or no later than '63 or we ain't gonna know it."

Eventually, the drunken band slid into a slow, funky jam of "Lucille," Lennon shrieking maniacally and McCartney trying to echo him with a harmony. It was less the remeshing of two great musical minds and more the sound of a pair of drunks shouting at each other over a slightly above-average pub band.

"Where's all that drink they always have in this place?" asked Lennon, sounding like he needed not one more drop. Then he vainly tried to get the group to tune up. "Someone give me an E," he said. "Or a snort."

Jimmy Iovine, a record producer turned Interscope Records boss, who was then an assistant studio engineer, witnessed the scene. "Paul chose to play drums," he reckons, "because he was alert enough to say, 'This is not how the Beatles are getting back together.' He was the one in the room who you could see got it."

McCartney, uncharacteristically, was taking a backseat, pitching in with the odd vocal interjection. An impassioned Lennon tried singing "Stand by Me" over a slurry of bum notes before freaking out at the hapless engineer in the control room: "Just turn the fucking vocal mike up! McCartney's doing the harmony on the drums, Stevie might get on it there if he's got a mike." They started up again before Lennon lost it once more. "I can't hear a fucking thing now!" On their third attempt at "Stand by Me," an angry Lennon gave up and just played guitar, as Paul scat-sang along and a gruff Nilsson joined in. Wonder, in typically fine voice, started to sing Sam Cooke's "Cupid" and "Chain Gang." Paul offered a halfhearted take on the old-time U.S. chain-gang folk song "Take This Hammer," an old Beatles jamming standby. The band, sounding knackered and clapped-out, finally fell apart.

Lennon offered Wonder a line of cocaine. "You wanna snort, Steve?" he said. "A toot? It's goin' round."

It was an inauspicious event, and, of course, those involved weren't so drunk that they didn't know it. Lennon later vaguely remembered of the blurry night, "There were fifty other people playing and they were all just watching me and Paul."

Four days later, early on Monday afternoon, Paul and Linda and the kids went to visit Lennon at the rented Santa Monica house. Like an overgrown teenager, John was still in bed. To pass the time, Paul sat down at a piano and tinkered around, even playing a medley of Beatles songs, to the lusty vocal accompaniment of Nilsson and Starr. Subconsciously, perhaps, he was awakening something in himself that had lain dormant for the four years since the demise of the group: the thought that he and John might write and perform together once more.

At one point Harry offered Paul a hit of angel dust. McCartney wasn't familiar with the drug, notorious for producing wildly unpredictable effects, from syrupy-headed nodding out to rage-filled hallucinatory delusions.

"What is it?" McCartney asked Nilsson.

"It's elephant tranquilizer," Harry replied.

"Is it fun?" wondered a doubtful Paul.

Nilsson paused and thought carefully about the question before replying, "No."

"Well, you know what, I won't have any," said McCartney.

In many ways, this incident summed up the dangerous peer pressure that was fueling the alcoholic and narcotic one-upmanship—the perceived wisdom being that taking anything was better than being straight.

Eventually, John got up. He seemed pleased to see Paul. "There was a very relaxed atmosphere," says Pang. "It wasn't heavy. It was about them just being them."

At one point, though, Paul gestured to John, indicating that he wanted to have a private word with him in another room. Before the McCartneys had left for Los Angeles, Yoko Ono had visited them in London. Clad in black like a mourning widow, she'd appeared shrunken, Paul had thought. She'd sadly informed Paul and Linda that John was in Los Angeles with Pang, the reality of the possible finality of their split sinking in.

Paul had asked her, "Do you still love him? Do you want to get back with him?" Ono said she did. McCartney told her that he planned to visit Lennon while in California, saying, "I can take a message. What would I have to tell him?" Ono laid out the conditions Lennon would have to meet if he was to return to her, which, given their unconventional relationship, were surprisingly old-fashioned. He'd have to move back to New York. They couldn't live together again immediately. He'd have to woo her, send her flowers, start over again.

In the Santa Monica house, Lennon absorbed all of this information. Before the month was out, he was back in New York. By November, he'd complied with each and every one of Ono's conditions. Only years later did Paul reveal the key role he'd played in the couple's eventual reconciliation. That spring in Los Angeles, there had certainly been reunion in the air. It just wasn't to be that of Lennon and McCartney.

As the afternoon slipped away in Santa Monica, the gathering moved to the pool, where Keith Moon's personal assistant, Peter "Dougal" Butler, took a series of Polaroids. Three of these pictures of John and Paul together survived—John in black peaked hat, pale blue denim shirt, and darker flared jeans, Paul sporting a wispy mullet and fashionably bushy Zapata mustache and wearing a brown patterned shirt and summery white clam diggers. They were caught by the camera lounging around and shooting the breeze. Neither, of course, could know that these casual, laid-back shots were to be the last taken of Lennon and McCartney together.

That gathering was a peaceful coda to a turbulent time. Not for nothing did Lennon nickname the Los Angeles of 1974 "Lost Arseholes."

Underlining the general messiness of the L.A. rock community, three days later Paul and Linda went to visit Beach Boy Brian Wilson—at the time hellishly acid-burned, paranoid, and a self-imposed prisoner in his Bel Air home. The McCartneys repeatedly knocked on his front door, waiting for over an hour. There was no response other than the sound of Wilson, hiding from them, softly crying.

8

GOING SOUTH

When people look back at a lot of your 1970s singles, they're seen as being light, compared to John's stuff and even what George was doing. Does that get on your nerves?

Pfff. Yeah. A bit. But I have to admit, some of it was. I don't give a toss. It was what it was. Yeah, some of my stuff was kinda lightweight, but a lot of it wasn't. The background stuff wasn't. There was enough good stuff to counter all of those accusations. But there's a lot of dubious stuff in there.

Which records do you think were dubious?

I'm not damning myself!

IT WAS TIME TO PUT THE BAND BACK TOGETHER AGAIN. Even if it wasn't the one that everyone really wanted him to put back together.

But if Paul was searching for more compliant musicians to help establish a more stable second incarnation of Wings, he seemed to be looking in all the wrong places.

First, he turned to a diminutive Glaswegian, Jimmy McCulloch, who had been transplanted to London at the age of twelve, rendering his accent a disorientating, vowel-chewing mush of Cockney and west-coast Scottish. McCulloch was only four months past his twentieth birthday when he found himself in a Mercedes van with the McCartneys, heading to Pathé Marconi Studios in Paris to play on a re-recording of Linda's "Seaside Woman." Like kids on a school trip, they horsed around on the ferry before driving immediately to the studio, where they all stayed up until eight the following morning. Clearly able to hang, Jimmy was instantly welcomed into the ranks. "It was a great loon," said Paul.

McCulloch had been a prodigy looking for a musical home. In thrall to Tommy Steele, the Shadows, and, of course, the Beatles, he'd picked up a guitar at the age of ten and instantly proved himself something of a boy wonder. A year later, in cahoots with his drummer brother Jack, he was playing Shadows numbers around the workingmen's clubs of Glasgow. At thirteen, he formed One in a Million, which cut a failed single for CBS and opened for the Who in Scotland. This cocky, precocious wee individual had caught the eye of Pete Townshend when he was helping an old friend, John "Speedy" Keen, with his nascent group Thunderclap Newman.

Pete asked Jimmy to join the band, completing an odd trio of individuals: McCulloch with his liquid rock-guitar runs, Keen with his yearning hippie vocals, and Andy Newman with his clumpy pub piano playing. In the studio, with Townshend at the desk, his head deep in *Tommy* at the time, McCulloch watched the Who guitarist molding and manipulating sounds on eight-track tape. Thunderclap Newman's first single and only hit, "Something in the Air," released in May 1969, when Jimmy was just fifteen, went to No. 1. Success didn't throw Jimmy, but becoming a pin-up did. He wasn't, he protested, into the "heavy pop angle." He hated it when girl fans would crowd or crush him, or dangerously wield scissors in an attempt to cut off a lock of his hair.

When the constantly bickering Thunderclap Newman musicians argued themselves into nonexistence, McCulloch moved on to the heavy blues circuit. He experienced an accelerated apprenticeship in John Mayall's Bluesbreakers: called up on Thursday, onstage with them in Germany by Sunday. The bandleader threw spontaneous calls for solos in his direction and put Jimmy on the spot in front of a paying audience. He then joined the tough Scottish soul-rabble band Stone the Crows, replacing guitarist Les Harvey, who in May 1972 at Swansea Top Rank had touched an ungrounded microphone with wet hands; the electric shock killed him instantly. The band struggled on with McCulloch for another year before, in the summer of 1973 in Montreux, their throaty, Janis Joplin–soundalike singer Maggie Bell walked out on them.

Disenchanted, McCulloch treaded water for a time in the forgettable, short-lived rock band Blue, whose members he found far too straight. "Not enough guts," he moaned. "I'd be all dressed up and ridiculous and they'd all walk on wearing jeans. From the start I was the odd one out. I just didn't fit in."

The problem was that Jimmy didn't seem to fit in anywhere. When he drifted into McCartney's orbit, he was thinking about going it alone and making a solo album. "I'm pretty lazy," he confessed. "I don't mind admitting it. It takes a long time to get to know people. So I tend to stay put until something comes along."

The connection to Wings was made through a mutual friend, roadie Ian Horne. McCartney invited McCulloch to the studio to hear the final mix of the *Band on the Run* LP. Then, months after the Paris session, Paul called Jimmy again and asked him to contribute to *McGear,* the album he was producing for his brother Mike at Strawberry Studios, in Stockport. "I agreed to give it a go," said McCulloch, before admitting that he'd been "slightly cautious because I'd heard people say [McCartney] was difficult to work with." During the sessions, when McCulloch was recording slide overdubs on the resonant, part-metal country-blues guitar known as a Dobro, an impressed Paul walked into the live room and on the spot asked Jimmy to join Wings full-time.

Jimmy was a bit starstruck. "It was like some kind of a dream," he recalled. "Paul was there chatting happily, and I just kept staring at him and thinking to myself, Christ, he used to be a Beatle. And here he is talking to me like I matter." Ultimately, though, even if he felt awed, McCulloch was far too hard-edged, Scottish, and proud to be fazed by the prospect of playing with a Beatle. Jimmy had always been more into John and George anyway, as he perhaps rashly revealed to the music newspaper *NME*. "Paul as well," he quickly added. "I've always admired his voice."

Before joining the band, McCulloch warned McCartney about his mood swings. Sober, Jimmy was a sweetheart. But once, as was his wont, he started tipping back the spirits and indulging in other intoxicants, he turned obnoxious. "There's a Jekyll and Hyde within me," he admitted. He explained to his new boss that he "got a bit funny sometimes."

Paul remembered the exchange: "I said, 'Don't we all, ducky?' and left it at that."

Then there was the problem of finding a drummer. In the last week of April 1974, Wings held auditions at the Albery Theatre, in the West End of London, hiring a band of session musicians to accompany the candidates while Denny Laine and the McCartneys sat in the front rows, judging them.

Among those queuing to try their luck was former Jimi Hendrix Experience drummer Mitch Mitchell, yet to find a decent gig five years after the breakup of the band, and almost four since the death of its leader. Denny Laine remembers that on the day, Mitchell was "on a head trip. . . . Maybe he resented the fact that we'd asked him to audition and he wasn't getting the star treatment."

After lunch, up stepped Geoff Britton, a sturdy blond Londoner who was a member of the U.K. amateur karate team, which had recently triumphed over its Japanese counterpart. Up to this point he had been grinding away on the pub circuit, most notably with the greasy 1950s throwback rock band Wild Angels. At the Albery, Britton sat down and settled behind the kit, looking every millimeter the rocker in his leather jacket and worn band T-shirt, and began hammering away with sticks so thick that even the heavy-handed Ginger Baker had deemed them unusable.

Britton sailed through the audition, even when he had to slip into the tricksy shuffle of Duke Ellington's "Caravan," having served his time in cabaret summer seasons. "Right up my street," he gruffly noted. "I did the business." Paul liked his soulful, frills-free drumming, and a few days later, the Londoner got the callback to try out with Wings itself, being told that he was on a short list of five.

"So, suddenly I'd gone from no chance to 25 percent chance," Britton told *NME,* his arithmetic temporarily failing him. "Anyway, had this audition, met the boys for the first time. Few days passed, another phone call. Scene is: come for the day, practice with them all, go for dinner. Now we're down to two people. So I'm on trial, right? They are going to suss me out. Everybody is charming to me but nobody gives away a thing. Couple of days go by, and then Paul phones and tells me I've got the gig."

Britton was thrilled, but there was a nagging worry in a corner of his mind. The Wild Angels band members had recently been caught skipping out on hotels in Glasgow—"jibbing," the drummer called it— and, as a result, were due in court. When McCartney called McCulloch and Britton to invite them on a Wings bonding trip to Nashville in June, the sweating, dithering drummer couldn't confirm until, with some relief, the court verdict handed down was the uniquely Scottish one of "not proven."

Wings was a five-piece once again, albeit a markedly disparate one, featuring a former Beatle, his musically naïve American wife, a devoted Birmingham-born guitarist, an unhinged Glaswegian, and a karate-daft, mouthy Cockney. Worse, it quickly became apparent that certain members of this new group really couldn't stand certain other members.

"He picked the wrong guys," Britton reckoned in the aftermath. "The chemistry was doomed."

Paul's idea was that the trip to Nashville would "break in" the band. In the end, it very nearly broke up the band.

The new Wings lineup, plus the McCartney family, flew into Tennessee on June 14, 1974. Even traveling under a cloak of relative secrecy, they were greeted at the airport by a gang of forty fans and assorted reporters. Asked about the new drummer, Paul said, "He has a black belt. I feel with those credentials he'll be able to whip the band into shape."

Their destination was a farm, set in 133 acres of land, in Lebanon, thirty-odd miles east of downtown Nashville. Its owner was songwriter Curly Putnam Jr., whose country hits included "Green, Green Grass of Home" and "D-I-V-O-R-C-E." He had agreed to vacate his home for six weeks in return for the princely rent of $2,000 a week, while he and his wife enjoyed an extended vacation in Hawaii.

At first the McCartneys settled in the main house, with the band living in a neighboring farmhouse, mirroring the living arrangements at High Park. It quickly became clear, however, that this sense of separation wasn't aiding the group's bonding. Only when the others moved into the big house did the rehearsal sessions in its converted garage become productive.

In their downtime, the musicians shot basketball hoops, enjoyed barbecues—including one four days in to celebrate Paul's thirty-second birthday—and rode motorbikes. McCartney treated himself to a Honda road bike, which he sped around on haphazardly and helmetless, much to the unease of one of the attendant security guards, who wryly commented, "The next headline he makes will be about a motorcycle wreck. He doesn't know how to drive that thing."

Elsewhere, Paul lived out his cowboy fantasies, sauntering around town in mirrored aviator shades and a Stetson. Lebanon, situated in the partly dry Wilson County, had restricted alcohol laws, resulting in moonshining in the surrounding hills. "Guys came into town in old pickup trucks and did their whittling with bits of wood," said Britton. "It was straight out of a movie."

As the weeks unfolded, visitors to the farm included Roy Orbison, whom Paul had first met during the early touring days of the Beatles, and such veteran Nashville musicians as guitarist Chet Atkins and pianist Floyd Cramer, who'd shared credits with Elvis Presley and the Everly Brothers. The McCartneys visited Johnny and June Cash, and were tickled that their daughters instantly began drawling in southern accents, copying the First Couple of Country's son, John.

At the home of music publisher Kevin Killen, Wings' fix-it man and gofer during their stay, the host was bemused to find the McCartneys allowing the kids to jump up and down on his new, all-white crushed-velvet couch, their fingers slick with Kentucky Fried Chicken grease. "They were very lenient parents," he noted. Ushering them out of the house while attempting to set his burglar alarm, Killen was horrified to hear the sound of a child bawling. Stella, now nearly three years old, had forgotten her shoes and dashed back inside, straight through a glass door, badly cutting her legs and arms. Linda ran into the house, grabbing towels to stem the bleeding. Stella was rushed to a hospital at nearby Donelson, where the doctors and nurses kept turning up to peek surreptitiously at her famous father. "A couple dozen people died at the hospital," Killen joked to Paul. "All the doctors were watching you."

It soon became public knowledge where the band were staying, and fans began congregating around the gates of the farm, requiring off-duty policemen to be positioned at the entrance twenty-four hours a day. The phones in the farmhouse rang constantly: TV and radio producers inviting Paul to appear on local shows, celebrities calling to say hello or ask favors. The peaking U.S. heartthrob David Cassidy repeatedly called McCartney at the Lebanon house. "The stars all came to Paul for help and advice," said Britton.

The McCartneys were clearly at ease in Tennessee. They indulged themselves with leisurely breakfasts of hot biscuits and country ham at the Loveless Motel; they motored to the nearest drive-in movie theater to catch double features at the end of the day. Linda bought a gob-smacked Paul the double bass used by Bill Black on Elvis Presley's "Heartbreak Hotel," one of the records that had made a formative impression on the teenage McCartney back in Liverpool.

One night out involved a visit to the fabled Grand Ole Opry to witness the third annual Grand Master Fiddler Championship. Stepping out of the car with the McCartneys, Kevin Killen noticed that as they approached the theater, people began to recognize the ex-Beatle and mouth his name in shock. One by one they gravitated toward Paul, forming a crowd. Killen admitted that he hadn't reckoned on the extent of McCartney's fame: "It just didn't dawn on me what an icon he was." Paul, meanwhile, was unruffled by the attention, having learned how to react to this kind of mob behavior in his Beatlemania days. "If you stay calm, you're okay," he told Killen. "But if you bolt and run, they'll tear you apart."

Another evening, at Nashville's vaunted Printers Alley, a thorough-fare designed for nightlife, threw up a song. The McCartneys had dinner at the Spanish-galleon-themed country music hangout the Captain's Table before moving to the Rainbow Room, where they bumped into a pinball-playing Waylon Jennings, who chatted with the rapt Paul about his early days with Buddy Holly. Later, in a boozy haze, McCartney was struck with an idea for a tune, originally to be titled "Diane," after country singer Diane Gaffney; he abandoned that name when he learned that she was in a particularly litigious mood and in the process of suing a newspaper reporter who had published an article without her consent.

Possibly distracted, Paul left the Rainbow Room that night without settling his $4.75 bill, resulting in his name being inked into the bar's "delinquent payments" book.

The next day, Britton found Paul sitting on a stoop at the farmhouse with his guitar, completing the lightly country-flavored song now called "Sally G." Set amid the previous night's shenanigans, the song has McCartney falling in love with the titular girl, who serenades him with Hank Snow's "A Tangled Mind" before breaking his heart. "That was my imagination, adding to the reality of it," he says.

Wings recorded the song at SoundShop Studios on Music Row in Nashville, despite the fact that they were essentially on holiday and didn't have work permits. At the same time, they committed to taping the chugging, "Get Back"–like pop rocker "Junior's Farm," an upbeat nonsense song written partly in tribute to their time spent lying low on Putnam's estate. On the recording, set to become the next Wings single, Paul sounds positively liberated, introducing McCulloch's melodic, slightly flashy guitar solo with the gleeful exhortation, "Take me down, Jimmy . . ."

The musicians even found time to record a jaunty, old-time swing instrumental written by Paul's father, Jim, entitled "Walking in the Park with Eloise." McCartney remembered sitting at the foot of the piano as a ten-year-old while his dad played this self-penned tune and standards such as "Chicago," thrilled and stimulated by the idea that his father had written an actual song of his own. During a dinner at the Lebanon farm, Paul told Chet Atkins about the tune and played it for him. The guitarist suggested that they record it, and the result was released under the name the Country Hams in October 1974; a perky, slight indulgence it failed to chart. Jim McCartney, quietly touched, was dismissive of his songwriting effort. "I said, 'You know that song you wrote, Dad?'" Paul remembers. "He said, 'No, I've never written one . . . I made one up.'"

These frivolities proved to be entertaining diversions, but ultimately, six weeks in, the band began to grow restless and testy. "If you're to-gether for six weeks, it's hard work and it begins to tell on you," reck-oned Denny Laine. "At one point I thought, I don't know what we've come here for—we should be at home gigging."

Geoff Britton was still trying to come to terms with being in a band with McCartney. During rehearsals, the drummer admits, he would catch himself staring at Paul, especially if—as the bandleader had de-cided to do—they were working up an old Beatles standard such as "Hey Jude." "It seemed like a dream," said Britton. "It was beautiful." Nevertheless, underprepared for the job, with his foot encased in plaster because of a karate injury, Geoff was having trouble playing some of the material. "I was put on the spot a bit," he said. "'Live and Let Die,' stuff like that. I hadn't really delved into the music much. I was goofing off. A poxy kit I didn't like, and I didn't think I was delivering the goods."

Worse, Britton was failing to gel with the others on a personal level, being a teetotaling fitness freak among a bunch of stoners. He began to irritate his bandmates, sitting there with his foot in a cast, not smoking or drinking. "So I'm not quite communicating on a social level," he said. "I knew it was gonna take them a bit of time to get off on me as a person, 'cause I'm gonna be a bit weird to them." In addition, the drummer was growing increasingly garrulous and opinionated: "I'd get a bit up-front about things. I'd bite my tongue but basically . . . no, I wouldn't."

One day a major argument broke out in rehearsals. According to Britton, "Everyone got a bit stoned, and then it got heavy." Jimmy insulted Linda, criticizing her playing, and there were tears. Britton turned on McCulloch, and the pair nearly came to blows. Paul told the angry Britton that he wanted to "reassess" the situation. The thunder-faced drummer stomped off to the crew room, determined to quit, asking the roadies for petty cash he could use while he took off and traveled around the States. In the end they talked him down, though he was still fuming and ranting, saying, "I'm not going back in there. I'm either the drummer in the band or I'm not." The incident punctured Britton's dreamy bubble. "I couldn't believe all the hassles," he said. "We were at each other's throats."

The next morning, Paul and Linda talked to Geoff, reassuring him that his place in the band was secure. An uneasy peace was established for the next few days. But in Britton's eyes, McCulloch remained the major problem—whether he was accusing Linda of playing the wrong chords or hassling the less fastidious guitarist Denny about his tuning. "It was very fragile," said the drummer. "If he came in wrecked and hungover, everything about him would be negative. If he was on an up, then we'd rock away for hours and it would be absolute magic."

Britton began to sympathize with McCartney, recognizing the difficulty of his position as a bandleader and peacemaker who was carrying the weight of a monumental reputation. "He was subject to so many pressures. His whole world was pressing in on him. And in those conditions, well, you are not a normal person." The drummer felt that, having replaced his formerly teenage buddies in the Beatles with what were effectively session players, McCartney was flanked by yes-men and, as a result, was isolated. "He didn't seem to have any old friends anymore," he said. "Paul didn't have anybody around who could tell him when he was out of order or to fuck off. You need that."

The elephant in the room, as always, was the financial agreement with the band. McCartney was keen to drop the idea of contracts and keep the group arrangement looser, and therefore cheaper, by paying the musicians session by session, performance by performance. The problem, once again, was that no one felt as if they were being offered any kind of monetary security. The original idea had been that everyone would travel to Nashville and sign contracts and seal their commitment to the new Wings. Now that they were there, and particularly in the light of the intraband hassles, this was looking far less likely.

The band faced up to McCartney and there was something of a showdown, during which the trio threatened to walk out. "It's not like these things hadn't been said before," Laine pointed out. "You're walking out. But the next minute you can be walking back." Somehow, fully employing his powers of persuasion, McCartney managed to talk the others round, convincing them that it would be better if their professional relationship was left non-contracted.

"I've signed so many contracts that got me into trouble," reasoned Laine, "I never want to sign anything again. It just didn't seem necessary to me."

"If you're a real pro and you've got a tour booked," argued Britton, "you don't phone up and say, 'I'm not going.' That's just not on."

McCulloch, who had been put on salary for a few months to secure his services after he joined the band, similarly decided that he'd rather operate on a freelance basis: "We'd just go on and get paid for what we do."

If the personality clashes within Wings Mark II were making Paul doubtful about committing himself to this group—especially legally, given the pain of his Beatles court battles—Denny Laine was feeling much the same way. "It was being a bit rushed," he reckoned. "I thought, Hang on, let's make sure that this is the right group." Having served his time as Paul's apprentice, Laine was clearly enjoying the reflected glow of being part of the core of the operation. "Me and Paul and Linda know exactly where we stand now, and you've got to inject that into the whole group," he stressed, verbally puffing his chest out.

Jimmy McCulloch was already proving a more gnarly proposition, however, beyond his combative behavior in the rehearsal room. In the SoundShop session he angrily threw a Coke bottle at the studio's control room window. Then he was arrested for some woefully reckless drunken driving, with Kevin Killen having to sweet-talk the authorities, who politely advised him that it might be better if this wayward Scottish rocker exited the country.

Luckily, the trip was coming to a close. On the day before leaving, the McCartneys met reporters in scorching ninety-degree heat at the gates of Putnam's farm. Paul seemed keen to underline his kinship with the Tennesseans, pointing out that he was basically a country boy at heart himself. "I've got a farm in Scotland," he said. "You're not the only people who have farms, y'know. Back in Scotland, we're country people in our own way."

Still, when the Wings musicians landed back in Britain, on July 17, their spirits were low. Britton felt as if he'd blown his big opportunity: "I said to my wife, 'Dream shattered . . . I should've fucking known better.'" The music press, meanwhile, picked up on the rumors of discontent within the band, ramping them up, with *NME* wrongly reporting under the headline "Wings Upheaval" that the band had split permanently: "The existing line-up of Paul McCartney's Wings appeared this week to have broken up, following what is understood to have been a major internal policy disagreement." A spokesman for Laine admitted that there had been "personal difficulties." The McCartneys' PR, meanwhile, underlined the open arrangement that Paul had agreed upon with the others. "Wings members are free to pursue their own musical careers," read their statement. "This will enable them to develop working relationships free of contractual ties. Wings will have a fluid concept, which will be adapted to suit current and future projects."

A vague plan was put in place to compile an album to be named *Cold Cuts*. It would mop up unheard recordings by the previous Wings lineup and introduce the new lineup with the material recorded in Nashville. That never happened. But Paul talked up the new band in *Melody Maker* while at the same time admitting that he felt there had been problems in the Denny Seiwell/Henry McCullough version of the group, since no one had dared to talk back to him. He cited "Mary Had a Little Lamb" as Exhibit A.

"No one would say, 'No, Paul, that's a mistake,'" he explained, without fully considering what his reaction might have been had the original drummer or guitarist questioned his wisdom in releasing the single. "It was all a bit ropey," he added. Further, he accepted that the other musicians had limitations, if compared to their peers, and recognized how hard it was to put a band together and nurture it. A touch defensively, he claimed that Wings was a purposely loose operation and that they were not attempting to "be cool and overreach ourselves and try to be Pink Floyd."

Instead, Paul reverted to *Let It Be* mode, gathering the band together at Abbey Road in August to record an hour-long TV special, *One Hand Clapping*, that in the light of the ructions to come was to remain unseen for many years. In it, the band turns in slick versions of "Jet," "Junior's Farm," the rattling rocker "Soily," and the loping, reggae-inflected "C Moon," sounding tight and strong. The musicians can be heard jamming the breezy if mawkish anti-war pop of Paper Lace's "Billy Don't Be a Hero," which earlier that year had knocked "Band on the Run" off the top of the U.K. singles chart, and which was conspicuously McCartney-flavored.

Paul was filmed alone at the piano, tinkling his way through an ad-lib medley of snatches of cabaret-style songs he'd constructed with other singers in mind, from the slightly bizarre "Suicide"—a Sinatra-fashioned ballad written in his teens and eventually presented to the legendary crooner, who wondered in bewilderment if it was a joke—to the drifty romanticism of "Let's Love," sung by Peggy Lee and produced by McCartney later that year.

Viewing the *One Hand Clapping* footage, Britton was surprised to discover that, "seeing us playing, we were a good band." But as smooth as the actual performances were, the film was revealing in other, less favorable ways: an impish McCulloch exits the room at a close-of-session rendition of "Bluebird," grinning and muttering that Paul is "flogging a dead horse." Later there is an appearance by an old friend of McCartney's from Liverpool, Howie Casey, five years older and a former member of Derry and the Seniors—the first band from the city to play in Hamburg, mapping out the territory for the Beatles. He is seen being conducted, a touch condescendingly, through a reprise of his improvised sax solo for "Bluebird." Paul, not a big drinker, had asked Howie if he could get him anything for the session, and the saxophonist had asked for a beer. A roadie was duly dispatched, returning, to the musician's amazement, with a single bottle of beer. "I'd been working with John Entwistle," Casey laughs, "and the place was full of booze, and then we'd go to a club afterwards."

Elsewhere in *One Hand Clapping*, Laine slurs through his voice-over, sounding staggeringly drunk. Britton unintentionally provides the comedy, bouncing behind his drum kit in his karate uniform. In one section, he enthusiastically slices and kicks his way through the choreography of a kata routine for the benefit of the camera. It is all too easy to see why he was becoming the butt of the others' jokes. Laine sometimes mocked the drummer mercilessly, asking him, "What are you gonna do? Play the drums or chop them in two?"

As one band was falling apart, the legal affairs of another, long dead, were finally being put to rest.

By the latter half of 1974, relations between the former Beatles were decidedly mixed. Paul and John were getting on better than they had done since the split. When Lennon first returned to New York from Los Angeles, and before getting back together with Ono, he shared an apartment with May Pang on East Fifty-second Street. The McCartneys were regular visitors whenever they were in town. "We would go out for dinner all the time," says Pang. Lennon said he and Paul enjoyed "Beaujolais evenings, reminiscing about the old times."

The main obstacle in the path of reconciliation was that George didn't want to have anything to do with Paul anymore. "How can we get together if George won't play with Paul?" Ringo asked a quizzing reporter. "Paul is a fine bass player," George said, not a little patronizingly, "but he's a bit overpowering at times. I'd join a band with John Lennon any day, but I couldn't join a band with Paul McCartney."

Still, by autumn, John was making encouraging noises about the Beatles working together again, saying they'd probably leave it until 1976, when their contract with EMI was due to expire. "I'd like the Beatles," he told a journalist, coolly sucking on a cigarette, "to make a record together again."

If he did, he had a funny way of showing it. In the second week of December, three of the ex-Beatles were by chance in New York at the same time. A plan was swiftly hatched to meet up for the signing of the recently completed 202-page document that would finally dissolve the band's partnership, freeing up millions in royalties. The papers were to be ceremoniously inked at the Plaza Hotel on Central Park South. On the morning of December 19, 1974, Paul and George arrived at a suite there, to be met with piles of contracts laid out on green baize tables.

Lennon didn't show, on the advice of his astrologer, revealing that the superstitious influence of Ono—she and John having begun the tentative process of reuniting—was back in play. Instead, he sent a balloon to the hotel bearing the enigmatic message "Listen to this balloon." Harrison hit the roof. He furiously rang Lennon, only across Central Park visiting Yoko at the Dakota, and bawled down the line, "You fucking maniac. You take your fucking dark glasses off and come and look at us, man."

It didn't work. An untypically huffy Linda later noted, "The numbers weren't right, the planets weren't right and John wasn't coming. Had we known there was some guy flipping cards on his bed to help him make his decision, we would all have gone over there."

"It was all quite far out," said Paul.

George was at the end of his first and only solo tour of the United States; he'd been criticized for his weak vocal performances, and for taking a haphazard, Dylan-like approach to radically rearranging his best-known songs. That night, Paul and Linda attended his show at Madison Square Garden, heavily disguised in shades, Afro wigs, and fuzzy fake mustaches, highlighting the sense of the ludicrous in the air.

Meanwhile, over Christmas in Florida, where he was on holiday with Pang and his son Julian, John finally signed the dissolution papers releasing the Beatles' money. Perhaps fittingly, given the cartoon reality of having been a Beatle, he put pen to paper at Disney World.

The following month, January 1975, Paul invited John down to New Orleans to get involved in the next Wings album. Lennon was seriously toying with the idea and had been sounding out various individuals for their opinions over the previous weeks. He asked Art Garfunkel, who had recently made up with Paul Simon, what he should do about the overtures from "*my* Paul." Garfunkel told him that he thought Lennon and McCartney should try to forget their personality differences and just make music together. John then wrote to former Beatles publicist Derek Taylor, saying that he was possibly going down to New Orleans "to see the McCartknees."

One evening in the East Fifty-second Street apartment, out of nowhere, Lennon asked Pang, "What would you think if I started writing with Paul again?"

She turned to him, open-mouthed, and said, "Are you kidding? I think it would be terrific."

Later that night, Lennon disappeared to the Dakota, enticed by Ono, who claimed to have discovered a foolproof smoking cure. Whatever happened that night, Pang says that Lennon returned to her changed. The reunion with Paul in Louisiana wasn't ever mentioned again.

The allure of the city's kaleidoscopically funky music scene had drawn Paul to New Orleans. Besides, there were tax advantages to be gained by recording in the States again—he'd be earning seventy cents on the dollar, rather than two pence on the pound. Added to this, McCartney loved the punchy drum sound captured on Labelle's lascivious 1974 hit "Lady Marmalade," recorded at Allen Toussaint's Sea-Saint Studios, which became the setting for the recording of the next Wings album, *Venus and Mars*.

Ironically, given the fact that McCartney had been attracted to the southern recording facility because of the drum sound, Paul felt Geoff Britton was struggling, both on a playing level and emotionally. The drummer's marriage was in trouble, and he had been dreading the trip. "I was so depressed," he admitted. "It should have been the happiest time of my life. But I was miserable and hated it. There was no sincerity in the band, and every day it was a fight for survival, a fight to reestablish yourself."

Britton noticed that, from the outset in New Orleans, Laine and McCulloch were distant with him, although he wasn't exactly trying to reach out to them with his talk of "thick northerners." "Well, they were thick northerners," he contended. "There's no hiding facts." He unequivocally considered Denny "a bastard." Jimmy, meanwhile, was "a cunt." For his part, Laine thought that Britton was only in it for the money: "He was always talking about 'When I get my big house . . .' The guy was an opportunist. It was a disaster, basically."

In Paul's measured, diplomatic opinion, "He wasn't quite like the rest of us. We had a sense of humor in common. He was nearly in with it all. But it's a fine line."

Two weeks into the sessions, one morning at their hotel in the French Quarter, the McCartneys turned up at Britton's room and told him that they were letting him go. "I got marched out and that was the end of it," he says.

"It was horrible because we really wanted it to work," said Linda. "It was another depressing period. We had started *Venus and Mars,* but it just wasn't working."

On many levels, Britton hadn't clicked. In his place came Joe English, a New Yorker blessed with natural swing, recommended by *Venus and Mars* trombone player and arranger Tony Dorsey. The drummer had played with an outfit called the Jam Factory, which had supported Jimi Hendrix and the Allman Brothers, but he had been on the skids for the previous two years. He was playing some sessions on the Macon-centered southern rock circuit, but he was broke and his wife had left with their two kids. It would be some time before it was revealed that English was expertly masking some serious demons of his own.

Floating above their worries, while in New Orleans the McCartneys were determined to enjoy the everlasting party. They took five days off for Mardi Gras and slipped into the crowds dressed as clowns. They threw a party–cum–press conference on a riverboat, the *Voyager,* and sailed up and down the bayou to the groovesome live R&B sounds of the Meters. The members of Wings turned out, looking resplendent in black top hats. They remained, for the meantime at least, a band projecting the illusion of unity, held together by mirrors and sticky tape.

9

LIFTOFFS AND LANDINGS

The mid-1970s seemed to become very intense for you. . . .

Well, yeah. But we did what we set out to do. Didn't cave in
under the pressure.

IT WAS JUST AFTER MIDNIGHT when the patrol car pulled them over. They
had been driving down Santa Monica Boulevard in their silver Lincoln
Continental when Paul took a right turn, missing a sign forbidding the
maneuver and running a red light. As the officer leaned into the car he
caught a whiff of grass. Everyone—Paul, Linda, and the three kids
asleep in the back—was ordered out of the vehicle.

According to the patrolman's report, a search of Linda's purse produced a plastic bag containing seventeen grams of marijuana, along
with a still-smoldering joint fished out from under the passenger seat.
Linda and Paul were immediately placed under arrest, before the
former—probably fearing ensuing U.S. visa problems—protested that
the dope was hers and that it had been her alone, not her husband,
smoking the spliff.

Paul insists to this day that the weed was planted by the police.
"They came up with a big bag of stuff that wasn't ours," he says.

Whatever the truth, the outcome was that Linda was detained for two hours while Paul drove the kids back to their rented house in Cold-water Canyon. He returned to the station where his wife was being held to discover that she had been charged with possession, her bail set at $500. Embarrassed, Paul had to confess that he was carrying only $200. In the middle of the night, he was forced to call former Apple executive director Peter Brown, who he knew was in town staying at the Beverly Hills Hotel, to borrow the rest.

Worse, there was the threat that a second and more damning charge—contributing to the delinquency of a minor—might be thrown at Linda, since she'd admitted to smoking weed while looking after her children. It all added to the couple's mounting feelings of harassment. "We were being targeted all the time," Linda groaned. "Maybe we were asking for it. Maybe we were a bit stupid. But we're not criminals."

The McCartneys were in Los Angeles enjoying something of a par-tying lifestyle; they'd lived it up at the Beverly Wilshire (where, Jo Jo Patrie noted, the normally thrifty couple put no limits on the hotel tabs) before moving into the Coldwater Canyon house. There was much to celebrate. Two nights earlier, on March 1, 1975—before an audience that included the reunited Lennon and Ono, who turned up with a tux-wearing, cocaine-emaciated David Bowie in tow—they had picked up two Grammys for *Band on the Run*. The album had steadily grown to become a towering success: five million copies sold, the bestselling U.K. album of 1974, named Album of the Year by the previously sniffy *Rolling Stone,* and so on and on.

Wings was in town putting the finishing touches to the initially troubled *Venus and Mars,* the making of which had become far easier with the introduction of Joe English and the move to California. To toast its completion, the McCartneys decided to throw a costly wrap party for the record aboard the RMS *Queen Mary,* a retired ocean liner docked in the waters off Long Beach. The two hundred guests included some of the top players in music and film at the time, including Joni Mitchell, Marvin Gaye, Bob Dylan, Cher, Led Zeppelin, Ryan and Tatum O'Neal, Dean Martin, and Tony Curtis. Guests were guided into the ship's Grand Saloon along a corridor bearing posters featuring the album's cosmic, cryptic slogan, "Venus and Mars are alright tonight." Later a woman, mistaking the planets of the album title as alter egos for the McCartneys, confounded them by walking up to them and saying, "Hello Venus, hello Mars."

Surprising everyone, given his recent put-down of McCartney in the press, George Harrison showed up, and he and his estranged bandmate were seen chatting. The party also marked the first time Paul and Michael Jackson met. Jackson remembered that he and McCartney were introduced and shook hands among a large crowd of people before the latter said, "You know, I've written a song for you."

"I was very surprised and thanked him," a thrilled Jackson recalled. "And he started singing 'Girlfriend' to me."

Paul didn't make quite such an impression on everyone. As the evening wore on, an utterly soused Dean Martin sat at a table with the McCartneys, repeatedly roaring, "Who the hell is giving this party? Do I know these people?"

With his star in the ascendant once more, Paul began planning a world tour befitting his status. There were signs, however, that he was doing so with some trepidation.

McCartney Productions had recently become the more ambitious MPL Communications, and moved its offices from Greek Street, in London's West End, around the corner to a five-story townhouse at 1 Soho Square. Paul fancied turning its sizable basement into a club, where he could play lunchtime gigs for office workers and serve up hot dogs, taking him back to the days of the cellar-based Casbah Coffee Club in Liverpool. MPL managing director Brian Brolly talked him out of the idea, pointing out that demand for tickets would be unreasonably high and the scheme would prove unworkable. If Paul was trying to shy away from the pressures of a big tour, this wasn't the way to go.

Instead, the Wings musicians got their heads down for an intensive rehearsal period lasting four whole months, highlighting just how determined McCartney was to get the band sounding right. There were rumors that the group was to play an outdoor show at Knebworth House in the summer of 1975. Instead, the slot was filled by Pink Floyd, which performed before an audience of one hundred thousand—too head-spinning a leap for the fledgling second lineup of Wings.

Venus and Mars, however, was a record built for touring. It even opened like a gig, with the gentle acoustic guitar picking of the title track finding the singer imagining himself in the audience at an arena concert, waiting for the lights to go down. This segued into the thumping "Rock Show," with its references to Jimmy Page, Madison Square Garden, and the Hollywood Bowl and, perhaps tellingly, scoring an entire ounce of dope, far more than the average long-haired punter could afford.

Rather than being Wings' New Orleans-flavored album, *Venus and Mars* was far more adventurous stylistically, from the floaty Californian FM sound of "Listen to What the Man Said" and the glassy-eyed hippie balladry of "Love in Song" to the tap-dancing music-hall frippery of "You Gave Me the Answer." The lyrical references took in the lowbrow ("Magneto and Titanium Man," inspired by a comic book found in Jamaica) and the high-minded (sci-fi writer Isaac Asimov influencing the futuristic couplets of "Venus and Mars—Reprise").

Yet having turned in a credible rock album in tune with the times, McCartney came close to blowing it with an oddball ending. "Treat Her Gently/Lonely Old People," a sensitive, if syrupy ode to old age and dementia, gave way to a rocktastic rendering of the theme from cozy U.K. teatime soap opera *Crossroads*. To Paul, it sounded like a show-stopping, Diana-Ross-is-leaving-the-building concert crescendo. To everyone else, it was a touch more cheese than was palatable, even if the soap's producers were subsequently moved to use the Wings version to soundtrack the program's end credits.

"One of the big things for lonely old people in England is to watch *Crossroads*," Paul argued, explaining the thinking behind this slightly strange finale. "That was it, just a joke at the end." Around the same time, more illuminatingly perhaps, when filling in the "weight" section of a teen-mag fact file, Paul wrote, "2 stoned."

Jokey ending notwithstanding, there were high expectations for *Venus and Mars*. Preorders alone for the LP exceeded 1.5 million. The cover was just as striking as the one for *Band on the Run:* red and yellow billiard balls, representing the planets of the title, expertly shot by Linda on a low-lit deep-blue baize.

Since they were spending most of their time getting ready for the tour, rarer now were the occasions when the McCartneys would all pile into their new green Rolls-Royce convertible and motor north to High Park. Instead, aside from a summer break in the United States when they stayed with the Eastmans in the Hamptons, the family was based for most of the time at Cavendish Avenue in London, where slightly aghast visitors would note that the indulgent parents allowed their kids to scribble on the walls.

To the horror of their snooty neighbors, over the years since Linda's arrival, the McCartneys' St. John's Wood abode had increasingly begun to resemble a city farm. The garden was full of weeds and, on wet days, mud. Alongside a glass geodesic "meditation dome," erected in the late 1960s and containing a large round bed given to Paul by Alice Cooper (who had originally been gifted it by Groucho Marx), it was home to a vegetable patch and a mucky menagerie of animals, from dogs and cats to ducks and rabbits. On one occasion Paul left the window of the Rolls-Royce open and, for a time, the chickens moved in, necessitating a reupholstering job costing £6,000. The family's cockerel would crow the long-suffering neighbors awake at first light. The McCartneys reinstated the stable blocks in the garden and kept four horses, which, donning hats and jodhpurs, they would ride on Sunday mornings.

All of this made the McCartneys less than popular in their exclusive urban locale. Once an irate neighbor phoned the RSPCA to complain that the dogs were left alone in the house all day when the family was elsewhere. A representative of the animal welfare charity visited, but left satisfied with the assurance that the family's part-nanny, part-housekeeper Rose Martin popped in once a day to make sure they were fine.

Inside, the living-room decor of Cavendish Avenue was millionaire boho with a hint of working-class. There were dark gray and brown carpets, and a green armchair and couch—with a rip that the kittens would disappear into—were arranged around a low coffee table covered with a checked Madras tablecloth. The furniture was cheap or second-hand, and matched with more expensive or antique items: Tiffany lampshades, a clock from the 1851 Great Exhibition, a robotlike sculpture by the Scottish artist Eduardo Paolozzi named *Solo*. Dotted around the walls were originals by Magritte and de Kooning.

At the same time, missing their bucolic Scottish retreat, the couple bought an unusual property for £42,000 in Peasmarsh, near Rye, on the Sussex coast. A circular, slightly cramped two-bedroom cottage with wedge-shaped rooms and over 160 acres of land, it mirrored High Park in being a small house set in an expanse of untamed nature. Its insides were soon filled with the McCartneys' clutter, and the couple shifted half an ark's worth of animals on to the land: horses, sheep, hens, pheasants, even an aviary of budgies. A stream that cascaded over a drop gave the property its name, Waterfall.

Back in London, at the same time, the pressures were piling up. In anticipation of the upcoming tour, a news story in *Melody Maker* carped, "Linda McCartney faces her sternest test yet." On September 5, Wings performed a dress rehearsal of the tour production at Elstree Studios for an invited audience of guests including Ringo and Harry Nilsson. According to Paul, even after the months of persnickety rehearsal, "it showed up a lot of holes in the show."

These were holes that needed to be filled, and quickly. This time around, Wings wasn't just a bunch of hippies jumping into a van. This time, there would be no room for mistakes.

"Just what keeps you going?" called out one reporter.

"Drugs!" replied a chipper McCartney.

It was September 11, 1975, the morning after the second date of the British leg of Wings' world tour, an ambitious jaunt expected to last a year and to sweep through Europe, Australia, Japan, and America. To fire up the excitement surrounding it, the band was giving a press conference at the Post House Hotel in Bristol, the city having been the scene of the previous night's show.

As much as Paul was attempting to draw a deep line in the sand between the Beatles and the newly streamlined Wings, he couldn't avoid the inevitable questions.

"Have you seen the Beatles lately?" quizzed another journalist.

"We run into each other and stuff," said Paul. "We're just good friends."

"Is Wings really a logical development from the Beatles?"

"Well, I've always written songs, but with the Beatles we only ever rehearsed for three days at the most. With this band, we rehearse a lot."

"Will Wings ever become as big as the Beatles?"

"I think it could be, funnily enough."

"How different is Wings from the Beatles?"

"They scream at our concerts, but they don't scream as much. People used to come and scream and didn't hear any of the music. Now they can."

"Do you want to bring back the Beatles?"

"It wasn't within my power to bring back the Beatles. It was a four-way split and we all wanted to do different things. We're all very good friends. John is keeping very quiet at the moment, while unfortunately I'm out working. I like it."

Later, Linda confessed to one journalist that the ex-Fabs were, unsurprisingly, sick of being asked over and over and over again about the possibility of the band re-forming. "They'll ask about the Beatles forever," she rightly pointed out. Even onstage, McCartney couldn't escape the relentless interrogation. Midway through the second of two sold-out shows at the Hammersmith Odeon in London a week later, one fan shouted, "What about John Lennon?" Trying to remain cheery and playfully dismissive, Paul responded, "What about him?"

Nevertheless, the set list for the tour proved that McCartney was confident about his post-Beatles output, comprising as it did mainly songs from *Band on the Run* and *Venus and Mars*. In a nod to his past, however, partway through, he offered up a crowd-pleasing medley of "Lady Madonna," "The Long and Winding Road," "I've Just Seen a Face," "Blackbird," and "Yesterday"—the last two performed solo, on acoustic guitar, literally spotlighting his formidable talents, lest anyone had forgotten. From the outside, Paul projected nothing but self-assurance.

Internally, however, it was another matter. If during a show, from the stage, he could see someone in the audience walking out or even lighting a cigarette, he would fret that he had lost their attention. He hated the fact that, at thirty-three, he was being cast as an old man of rock by the music press or, denting his ego, a throwback to the 1960s. "I suppose I am from another age," he ruminated wistfully.

Still, in perhaps the first wave of rock nostalgia, there was enormous demand for tickets for the tour. Fanning the flames of anticipation, in its review of the show, *Melody Maker* deemed it to be "excellent," going on to say that it would "awaken Beatlemania across the Atlantic."

As the tour progressed, this didn't seem like hot air. In Melbourne, fifteen hundred hardy and determined souls queued for tickets overnight under skies filled with rain, thunder, and lightning. Displaying less dedication, on October 27 the McCartneys slept in on the morning of the flight down under, forcing a Qantas jet filled with their tetchy fellow passengers to idle on the tarmac for forty-five minutes while the family rushed to Heathrow. Hitting him precisely where it hurt, the airline fined Paul $9,000 for holding the plane up—$200 for every minute of the delay.

A cartoon that appeared in *The Sun* two days later, sketched by the paper's regular satirist Stanley Arthur Franklin, depicted a planeload of furious passengers spitting out their Foster's lager, chewing the seats, suffering heart attacks, and, in one instance, pulling out a revolver, as a grinning, laid-back Paul, reclining with his hands behind his head, receives the cabin PA announcement: "We regret having to turn back, cobbers, but Mr. McCartney has forgotten his toothbrush . . ."

It had been eleven years since Paul had toured Australia with the Beatles, and once Wings landed in the country, the response was no less overwhelming. Beatlemaniacal scenes met the McCartneys at Perth Airport, with Paul walking along the front row of fervent fans, shaking hands, while carrying a bemused, four-year-old Stella.

One television reporter touched a recently exposed nerve when he pointed out to McCartney, "Thirty-three, that's a bit old for rock'n'roll."

"Ancient . . . ancient," Paul responded, fiddling with his hair, annoyance clearly bubbling just below the surface.

"Do you think you're past it?" asked the hack.

"I don't know," Paul replied, visibly ruffled. "I wouldn't be here if I thought I was. But you come and see the show, and if you like the show, you tell me if I'm over my peak after it, okay?" Before he broke away, he added, "And if you tell me I am, it's coats off outside, cobber."

Wings quickly settled in Australia, throwing a thirty-first-birthday party for Denny Laine on October 29, in which the musicians and their friends cruised around the Perth waters on a hydrofoil. As was fast becoming their routine, they threw a press conference in the city to meet the media. Arriving in a room filled with two hundred representatives from newspapers, magazines, and TV channels, the group found a figure—in a cheap brown suit, his thinning hair greasily slicked forward, a piece of toilet paper sticking to a shaving cut—apparently asleep in one of their chairs.

It turned out to be the Aussie comic creation Norman Gunston (in reality, actor Garry McDonald), who awoke and immediately hijacked the proceedings, turning them into a two-way ribbing routine between himself and the band. Was Paul planning to open another fruit shop after the failure of Apple? Was there any truth in the rumor that he'd been dead? As a wedded couple in a band, did Linda ever feel like telling her husband that she couldn't perform that night due to a headache? How, indeed, was the marriage going?

"It's all right," Paul responded, as gales of slightly nervous laughter blew around the room. "But you're not helping it, Norm."

McCartney was in a jocular mood throughout the tour. During his solo portion of the set, he took to introducing "Yesterday" by saying, "Tell you what, see if you remember this one." Then he'd pick the opening chords of his most famous song to thunderous applause before atonally singing, "What a jolly swine." The audience, teased, would howl with laughter. He'd pause and begin again to a deafening chorus of female screams and male roars.

The news that arrived on November 11 temporarily wiped the smile off his face, however. The Japanese authorities, citing the Scottish marijuana conviction of 1973, were refusing Wings entry to the country. The gigs there had to be scrapped. Paul was initially angered by the ban: the Japanese embassy in London had already approved his visa. "They're still old-fashioned out there," he reasoned. "The older folks see a great danger in allowing in an alien who has admitted smoking marijuana and they're trying to stamp it out, using all the wrong methods, as usual."

The Melbourne show, having been filmed for Australia, was sent to Japan to be screened as an apology to fans, along with a televised Japanese debate about marijuana. Paul lamented the fact that he and Linda "had become martyrs for the cause." Interviewed in Australia on the daytime chat program *The Mike Walsh Show*, as Linda, Jimmy, and Denny lolled around him, Paul, looking and sounding lightly refreshed, pointed out that it was a two-year-old charge and that, after arguing their case, the authorities in both Australia and the United States had agreed to let him in. It was the Japanese minister of justice alone who had nixed the visit.

"He's no friend o' mine!" joked Paul, in a passable Scottish accent, eyeballing the viewers at home.

"The first chance I get, I'll put him doon," added Denny Laine.

"You could put him doon, I'll stick the heid on him," slurred the genuinely Scottish Jimmy McCulloch, looking as if he just might, given the chance.

As a postscript, Paul filmed a message of apology to the Japanese fans. But it was a smirking McCartney who faced the lens to say, "We're very sorry that we can't come to Japan to play our music to you this time. But if the minister of justice says we can't come in, then we can't come in. Don't worry, we'll see you when we come back to your beautiful country . . . *sayonara.*"

He put his hands together and bowed his head, spread them into a W shape to represent the Wings logo, and then smiled knowingly.

A certain cockiness now evident in the McCartneys' demeanor was noticed by others. In New York, a longtime friend of Linda's, the writer Danny Fields, was gobsmacked when the couple visited him, got stoned, and then asked to borrow money from him for the cab fare back uptown.

"We don't bother carrying money in New York," Linda told him. "We just tell the cab driver who we are, and then we sign autographs for him and he says we should forget what's on the meter." On this occasion they needed cash for the return journey since, on the way down to Fields's apartment, they'd encountered a driver who hadn't recognized them. "Sure enough, he wanted money," Linda moaned. "I had some coins in my purse. We told him it was a lot of money in New Zealand or something."

Eight days before Christmas 1975, Paul and Linda turned up unannounced to see John and Yoko at the Dakota. The Lennons were sitting in their bedroom with photographer Bob Gruen when they heard voices directly outside their apartment door. Lennon was instantly freaked, since the arrangement at the building was that any visitors first had to pass by the doormen at the gates and introduce themselves to the concierge, who would then call upstairs.

The Lennons nervously asked Gruen to check who it was. He walked into the hall and unlocked the inner door, leaving the outer door closed. Hearing the sound of voices harmonizing, he shouted back to John and Yoko in the bedroom, "Don't worry, it's just kids in the building singing Christmas carols." When he opened the second door, there before him stood Paul and Linda singing "We Wish You a Merry Christmas." The photographer, taken aback, said, "I think you're looking for the guys in the bedroom . . . come on in."

As Gruen remembers, "It was like old friends meeting by surprise and really glad to see each other. We sat around and drank tea." Paul and Linda griped to a sympathetic John and Yoko about the Japanese dope ban. "They were talking about what a small thing it was. They were very sorry that they couldn't go to Japan for such a seemingly trivial reason."

As Lennon and McCartney began to rebuild their friendship properly, in February 1976 a U.S. promoter named Bill Sargent made them an offer that seemed irresistible. He was willing to pay a re-formed Beatles $50 million for a one-off show. When, by March, there had been no response, he doubled the offer. At the same time, a U.S. industrialist, Mike Matthews, the head of the guitar effects pedal company Electro-Harmonix, offered them $3 million, with an additional cut of pay-per-view TV revenue that would up their share to more than $30 million. Lee Eastman, speaking for McCartney, stated that these offers weren't "even being considered."

Privately, Paul asked the other ex-Beatles if they should put out a joint statement turning down the offers. No one would commit to it. Going it alone, McCartney began to contradict himself in the press. One minute he was saying that his response to the offer was a "positive maybe," the next that any Beatles reunion would only happen "if we wanted to do something musically, not . . . just for the money." It came back to that familiar fear that they might desecrate their legacy. Around this time, Paul in London and John in New York had a long chat on the phone. Never once were the offers or the specter of a re-formation even mentioned.

Still, with the Wings tours of Europe and the United States looming, the Beatles once again threatened to overshadow everything as Parlophone/EMI reissued all twenty-two of their U.K. singles at once, along with a 45 of "Yesterday." *Reveille* magazine, in Britain, reported that this had created a "Beatles Boom!," particularly among a new generation of teenagers discovering the group for the first time. At one point, in the U.K. Top 100, the Beatles occupied twenty-three places. Accordingly, EMI's profits for the period rose by a third.

But Paul, who had just released the chirpy, critic-challenging "Silly Love Songs" with Wings, was riled by the idea of having to compete with the ghost of his younger self. "I wouldn't want 'Silly Love Songs' kept off the top by 'Love Me Do,'" he noted, bristling.

Linda, Heather, and Paul arrive at JFK Airport, New York City,
March 17, 1969, five days after their London wedding. Paul: "She had a child.
I was genuinely impressed by the way she handled herself in life."

Promo shot of Paul used to promote the release
of *Let It Be,* in May 1970.

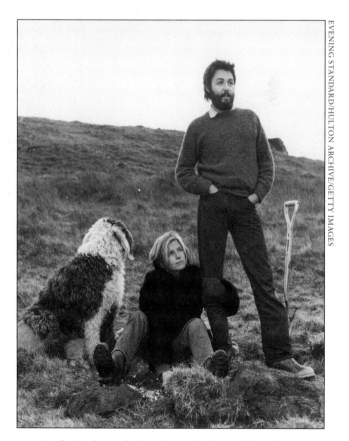

Paul, Linda, and sheepdog Martha at High Park,
Argyll, Scotland, January 1971, only days after
McCartney filed his lawsuit to sue the other Beatles.

McCartney the family man: (left to right) Mary, Paul, Linda, Heather, in 1970.

Paul and Linda emerge from the High
Court in London on February 19, 1971,
on the first day of the proceedings to
untangle the Beatles' legal affairs.
Paul: "I was having to fight my mates.
It was just fucking awful."

Allen Klein, the master of
casual intimidation, March 1971.

Wings Over Europe sound check, Châteauvallon, France, July 9, 1972.
Paul and Denny Seiwell go over keyboard parts with a nervous Linda.
Seiwell: "She was unhappy and frightened. But she had a lot of chutzpah."

Paul the bed-headed businessman, behind the desk, 1972.

The fivesome with the trundling, freakadelic, open-topped bus used for
Wings Over Europe, July 1972.

The McCartneys peer out of the back of a police car after the Swedish dope bust,
Gothenburg, August 10, 1972. Linda to photographer Joe Stevens:
"Just get the pictures."

December 1, 1972, the day "Hi Hi Hi" was released and instantly banned by the BBC.
Paul: "I think the BBC should be highly praised, preventing the youth
from hearing my opinions."

Outside Campbeltown Sheriff Court, March 1973, trying to keep straight faces, after being fined for growing marijuana in Scotland. Paul: "We got a load of seeds. . . . We didn't know what they were. [We] planted them all and five of them came up . . . illegal."

The McCartneys—with Paul's mullet in full flow—fly out from London to Jamaica for a vacation before the release of *Red Rose Speedway,* April 1973: (left to right) Heather, Linda, Stella, Paul, Mary.

Surrounded by sheep, filming a clip for the maligned
"Mary Had a Little Lamb" (released the year before) as part of the
James Paul McCartney TV special, March 10, 1973.

Linda snaps Paul during the making of the *James Paul McCartney* TV special,
Elstree Studios, England.

Dressed up in La-La Land. At the 46th Annual Academy Awards, April 1974.
"Live and Let Die" was nominated for Best Original Song but lost out
to Barbra Streisand's "The Way We Were."

On the porch of songwriter Curly Putnam Jr.'s house,
Tennessee, July 1974, toasting the end of the troubled
preliminary rehearsals with Wings Mark II.

The McCartneys and their horses: (left to right) Heather, Mary, Paul, Linda, Stella.
Paul: "It was more like gypsies than anything else."

All together now: the extended McCartney family reunites in Liverpool, including Paul's brother, Mike (in hat), and his father, Jim (far right), with second wife, Angie.

Paul making a sandwich at the back of the Wings tour bus in 1975. Note the two Rolls-Royces following behind the coach for added comfort.

Paul and Linda with their daughters, Heather, Stella, and Mary, on the grounds of their house in Peasmarsh, near Rye, Sussex, England, April 4, 1976.

The record-trouncing, critics-bowling, all-conquering Wings lineup of 1976:
(left to right) Joe English, Linda, Jimmy McCulloch, Paul,
and Denny Laine.

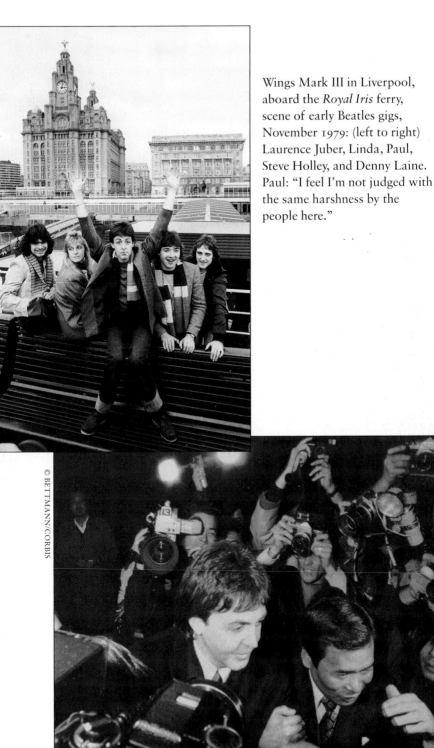

Wings Mark III in Liverpool, aboard the *Royal Iris* ferry, scene of early Beatles gigs, November 1979: (left to right) Laurence Juber, Linda, Paul, Steve Holley, and Denny Laine. Paul: "I feel I'm not judged with the same harshness by the people here."

Still smiling amid the crush and chaos, in spite of the potential seven-year jail sentence hanging over his head for carrying nearly half a pound of weed into Japan, January 1980. Paul: "It was like a sort of mad movie."

Greeting the British press at the Sussex farm after being deported from Japan, January 28, 1980. Asked whether he was planning to spend time with his family, Paul responded: "Yeah, if you fellas would leave me alone, that *would* be possible."

© DAVID HARRIS/HULTON ARCHIVE/GETTY IMAGES

———

On March 18, 1976, Paul's father, Jim, died, from a combination of bronchial pneumonia and heart failure, at home in Rembrandt, the house his famous son had bought for him in the village of Gayton on the Wirral, Merseyside. Paul received the news from Jim's second wife, Angie, in a telephone call to the Royal Garden Hotel in London, where the Wings band members were staying prior to leaving for the European tour.

"I'm sorry, son, it just happened," said Angie.

"Are you sure?" Paul asked her, shocked.

To the astonishment of outsiders, McCartney didn't attend the cremation, held four days later at Landican Cemetery, near Jim McCartney's home. The idea that a son wouldn't attend his own father's funeral was, of course, unthinkable. In the end, there were two reasons for Paul's decision: first, the media attention would mar the service—Angie said "it would just be a circus"; second, he couldn't face the emotional trauma of grieving in public. His brother, Mike, admitted, "Paul would never face that sort of thing. As Dad would say, 'It's just the way you're made, son.'"

Instead, Paul threw himself back into work. "That's just my character. I suppose I coped by remembering him as he was. He used to hate funerals and all of that sort of stuff, so I didn't get involved. I sort of thought, Well, he hated it, so it would be kind of hypocritical to go and do all the weeping and wailing."

Linda admitted to Danny Fields that going to the funeral would have "caused problems," but she worried that she and Paul were being criticized for not attending. Paul was later to become estranged from Angie and his stepsister, Ruth, who he believed had profited from selling memorabilia from his dad's home.

Weirdly, however, even though Lennon was among the first to hear the news and called McCartney to offer his condolences, Paul didn't tell the other members of Wings. The first Denny Laine knew about it was when Paul was randomly asked in a press conference in Paris whether either of his parents were still alive. McCartney flatly replied, "No." Laine was gobsmacked. "Paul is . . . quite privately shy," he reasons. "It's just his personality."

Meanwhile the group was on a roll, having swiftly completed their fifth album, *Wings at the Speed of Sound,* released a mere ten months after *Venus and Mars.* This increased productivity was partly due to the fact that this was the band's first "democratic" album, opening up the lead vocal performances to all members in overtly trying to prove that Wings was a real band and not merely a construct of session musicians built to prop up McCartney's ego.

In both this open band arrangement and its mellow West Coast characteristics, *Wings at the Speed of Sound* went some way to emulating the Eagles, then a dominant force on the U.S. charts. The record opened with the literally inviting "Let 'Em In," in which a languid-voiced Paul acted as welcoming host to an imaginary parade of guests, including the Everly Brothers, his brother, Mike, and his Auntie Gin. Elsewhere, Denny Laine turned in an aching performance on "The Note You Never Wrote," Joe English was cast as a brokenhearted country singer on the lonesome "Must Do Something About It," and Linda played it for laughs with the proto-rock'n'roll of "Cook of the House," which depicted her getting busy-busy in the kitchen and closed with the sound of chips frying, sounding like applause.

Jimmy McCulloch, meanwhile, in cahoots with the former Stone the Crows drummer and lyricist Colin Allen, offered another of their anti-drug songs, mined from the same vein as the cautionary "Medicine Jar" from *Venus and Mars.* "Wino Junko" closed the first side of *Wings at the Speed of Sound* with a lilting melody, finding the "pill freak" narrator addressing his addictions and even noting that he was unafraid to risk his life for his beloved highs. Even if the words weren't his own, McCulloch might have been advised to listen closer to the song he was singing, since he was increasingly becoming a worrying and unstable element of Wings. At the outset of the European tour, photographer Robert Ellis noted that Jimmy was becoming "really hard to handle. . . . He was constantly paranoid and constantly out of his head."

This was proved in ludicrous fashion on March 26, 1976, in Paris, where Wings had taken up residence at the swish Hotel George V. After the show at the Pavillon de Paris, the band and entourage, sans McCartneys, sprawled out in the bar, where they began drinking heavily, pulling teen idol David Cassidy into their orbit. At some point the party repaired upstairs, where a fight broke out when a spectacularly leathered McCulloch accused Cassidy of being a "fag" and took a swing at him.

Cassidy went to block McCulloch's punch, accidentally knocking him to the floor. The heated and chaotic scene quickly cooled when it became apparent that McCulloch had injured a finger, fracturing the bone.

The much trumpeted upcoming U.S. tour—due to be the first time McCartney would appear live in America in a decade, before an expected audience of half a million, yielding an estimated $4 million in profits—was postponed, at great expense, for three weeks, because of McCulloch's drunken antics. Talking to reporters, Jimmy and Paul tried to laugh off the incident. The guitarist fibbed and said he'd broken the finger after slipping on a wet floor when getting out of the bath.

"Yeah," Paul added darkly. "We're gonna break his arm next week."

10

HIGH OVER AMERICA

*It's tempting to snip up those solo Beatles LPs and picture maybe
"Jet" on the same album as "Imagine" and "My Sweet Lord" . . .*

That's right. Could've been all right. Let's do that then and we'll call
it the Beatles. It would have been good, I suppose, from that point of
view. But we just decided we'd done it. We'd come full circle and
enough was enough. It would've been a calculated move to put the
Beatles back together, just 'cause some guy offered us millions.
Between us, at various moments, one of us would get hot on the idea
and the big offer would come in, but it was like, Nah. That was one
good thing about the Beatles—it just all flowed, it just came shooting
out of us. And it was like, Let's leave it. Let sleeping dogs lie.

S ITTING BEHIND A DESK, adopting an air of mock seriousness, Lorne
Michaels, the producer and occasional presenter of NBC's comedy
and music revue *Saturday Night Live,* faced the camera, twelve items
into the show's broadcast of April 24, 1976. The starring guests that
week included the voluptuous film star Raquel Welch and John Sebas-
tian, founder of the feel-good 1960s pop band the Lovin' Spoonful,
plugging his theme song to the high school sitcom *Welcome Back, Kot-
ter,* set to become the U.S. No. 1 single the following month. Comedian
Chevy Chase had opened the show, in a skit where he'd presented an
award to the best "political actor," the nominees including presidential
candidates Jimmy Carter and Gerald Ford. There had been a spoof ad
for Purina pet food for rats, and John Belushi had turned in his uncom-
fortably grimacing impersonation of British singer Joe Cocker.

Now, in what appeared to be a break in transmission, Michaels
looked set to make an important announcement.

"We're being seen by approximately twenty-two million viewers," he began. "But please allow me, if I may, to address myself to four very special people . . . John, Paul, George, and Ringo . . . the Beatles. Lately there have been a lot of rumors to the effect that the four of you might be getting back together. That would be great. In my book, the Beatles are the best thing that ever happened to music. It goes even deeper than that. You're not just a musical group. You're a part of us. We grew up with you.

"It's for this reason that I'm inviting you to come on our show. Now, we've heard and read a lot about personality and legal conflicts that might prevent you guys from reuniting. That's none of my business. You guys will have to handle that. But it's also been said that no one has yet come up with *enough* money to satisfy you. Well, if it's money you want, there's no problem here. The National Broadcasting Company has authorized *me* to offer *you* a certified check for three thousand dollars. Here, can you get a close-up of this?"

Michaels held a check up to the camera, clearly inked out to the Beatles.

"As you can see," he went on, "verifiably, a check made out to you, the Beatles, for three thousand dollars. All you have to do is sing three Beatle tunes. 'She loves you, yeah yeah yeah'—that's a thousand dollars right there. You know the words, it'll be easy. Like I said, this check is made out to the Beatles. You divide it any way you want. If you want to give Ringo less, that's up to you. I'd rather not get involved. I'm sincere about this. If it helps you to reach a decision to reunite, well then, it's a worthwhile investment. You have agents. You know where I can be reached. Just think about it, okay?"

Unknown to Michaels, only twenty-two blocks north of the TV studio at Rockefeller Plaza, Paul and John, together with Linda and Yoko, were sitting up late at the Dakota—watching the show, laughing their asses off, and, just for a minute, actually considering his offer.

"Wouldn't it be funny if we went down?" said John. "We should go down there. We should go down now and just do it."

The pair toyed with the idea of jumping in a cab and making it to the studio before the end of the ninety-minute broadcast. Then, once their laughter had subsided, the cold reality of the prospect set in, and they decided they were too tired. When the show was over, in the small hours of Sunday morning, Paul and Linda left John and Yoko settling down to watch a screening of the 1960 film adaptation of H. G. Wells's *The Time Machine.*

As jokey as it was, Michaels's offer obviously planted a seed in McCartney's mind. That evening, he returned to the Dakota, this time carrying a guitar. But John, who had been looking after baby Sean all day, was in a very different mood from the previous night and bluntly snubbed him. There was likely some jealousy at play on Lennon's part— the previous day had seen *Wings at the Speed of Sound* rise to the top of the U.S. album chart for a seven-week run; he had recently read that Paul, because of Wings' newfound earning power, was worth $25 million and had moaned to Yoko that he would never earn that kind of money.

"Please call before you come over," he snapped at an upset McCartney. "It's not 1956, and turning up at the door isn't the same anymore."

Later, a contrite John stated, "I didn't mean it badly." But the damage was done. Paul turned and left, and in the morning he flew to Dallas to hook up with Wings and begin rehearsals for their American tour. Lennon and McCartney would never see each other again.

Eight nights later, on May 3, Paul stood in the wings at the Tarrant County Convention Center, in Fort Worth, Texas. The venue had been chosen as the best location for the opening night, to ease the band into the tour as far out of the way of the major cultural capitals as was reasonable. It was to be McCartney's first live performance live in America since the frazzled, road-sick Beatles had retired from touring, just under ten years earlier, before vanishing into the studio. Stepping back into the light, Paul was stunned by the response: fifteen minutes of ovation from the 13,500-strong crowd before Wings even struck the opening chord.

After months of rehearsals and the preliminary legs of the tour, the Wings over America show was by this stage a very polished presentation, if still edging toward the softer end of the rock spectrum when held up against the likes of the Who or Led Zeppelin. Nevertheless, it had a suitably dramatic, audience-stirring opener, with McCartney emerging alone from the darkness, lit in red, in a cloud of dry ice, for the gentle "Venus and Mars" introduction that slammed into "Rock Show." The band, long-haired and in fashionable shirts and waistcoats,

looked very 1976, with the black-clad, white-scarf-draped singer front-
ing them in assured, grinning form as, stage left, his wife, in her feather-
collared dress, shifted from Moog to Hammond to Mellotron and
heartily sang and clapped along.

One new feature of the live production was a laser display, of which,
Paul comically states, he was initially a touch nervous. "I'd seen lasers at
Led Zeppelin's concert at Earls Court [in 1975] and the only thing I
knew about them was from the Bond movie where the baddie was about
to slice Mr. Bond with a laser. So, I literally thought that Robert Plant
was being really courageous and endangering his life dancing around in
front of these lasers. I was like, 'God, that's amazing, what he does for
his art, y'know.' I fully expected to see Planty sliced up by the end of the
show."

This new, cutting-edge Wings show was a far cry from the sham-
bling U.K. university tour of four years before. The quintet, with added
drama and swing supplied by their four-piece brass section, threw themselves into a set that showcased the strength of Paul's post-Beatles catalog, from tougher-sounding numbers such as "Jet" and "Let Me Roll It"
to grandstanding ballads "Maybe I'm Amazed" and "My Love," which
were complemented, rather than overshadowed, by the selection of Beatles songs reclaimed by McCartney.

For once the critics were, as one, bowled over. "When the house
lights dimmed," wrote the reviewer from the *Los Angeles Times,* getting
caught up in the sense of occasion, "virtually everyone in the arena
stood in anticipation of what was clearly the most notable return to
rock concerts since Bob Dylan's 1974 appearance in Chicago. Not only
did the two-hour concert demonstrate McCartney's ability to satisfy
audiences with his post-Beatles work, it also enabled many in the audience to relive some of the magic of the heralded Beatles era. A double
triumph." *The New York Times* enthused, "Mr. McCartney established
himself and his band, Wings, as concert artists in their own right . . .
and he did so triumphantly."

The U.S. tour was run on an enormous scale. Three articulated
trucks lugged twelve and a half tons of gear, each vehicle's roof stenciled in red with one of the words from the phrase "WINGS . . . OVER . . .
AMERICA." Their drivers communicated via CB radio, as a helicopter
rotored overhead, filming the progress of this showy cavalcade. The ex-
panded tour personnel stretched from new guitar tech John Hammel

(later to become Paul's personal assistant) and the McCartney brood's nanny Rose Martin to ex-FBI-agent turned security man Orrin Bartlett, who was employed to oversee a sweep of each venue and grill the staff about potential bomb threats, weapons screening, and any strange calls they might have received. In America, the atmosphere felt heightened and possibly more dangerous. According to *Time* magazine, Paul "worried about snipers." At the same time, McCartney was being more upfront about his wife's role in his professional organization. He needed her, he admitted, "for my confidence."

The centerpiece of the traveling circus was a rented and customized BAC One-Eleven jet with the obligatory tour logo painted on the fuselage. Inside, the plane was equipped with the usual comforts and distractions of the premier-league touring 1970s rock band: video machine, table-tennis setup, and, hidden behind a curtain at the rear, a minidiscotheque, painted with stars and dotted with fluorescent lights, which was much loved by the McCartney girls. The rest of the interior was kitted out like a lounge, where the band could laze around and be served endless drinks from the corner bar by stewards, before retreating to one of the sectioned-off bedrooms.

Attempting to replicate some sense of familial normality, rather than stay in hotels, the McCartneys had four bases for the American tour: rented houses in Dallas, Chicago, New York, and Los Angeles, which they would fly to directly after each show, depending upon where they were in the country. As ideal as the arrangement sounded, the time spent in those lavish houses only served to fuel Linda's homesickness. "I felt very empty and very lonely," she admitted.

Her pining was temporarily ameliorated on a day off in Texas in the first week of May, when she spotted a chestnut Appaloosa stallion in a field by the side of the road. Turning off and taking a detour into Lucky Spot Stables, she asked the owner, "Could we look at that horse out in the field?" He insisted that the horse wasn't for sale but allowed Linda to take it for a ride. Afterward, and with some persuasion, the owner caved in and agreed to a price. The horse, named Lucky Spot, was shipped to England, where the McCartneys began successfully breeding Appaloosas.

Meanwhile, the tour powered onward. On the second date, in Houston, Paul was nearly injured by a piece of scaffolding that fell from the elaborate rigging during the set, the metal pole instead hitting tour

manager Trevor Jones on the head, causing an injury that required thirteen stitches. In Detroit, McCartney was ratty onstage, coping with
feedback and a pizza-slicing cut on his finger that caused him to mess
up the complex guitar picking of "Blackbird" and, later, to lash out at
one reporter who dared to ask the Beatle question. "Look, mate," he
retorted, "it's 1976, and I don't think most people care about what happened ten years ago." In Toronto, Ringo and George turned up, sitting
in the audience and appreciatively nodding along.

In Boston, Paul and Jimmy McCulloch suffered their first serious
bust-up. After closing the main set, Wings jogged to the side of the stage
for a breather in preparation for their first encore. Jimmy had left his
guitar resting on his amp, volume up, causing it to howl with feedback
through the state-of-the-art PA. Then the inexplicably balky guitarist
announced that he wasn't going back on and swaggered off in the direction of the dressing room.

McCartney remembers: "It was like, '*What?*' I mean, I'd never had
anyone decide that ever before. So I just ran off and sort of grabbed
him." According to saxophonist Howie Casey, McCartney did more
than just "sort of grab" McCulloch. "Paul came flying in and smacked
him," he says. The four members of the horn section quickly waded in
to separate the pair, with trombonist Tony Dorsey taking it upon himself to hold McCartney back.

"There was violence involved," Paul concedes. "I gave him what he
understood, really. Now obviously that's not the way you want to operate. But at that moment there was no alternative. He probably would
have done the same to me if he'd have been the leader of the band."

"Jimmy was acting up big-time," says Casey. "And it's Paul's
show . . . he's the leader, he's the star and all that. You don't do that. But
Jimmy had that thing in him."

"Jimmy was his own man, shall we say," says Paul, who noted that
the guitarist returned to the stage in top form and played "a blinder"
following the confrontation. From this point on, McCartney would
sometimes take McCulloch aside on the plane for pep talks meant to
steer him away from the self-destructive habits that were intensifying his
roller-coaster moods. "He was always a little dangerous. I did try and
warn him a couple of times. Like, what's going to happen when you're
thirty? You've got your whole life ahead of you. But he liked partying
too much and was getting into too many things."

Jimmy wasn't the only one. The Wings musicians were far from clean-living and willingly surrendered to the many temptations on offer. In the tour-planning stage, each member of the band was asked what their favorite tipple was and, accordingly, a bottle of whiskey or vodka or whatever spirit they preferred would be waiting for them in the dressing room before the sound check. The bottles would immediately be cracked open, joints would do the rounds, and some of the more likely suspects might chop out a preshow line of coke. Unsurprisingly, by the time the gig began, they were all were pretty loaded. Backstage afterward: more spirits, more spliffs, more lines. It's no surprise that a TV crew who came to the dressing room of the Chicago Stadium to interview the non-McCartney members found them to be conspicuously wasted.

"There's a lot more going for this band than you actually see," argued a heavy-lidded Denny Laine, finding it hard to focus.

"It's a question of everybody just putting a lot into it," Jimmy McCulloch offered vaguely.

Elsewhere, Joe English was in notably chatty if visibly glazed form. "It's an easy gig, it's a good gig, it's the easiest gig I've had. I mean, it's easy meeting people I'm working with and getting along." He paused to think about what else to say, then added, "Good gig."

The drummer, it transpired, was something of a dark horse. Howie Casey was the first to notice that, on the U.K. tour, the genial New Yorker had taken a keen interest in the wares available in British chemists' shops, particularly cough medicines containing active ingredients banned from over-the-counter sale in the States. "He'd drink bottles of it," says Casey. "He'd get out of it on stuff like that. He might have been a little distant at times, but he was all right. Most of the time he seemed on top of it. He was a bloody good drummer."

Secretly, Joe English was battling a serious drug habit, including heroin addiction. While he never missed a gig, he was prone to becoming utterly zonked and falling unconscious for twenty-four hours at a time, then waking up not knowing exactly where he was. He later admitted that there were two or three occasions during his time in Wings when he overdosed on smack. The money he was earning from being in the group was essentially fueling his addiction and dragging him down.

Whatever state everyone was in, a post-show routine was established where the band immediately left the venue in a fleet of limos and returned to the airport and the waiting BAC One-Eleven. There, they'd typically wind up waiting for Paul and Linda, who were always running late or otherwise detained by fans, well-wishers, or hangers-on. Once the plane's doors were closed, the group and their entourage found themselves in what tour photographer Robert Ellis calls "a superbubble."

A photograph taken during the 1976 tour perfectly illustrates how being a member of the McCartney family must have been, in some ways, completely normal and at the same time utterly surreal. In it, Linda and the four-year-old Stella are seen settling down to dinner in their lounge, the former perched on a sofa while balancing a tray on her lap. Across from them, Paul sits playing a bass guitar as Mary, only six, leans in to listen. It appears to be a fairly typical, cozy, slightly boho picture. Except for the fact that it found the McCartneys aboard their private jet, high in the skies above America.

"That became normal for us," says Paul. "In our minds, we were giving the kids a normal upbringing. While at the same time we knew it was not."

Somehow, the delicate balance the McCartneys had created between family life and band life seemed to work. Even the more decadent tendencies of certain members were successfully hidden from the kids. "Anyone who was likely to get crazy," says Paul, "it would be on their own time, in a hotel room. It would be somewhere where the kids weren't. They were very respectful, and the kids never really saw any kind of hedonistic behavior."

"You've got this weird mixture of little kids bounding about the plane and all these hard-arsed musos swilling whiskey and smoking fags," says Howie Casey. "Maybe we were like uncles. They could be cheeky to us, they could ask us things. It was really nice." But even if Wings seemed like an egalitarian setup, from Casey's point of view there was an obvious pecking order. "We socialized totally with them, but they were the bosses. You knew your place a little bit."

As much as McCartney wanted to be one of the boys, sometimes the dividing line between him and the others was all too obvious. On the plane, to fritter away the time, the musicians would often dig out cards and play a few hands of ten-card brag, gambling with nickels and cents. During one flight, Paul heard the others laughing over a game and asked if he could join in. He was quickly taught the rules, and play continued.

McCartney nearly won a couple of hands before Casey scooped the pot with a game-ending four of a kind. Paul, Casey recalls, "did his nut" and stormed off in a huff.

"See, that shows something," Casey reckons. "It's not the money. It's the *winning*. He's used to winning."

Another, far more serious incident caused Paul's anger to explode. In flight, inebriated members of the band and entourage would sometimes enter the cockpit and hang out and chat with the laid-back Texan pilots charged with handling the tour plane. On one occasion, trumpeter Steve Howard, holder of a pilot's license for smaller aircraft, was given a turn at the controls of the jet, acquitting himself admirably. Denny Laine, at the time perhaps worryingly reading a book entitled *Anyone Can Fly,* was also given a go in the pilot's chair. After a few minutes, the real flight crew's attentions having drifted, a call came through from air traffic control warning them that the plane was cruising several thousand feet below its agreed-upon altitude. According to Laine, "When you take anything off automatic pilot, it goes all over the place for a moment or two."

During another flight, one member of the miles-high party—reports differ as to the identity of the culprit—sent the plane into a dive, throwing everyone around the cabin. It was at this point that a furious McCartney discovered that, for some weeks, drunken members of his group had been taking turns flying the plane, with his wife and children on board. Never the most comfortable flier, Paul blew his top. From here on in, everyone in the touring party was banned from the cockpit. "Which is fair enough," Howie Casey notes. "Even though I was pissed, I'd think, No, that's silly."

Upon realizing that his meticulously plotted tour was veering dangerously off course, Paul called everyone to a meeting and read them the riot act. "It was a question of 'We've got to keep this on the straight and narrow, we've got to keep this going,'" says Robert Ellis. "Control was the point."

These days, though, Paul remembers it differently. "That's the legend," he says. "In actual fact, the pilots were on autopilot, and so they let you sit up there and wiggle the joystick a bit, 'cause it's not operational. And when you're pissed, you think you're flying the plane. There's no way I would let that really happen, y'know. You're kidding me? But I wasn't going to be the one to tell them they weren't flying the plane."

Whatever the truth, as relatively tame as Wings outwardly appeared in terms of 1970s rock groups, with their many and varied excesses, at times McCartney must have felt like he was trying to orchestrate chaos.

"Everything I've done since the Beatles split has been leading up to this show," Paul told a reporter backstage at Madison Square Garden on May 24, the start of a sold-out two-night stint at the prestigious, star-making New York venue.

Inside the arena, the mood of the crowd was rising toward hysteria. Word spread—fanned by a quote from McCartney refusing to rule out the possibility—that John Lennon was to make an appearance onstage. Fans crushed at the lip of the stage, while others in the bleachers mindlessly set off flares and fireworks. Arriving onstage, the Wings band members walked tall and were met with scenes reminiscent of the Beatlemania McCartney must surely have felt had been consigned to the past. Boys ripped off their shirts. Girls sobbed, overwhelmed. Launching into their set, the band rose to the occasion and, well oiled as they were on more than one level, easily surpassed expectations. Even if Lennon was a no-show, for now all talk of Beatles reunions was irrelevant.

On the second night, having insisted on a backstage press ban, Jacqueline Kennedy Onassis showed up with two of her children, John and Caroline Kennedy, and hung out with the McCartneys in their dressing room, signifying just how far their star had risen. Following the modest early days of Wings, Paul found himself back in the full glare of the media spotlight. "Yeah, it was interesting," he says. "Because we started so small, it was like I wasn't famous. But then, suddenly, all that fame came back. You were suddenly on prime-time news." A week later, *Time* magazine featured Paul on its cover, in a live shot of the singer rendered in fuchsia and wiggly daubs of blue and green, with the blaringly triumphant headline "McCartney Comes Back." Even Linda's confidence seemed to have hit an all-time high. Initially fearing that she would be eviscerated by the American press, when asked by a *Rolling Stone* reporter if she had a message for her critics, she replied, "My answer is always 'Fuck off.'"

"A fairly unequivocal answer," Paul laughs today.

Having through the years graduated from university bars to theaters to arenas, Wings arrived as a stadium act on June 10, selling out every last ticket of the 67,110 released for their show at the Seattle Kingdome. Sweetening the satisfaction, this trumped the record set by the Beatles at Shea Stadium by a comfortable 12,000. The Kingdome, opened only three months earlier, was so vast that it had its own internal temperature-controlled microclimate. Even with the erection of two video screens above the stage, the gigantic venue seemed to dwarf Wings' setup.

After the sound check, Robert Ellis photographed the band standing in the upper tier at the back of the empty stadium. "It took us half an hour to get from the stage to where the picture was taken and back again," he says. The Seattle gig was filmed and eventually released as part of the 1980 film *Rockshow,* which revealed the Wings over America tour in all its victory-lap glory.

"There probably were nerves involved, which I've forgotten now," says Paul. "I tend to sort of block them out of memories. I'm sure we were a bit nervous, but by then we'd kind of got a lot of the kinks worked out of the show and felt really good about it. It was very exciting. I remember looking out at the lines of people snaking around the Kingdome. It was really cool to see that. The tour was a special tour, but something as huge as the Kingdome meant we were right back up to the level where I'd left off."

Into its final furlong, the tour reached California as its participants found themselves close to burnout. "The drugs were taking over," says Robert Ellis. "I had extreme difficulties keeping myself straight enough to do the work I had to do." In San Francisco, backstage, the increasingly feral Jo Jo Patrie stole a bunch of complimentary front-row tickets from the tour manager's briefcase before disguising herself to go out to the front of the Cow Palace to sell them. She returned with enough cash to buy an ounce of cocaine, a sizable amount. This lasted her, Laine, and McCulloch for the rest of the tour. But while she didn't dare snort the drug around Paul, who had dabbled with coke in the 1960s and stopped when it "got too fashionable," Patrie claimed that on one occasion she offered some to Linda during a flight and the two women sneaked into the toilet for a toot.

The tour diverted to Arizona on June 18 for a show at the Tucson

Community Center. There, a surprise birthday party for Paul's thirty-fourth saw him being serenaded by a mariachi band and, blindfolded, bashing a goat-shaped orange piñata with a stick. At a trio of tour-closing shows at the Los Angeles Forum beginning three days later, Wings drew a star-stuffed audience that included Diana Ross, Cher, Elton John, Jack Nicholson, and Dustin Hoffman.

Outside the venue, a marching band led by someone in a chicken suit tooted its way through a version of "Listen to What the Man Said." Inside, at the end of a rollicking set, Ringo appeared onstage to present Paul with flowers. Then Starr picked up and pawed a guitar that had been left in a stand, as if prompting a spontaneous Beatles reunion. Backstage, the air surrounding McCartney and Starr, perhaps since they were being watched by a roomful of people, was one of slightly forced jollity.

"Well, it wasn't bad," Ringo said. "Eight out of ten."

"Let's see you bloody get up and do it then," Paul responded in a comedic challenge, mugging nose to nose with his former bandmate.

Two nights later the McCartneys threw a party, costing a dizzying $75,000, at the estate in Benedict Canyon that had belonged to silent-movie comedian Harold Lloyd. "That was a blowout," says Paul. "We said afterwards, 'That was an exercise in how to spend the entire profits of the tour.'" Money was no longer an issue: in seven weeks, the Wings over America jaunt had grossed $5 million, a mind-boggling amount for the time, and considerably more than anyone had estimated.

This uncharacteristic display of extravagance—more on the level of a society wedding than a show-business party—served to attract the usual musical suspects, including the Eagles, the Jacksons, and Bob Dylan, but it also drew such key figures from Hollywood as Henry Fonda, Tony Curtis, Roman Polanski, Steve McQueen, and Warren Beatty. Guests were met at the gates of the estate and ferried to the house in a fleet of golf buggies. All partygoers had been urged to wear white, since Paul and Linda had arranged for a troupe of Hawaiian artists to wander through the gathering, splashing and spraying people with paint. Everyone took to scribbling their signatures on one another's T-shirts. There was a palm reader, appearances by the Los Angeles Ballet and the Nelson Riddle Orchestra, and even, in the pool, a Busby Berkeley–style routine performed by faux starlets.

Everyone got into the swing except for Bob Dylan, who, according to some accounts, sat in a tree, musing, for much of the party. Leaving at the end of the evening, he was pursued by Robert Ellis, who had been instructed by McCartney to take shots of all of the guests. Ellis caught up with Dylan while the star was trundling along in a buggy, and kept snapping away until the singer hopped out and leaped on the photographer, demanding to know why he was taking pictures. "I was going, 'I'm Paul's official photographer,'" Ellis recalls. "He says, 'I don't want my picture in no magazine.'" Back up at the house, many of the revelers jumped into the pool. Those who wandered back down the hill to their parked cars found a single white rose on the dashboard, along with a note: "Thank you for coming, Paul and Linda."

"After the Beatles," Paul reasoned to one journalist in the aftermath, as he came down from the highs of the tour, "you would have thought it would have been pretty much impossible for me to follow that and to get anything else going. At least, I thought that. This tour has convinced us that we're a group and I think it has convinced audiences, too. This wasn't just a one-time trip. This is going to be a working band. We'll be back."

Success seemed to have restored McCartney's equilibrium, too. "He's very much back to his old self again," said Linda, no doubt meaning the peacocking, funny, creative individual she'd first met nearly a decade earlier, before the years of self-crisis and doubt and grind.

It had perhaps also brought back some of his less appealing traits, though. In an interview with U.S. TV presenter Geraldo Rivera on *Good Night America,* Paul came across as smug, evasive, and contentious. At one point, when McCartney addressed him as "Freddie," Rivera bravely reached over and gave his face a playful slap.

Back in Europe, inevitably, the comedown kicked in. Paul grew an ill-advised mustache that was less *Sgt. Pepper,* more used-car dealer, and Wings mopped up the last remaining dates in Austria, Yugoslavia, Italy, and West Germany. In Vienna, the lighting techs bounced laser beams off ancient buildings to dazzling effect. In Zagreb, for the first time, the audience took over from Paul and sang "Yesterday" on their own, deeply moving its composer. In St. Mark's Square in Venice, performing a benefit for UNESCO to raise funds to help restore the decaying city, the group provoked mild controversy when it was revealed that—irony of ironies—their heavy equipment trucks had wrecked some centuries-old paving slabs.

At the end of a three-night October run at Wembley Empire Pool in London, EMI threw a party populated by B-list guests such as singer Kiki Dee, members of the art-pop group 10cc, and *Old Grey Whistle Test* host Bob Harris. At the end of the night, the guests grew boisterous and pelted one another with cream cakes.

It certainly wasn't hanging around in the Californian sunshine with Henry Fonda and Steve McQueen as hummingbirds flitted beneath the palm trees. A sense of anticlimax hung in the air, along with uncertainty about the future. Robert Ellis felt that ultimately it was "an uncomfortable tour. There were changes afoot. Paul was restless about everything." Despite the undeniable success of the U.S. tour, the photographer says, "It was always a question of, What's next? Which made it all a bit insecure. There was the sense of the end of an era about it."

McCartney retreated to the cocoon of the studio, holing up at Abbey Road to sift through the ninety hours of live tapes from the U.S. tour for the triple *Wings over America* album, due out in December 1976. Acknowledging the significance of his touring achievement, Paul drove himself hard in the polishing and mixing of the record, becoming a touch obsessive and working fourteen-hour days, seven days a week, for a six-week period. "Well, it's always intense mixing something when you've got so much stuff to go through," he points out. "But it was my baby, and I was very hands-on with it. It was a very personal project, 'cause I knew it had all gone well. I wanted people who hadn't been to the concerts to hear what had gone on." Before the year was out, Linda was pregnant again, putting an instant dampener on the notion of any future touring. The couple began to argue about Paul spending so much time in the studio.

Bizarrely, at the same time, spinning off from the sci-fi elements of *Venus and Mars* and reflecting Wings' newfound U.S. celebrity, *Star Trek* creator Gene Roddenberry approached the band members with a view to them playing themselves in his planned sci-fi musical, plotted around an invasion from outer space. As tempting as the offer seemed to the cosmically minded Paul, the project was never to make it past the planning stage, even with McCartney's name attached, since Roddenberry was struggling in his career and unable to convince any of the television or film companies to supply the financing.

With time on his hands, Jimmy McCulloch had formed the tellingly named group White Line, along with his drummer brother, Jack, and his friend Dave Clarke. The trio released one single for EMI, the gutsy, harmonizing pop rock song "Call My Name," performed under a shower of silver balloons on the ITV music show *Supersonic,* before the ongoing factory production of additional copies of the record was mysteriously, according to the band members, halted by EMI.

Hanging around the record company's London offices in Manchester Square one day, McCulloch and Clarke sloped off to a nearby pub, which they found themselves sharing with another recent act signed to the label, the Sex Pistols. "Jim started gobbing off," says Clarke, "telling them how crap they were. So this fight started between Jim and I forget which one of them. Me and the bass player of the Sex Pistols [Glen Matlock] managed to drag them apart."

Clarke says McCulloch had grown cocky during his tenure with McCartney: "Jim was young and headstrong and had everything that he wanted when he was in Wings, and it's difficult to deal with. I think it went to his head a bit. He could be really charming. But when the drink took over big-time, it was awkward." It's perhaps no coincidence that, at this point, rumors began to circulate that Eric Stewart, from the recently fractured 10cc, was being groomed to replace Jimmy in Wings.

Wings over America was released in time for Christmas, and by January 1977, it was sitting at the top of the U.S. chart, completing a remarkable straight run of American No. 1 albums that had begun with *Red Rose Speedway.* "I couldn't believe it," says Paul. "I mean, you were always advised not to do double albums, and suddenly there we were doing a triple. That was pretty cool, I must admit."

In the spring, Paul took the opportunity to release a slightly strange project that had been in the can since 1971. Upon the completion of *Ram,* six years earlier, McCartney had hired arranger Richard Hewson to put together an instrumental pop-orchestral version of the album, not a million miles away from the easy listening sounds of German bandleader James Last.

The album was finally released in April 1977, under the masquerading name of Percy "Thrills" Thrillington, an alter ego McCartney had been cultivating for some time. Supposedly a posh society figure, born in Coventry Cathedral in 1939, the fictitious Thrillington had theoretically traveled to Louisiana to study music and to California to learn arranging and conducting, before returning to London to form his own orchestra and becoming friends with McCartney, who'd helped him secure a record contract. In return, Thrillington had been inspired to pay homage to *Ram*.

To bolster the ruse, over the previous year Paul had been taking out ads in the personals columns of *The Times* and the *Evening Standard* in which Percy Thrillington announced his visits to Geneva or Mustique, or excursions to the Torbay Relaxation Center or the Badminton Horse Trials at Newbury. One read, "Percy Thrillington wishes to advise friends that he is feeling thoroughly invigorated by the crisp and brisk ski-ing conditions in Gstaad." Another made known the fact that "Percy Thrillington is delighted with the efforts of those concerned with The Yellowplush Gallery to humour his aesthetic needs."

Letters from readers began to appear in the papers' columns, seeking more information about the witty and mysterious Thrillington. Of course, the tongue-in-cheek tone of the missives suggested that they were probably the work of a prankster. Then a revealing small ad was printed, noting that Mr. Thrillington was to be "taking an extended holiday in South America following the rigours of launching his first record album." In March 1977 the *Evening Standard* ran an investigative piece, under the headline "The Perambulations of Percy Thrillington," that knowingly followed the trail of clues back to McCartney's PR man Tony Brainsby. Brainsby denied that Thrillington had been created by Paul as a publicity stunt.

Upon the *Thrillington* album's release, the liner notes went one step further, quoting an EMI press officer as apparently saying, "Percy Thrillington certainly isn't Paul McCartney as some people seem to think." In an attempt to throw pursuers off the scent, Paul and Linda, traveling around Ireland, found a young farmer in a field and asked him if he fancied doing a spot of paid modeling for them. The bemused youth— "someone no one could possibly trace," according to the McCartneys— posed for them first in a sweater and then in an evening suit. But, says Paul, "he never quite looked Percy Thrillington enough," and the session was shelved.

Hearing his songs given such straightforward, light-entertainment arrangements must have tickled McCartney, but beyond being a bit of diverting fun for its creator, it was hard to see the exact point of *Thrillington*. It would be another twelve years before Paul would finally admit, in a press conference, that he was behind this daft hoax. "We kept it a secret for a long time, but now the world knows," he laughed.

On an altogether more serious level, the first months of 1977 saw Apple finally sever all remaining ties with Allen Klein, following a stinging $5 million settlement. McCartney, though, insisted that there was still a massive, unexplained hole in the Beatles' earnings. Though he never liked to talk about money, Paul felt moved to point out to the *Daily Express* that with Wings, between 1974 and 1976, he had "earned more money than I ever earned in all those other so-called boom years." He said the Fabs had been told that they'd sold somewhere in the region of three hundred million records. "If you compute that," Paul reckoned, roughly crunching the numbers, "and say the group should have had 10 pee a go, then where did that money go?"

Meanwhile, the *Saturday Night Live* joke had run and run. Having had no response from the former Beatles since his spoof reunion appeal, and unaware that John and Paul had watched it live, Lorne Michaels upped his offer to $3,200 and promised to throw some hotel accommodations into the deal. Five months later, he used the ongoing stunt to introduce the first footage of the Rutles, the uncanny, parallel-universe send-up of the Beatles created by Eric Idle of Monty Python and Neil Innes of the Bonzo Dog Doo-Dah Band.

According to Innes, who bumped into an apparently "edgy" McCartney at a party at George Harrison's house, Paul wasn't entirely enamored of the clearly affectionate fan-boy parody, which featured Idle's portrayal of him as Dirk McQuickly, a wide-eyed showbiz opportunist with a knack for writing light, frothy tunes. In truth, the crux of the problem seemed to be that an increasingly irritated McCartney was being asked his opinion of the Rutles in virtually every interview.

Later, George Harrison, always the most comedy-friendly ex-Beatle, not least in his endorsement and financing of Monty Python, appeared on *Saturday Night Live*. In the opening minutes of the episode, he could be seen muttering to Lorne Michaels in a corridor of the NBC building, asking Michaels if he could have the check for $3,000 and being told he could have only his $750 share.

"I've come all this way," Harrison pretended to protest. "It's three thousand dollars. That was the deal."

"How do you think I feel?" spluttered Michaels. "I feel terrible about it. But it was just one of those mix-ups."

All frivolities aside, only a year after they'd sat together laughing at the *SNL* appeal, in their increasingly strained and infrequent telephone conversations, Paul and John were once more growing painfully estranged. April 1977 found Paul and Linda in New York, staying at the Stanhope Hotel, across the park from the Dakota, in town to do some business and catch some Broadway shows. McCartney called Lennon up, even though he felt that, from his former partner's point of view, there was "so much suspicion."

Paul remembers that he started the conversation by saying, "Hey, I'd really like to see you."

"What for?" Lennon replied. "What the fuck d'you want, man?"

Paul later confessed that at this stage John still made him nervous, even after all the years and their times of apparent brotherly closeness. "I actually used to have some very frightening phone calls with him," McCartney admitted. Paul told John what he'd been up to: eating pizza with the kids, reading them fairy tales.

"You're all pizza and fairy tales," Lennon retorted bizarrely.

Another time, John raged at Paul in an accent that was becoming more Americanized, and reminiscent of a bald-headed, lollipop-sucking TV detective who was big in the mid-1970s.

"Yeah? Yeah? Whadda ya want?" snarled John, answering the call.

McCartney was suddenly sick of this "vitriolic" Lennon.

"Oh, fuck off, Kojak," he barked, and slammed the phone down.

11

FLOAT ON

Did you feel a sense of vindication after the 1976 tour?

Well, yeah. That really was the kind of payoff tour. I remember that being what I saw as the turnaround where Wings were now, like, very successful. We had the American tour, and "Silly Love Songs" was a big hit. The great thing happened, which was always a fun thing that used to happen with the Beatles, was you'd put a record out and you'd start playing it live and no one would know it. And it'd be, "Hold your nerve, boys, we're okay, just keep playing it." And by the end of that tour, it was the big hit. It was really lovely, that. The nice thing that was happening on that tour, because of the level, was there were a lot of things that were reminiscent of the Beatles days.

IT COULD HARDLY HAVE SOUNDED MORE IDYLLIC. Wings was six weeks into the sessions for their sixth album, in the gray London of February 1977, when Geoff Emerick began regaling them with tales of his recent recording expedition to Hawaii. The seasoned sound engineer filled their heads with sunshine, just when they were stuck back in the all too familiar environs of Abbey Road, digging themselves into a rut.

Two months later, with McCartney having decided to indulge a rock-star whim, Wings landed in the U.S. Virgin Islands. During the intervening weeks, an apparently simple if potentially troublesome plan had been formulated. In yet another bid to take flight to another location and free up the recording process, the band planned to make an album aboard a yacht—its punning working title was *Water Wings*.

The original idea came from Denny Laine, who had a passion for boats. In the early 1970s, he'd lived on the *Searchlight,* a barge moored on the Thames between Shepperton and Chertsey, the vessel later sold to Viv Stanshall of the Bonzo Dog Doo-Dah Band. Recently, he'd treated himself to a forty-foot cabin cruiser he'd named the *Louis Philippe;* he kept it in the harbor at Rye, near Paul's house, and sailed up and down England's south coast, sometimes with McCartney aboard.

But the real spark of inspiration had come to Laine when he'd visited Rod Stewart, who was recording on the Record Plant's floating studio in the Pacific waters off Los Angeles. "I've always loved boats and thought it might be an interesting way to record an album," said the guitarist, although he wasn't entirely convinced that McCartney would buy into the idea, having had such trouble in Lagos when deciding to go off-road with *Band on the Run.* "To be honest," Laine admitted, "I was surprised when Paul said we should give it a try." But having just completed the intensive mixing sessions for *Wings over America* and gone straight into the making of the next studio album, McCartney was looking for a break from the routine. He viewed this Caribbean jaunt as "an experiment to see if we could work better in a holiday atmosphere."

An advance party of five techs, including Emerick, John Hammel, and assistant engineer Mark Vigars, was sent out to the Virgin Islands at the end of April to oversee the setting up of the studio. Upon their arrival on St. Thomas, they began kitting out a charter yacht named the *Fair Carol* as a waterborne recording facility. It proved not to be the easiest of tasks.

The boat was one hundred feet long but narrow. When its captain saw the amount of equipment the team was hoping to install, he freaked. The heavy mixing desk and washing-machine-sized twenty-four-track tape machine were bad enough, before factoring in the weighty amps, the cumbersome Mellotron, and so on. In the end, an ergonomic plan was agreed upon in which the gear would be lined up on either side of the boat's lounge turned live room and thus equally balanced, in order to avoid difficulties in the water. Carpenters were brought in to build a structure on the open deck to house a control room.

On April 30, 1977, the *Fair Carol* set out for Francis Bay, on the neighboring island of St. John, in anticipation of the arrival of the McCartney family, the band, and MPL's Alan Crowder and Brian Brolly. Completing the Wings flotilla was a converted minesweeper called the *Samala,* providing the band and crew with accommodations and catering (simple English grub such as steak and kidney pie), and a trimaran with a huge living space and lower-deck bedrooms, named the *El Toro,* that was to be home to the McCartneys.

The daily routine was a suitably leisurely one: rise around nine, breakfast at ten, followed by a fifty-yard commute to the *Fair Carol* in a motorized rubber dinghy. Record until lunchtime, laze around for a while in the afternoon, and then work into the evening, until it was time for dinner and cocktails on the *Samala*. Unsurprisingly, this low-gear approach suited Paul: "I like to record and not have to feel like it's too much work. I hate to think, I'm going to work now . . . I'm going to grind out some music." Of course, Jimmy McCulloch was much enamored of this lifestyle, which entirely zoned in on making music and getting high. "You don't have the gas man coming in or mail that you have to act on," he pointed out.

The party would anchor the three boats in bays or harbors at St. Croix, St. John, or St. Thomas. Then, whenever the mood took their fancy, they would up and sail away to a new location. As time went on, the motor dinghies were abandoned altogether and the musicians would just jump off one boat and swim to another. In the manner of a rock-star stag party, they had corny white T-shirts made up, bannering their names in black letters, along with the legend M.Y. SAMALA, VIRGIN ISLANDS, MAY 77. ("M.Y." is the merchant ship designation for a motor yacht.) For all involved, this working holiday was an entirely liberating experience. "No one wore shoes the whole time," noted visiting photographer Henry Diltz.

"The mornings were really beautiful in the bay," wrote Alan Crowder in his diary, "with jumping fish called 'Jumping Jacks,' laughing seagulls, pelicans and very large birds called frigates."

Initially, Paul worried about the logistical realities of recording on the ocean waves. Day one saw the group taking baby steps, reviewing the tapes from Abbey Road and jamming. "The big problem with recording on a boat," Paul said, "was that maybe once we got out there, we might find that salt water had gone through the machines and the equipment, or that they just wouldn't work." In the end, to his relief, the sessions progressed remarkably smoothly: "We didn't have any problems with salt water or sharks attacking us."

They conducted one slightly dippy experiment, attempting to record a jam while the boat was in motion. Of course, given the engine noise, it sounded terrible. "It was silly and fun, and I don't think it was very good music," says Paul. But, still, in this environment Wings was stretching out in unexpected ways—instead of hammering out old chestnuts such as "Lucille" or "Twenty Flight Rock" in their musical downtime, they might pick their way through Irving Berlin's "Easter Parade."

In the afternoons, the McCartney girls would lounge in a hammock or swing from ropes before free-falling into the blue water. Mary and Stella pestered their father to repeatedly throw them over the side of the boat. There was a mini-piano on the *Samala,* and Paul played it as the girls danced around the cabin. Absent from school once again, the kids were tutored, though in this environment it took a lot of effort to drag them out of the sun and get them to concentrate on their studies.

The musicians would idly snorkel in the water, spotting sea urchins and starfish and small, harmless barracudas. One day Denny spied a dolphin's fin moving through the waves and shouted, "Shark!," terrifying a swimming Joe English. On another occasion, Paul sat on the stern deck of the *Fair Carol* recording an acoustic guitar part as another of the curious creatures circled the boat, surfacing and diving.

Come evening, everyone sat on the deck of the *Samala* drinking rum, the boat twinkling with fairy lights. Bats swooped around in the moonlight, trying to catch flying fish. There was much merriment as the more spirited participants took turns, Paul remembers, "leaping from top decks into uncharted waters and stuff." He says, "I had a couple too many one night and nearly broke something jumping from one boat to another."

He escaped with a bruised leg and cut knee. But it was clear that his colleagues weren't entirely seaworthy, and soon there were other mishaps. McCulloch limped around after sustaining a mysterious injury, while Denny, ever the sailor, took off in a one-man Sunfish sailboat to explore the coves around St. John. "I got lost for five hours," he admits. Upon his return, he had to be taken to Caneel Bay, on the island, and treated by a doctor for severe sunburn. Meanwhile, the injury count kept rising: Geoff Emerick managed to electrocute himself in the foot, and Alan Crowder slipped down a set of stairs and broke his heel; he returned from the hospital hobbling around on a crutch that made him resemble Long John Silver.

Since all of the wives and girlfriends except Linda had been excluded from the trip, left back home in Britain or the States, the musicians were soon talking like a bunch of randy sailors. "The conversation turns to women every other word," said Joe English. "If the word isn't *women,* it's *girls.*" A sulky Jo Jo Patrie blamed the ban on an insecure and pregnant Linda. "I think she was intimidated by the girls perhaps wearing a bikini around Paul," she huffed. "Jimmy's girlfriend was the [*Playboy*] Playmate for February 1976, so we would have both gone down there looking pretty terrific."

To blow off steam, and in a further display of jet-set extravagance, McCartney had an MPL employee fly over from London with a video-tape of the 1977 FA Cup Final between Liverpool and Manchester United (United triumphed 2–1). In the moonlit early hours of the morning following the screening, there were races in the dinghies as calls of "Pursuit, pursuit!" rang out, along with the more fate-tempting inquiry "Who's next for the medicos?"

Dropping anchor in the harbor at St. John one night, the band cranked up and jammed at full volume. Unbeknownst to them, there was a ban on amplified music in the area after ten P.M. McCartney remembers discovering that the rules were so strict that even the use of transistor radios was forbidden. And here was Wings, banging away through a PA. "We had a whole thing going," he says. "You could hear it for miles." The noise quickly attracted the attention of rangers from the national park, which covered 60 percent of the island. Once aboard the rock-star-annexed fleet, they began snooping around, sticking their noses into ashtrays, several of which inevitably contained joint roaches. In the end, Wings was lucky to escape with a fifteen-dollar fine for disrupting the tropical peace. But after the rangers left, the group defiantly struck up again as they sailed around to the nearby Waterlemon Bay.

This kind of behavior perhaps unavoidably drew more in the way of unwanted attention. Soon after, doubtless tipped off by the St. John rangers, three U.S. Customs officials made a surprise visit to the boats and, incredibly, left without finding any evidence of drug use. The incident did, however, bring to a head a growing disagreement between McCartney and the captain of the *El Toro,* who had smelled marijuana smoke on the boat the night the band had arrived and threatened to report them to the authorities. Now, after this latest development, he turned menacing.

"He was a little sort of heavier than the other captains," says McCartney. "He took it a little more seriously. We had an argument with him, and I said, 'Y'know, we don't need all this aggro.'" The owners of another boat located in the harbor, the *Wanderlust,* had already offered the use of the catamaran to the McCartneys, and so, before they ended up in trouble again, they took this opportunity to literally jump ship. Paul wrote a song about the experience, giving it the title "Wanderlust" and referring in the lyrics to a captain out to make his mark and warning of a bust. The craft seemed, he says, "a symbol of freedom to me . . . breaking away from oppression . . . let's get out of here."

On May 22, a letter was sent to Alan Crowder from Peter Baker, the agent who'd arranged for the charter of the boats. In it, he informed him that he knew the yachts *Fair Carol, Samala,* and *El Toro* had recently been visited by U.S. Customs officials.

"I must emphasize to you and the group that the possession or use of mariahuana [*sic*] is illegal in the Virgin Islands," he wrote. "And that includes possession or use onboard a boat in territorial waters." He went on to essentially warn Crowder that use of illegal drugs on the boats might result in "us . . . advising the owner to conclude the charter."

In a rebellious mood, the band asked photographer Henry Diltz to take a picture of the letter, ornamented with a pack of Bambu rolling papers and the butt of a spliff.

The bandmates returned to the United Kingdom reenergized, their heads buzzing with thoughts of other unusual locations they might record in. They talked about putting a studio on a train and traveling across Canada. "Next year, darling," Paul jested, "I was thinking of hiring a string of cable cars in the Bavarian Alps."

Back home, however, the music scene was changing, with the dawning of punk having made the soft rock of bands like Wings sound outdated virtually overnight. McCartney, perhaps to his credit, stuck to his guns musically, even if he recognized that it might find him being labeled a dinosaur. "The hard nuts of the music business, the critics, are gonna hate me because I'm not writing about acne," he moaned. Still, this extreme shift in musical fashion, he stressed, now made the Beatles seem as if they were from another age entirely, even if it had been only seven years since they'd broken up. No one, he argued, could "think of the Beatles as a current group, no matter which way you looked at it."

In private, Paul and Linda joked about going punk, giving themselves the suitably snotty nicknames Noxious Fumes and Vile Lin.

Writer and broadcaster Paul Gambaccini, visiting the recording sessions in the Virgin Islands, had been surprised to hear Linda singing the Damned's "Neat Neat Neat" to herself one day aboard the *Fair Carol*. It turned out that Heather, now fourteen, was into punk. Paul—no stranger to the compelling powers of primal rock'n'roll after the days of his youth in Hamburg—noticed a remarkable transformation in his daughter after she had gone to see the Stranglers. "She came back a changed person, over the moon, just loved it," he said.

At Abbey Road, on his return from the Caribbean, McCartney even knocked off a comedy punk song, as a jokey gift to Heather, entitled "Boil Crisis." He revealed to one journalist the opening lines of the jokey lyrics: "One night in the life of a kid named Sid, he scored with a broad in a pyramid." McCartney realized, of course, that he couldn't put the song out, no matter how tongue-in-cheek it was intended to be. "If I release it," he rightly pointed out, "people will only slag me off." Instead, his typically whimsical, typically eccentric response was to go in entirely the opposite direction, with a song in the traditional Scottish folk style extolling the beauty of the southwestern tip of the Kintyre Peninsula.

Summer 1977 found the McCartneys spending a lot of their time back in Scotland. This arrangement didn't please either Jimmy McCulloch or Jo Jo Patrie, though Denny Laine and Joe English seemed happy enough to rough it in the countryside. The barn at Low Ranachan had by now been professionally converted into a rehearsal and recording studio and basic living quarters for the musicians. McCulloch sneeringly nicknamed it the Bunker. Patrie turned her nose up at the small cottage provided for Denny and her and their two kids, Laine and Heidi; she disdained its cement walls and bare furnishings, comprising, as she saw it, "a couple of old chairs and some ragged, pee-stained mattresses."

Those who couldn't take to rural life found the existence in Scotland hard going. In a surreal protest, the bored, stoned instrument techs drew the image of a television set on their cottage wall and pretended to watch it. Stuck out there on the farm, Jimmy McCulloch, his drinking and drugging beginning to intensify, started to crack up. Jo Jo Patrie later wildly stated that this led to the guitarist sneaking into the High Park cottage in the middle of the night and pointing a gun at the McCartneys while they slept, before suffering a breakdown and attempting to shoot himself. No one else, though, has ever backed up her story.

The truth appears to have been far less melodramatic, and a touch more daft. Revealing the depth of their devotion to their chickens, left home alone in London, the McCartneys arranged to have their brood driven in a taxi from St. John's Wood to Argyll, at a cost of over £100. Then, one evening on the farm after a binge, a drink-maddened Jimmy took two dozen of the eggs produced by the hens, carefully collected each day by Linda and Paul, and angrily splattered them on the interior walls of the roadies' cottage.

As trivial as this might have appeared to outsiders, it was seen by the McCartneys as a final act of abuse. Linda cried when she saw the mess. Paul, for the last time, lit into Jimmy, grabbing him by his skinny neck and telling him to get the fuck off his farm. "It got a bit fraught up in Scotland," McCartney later admitted, with no little amount of understatement.

One morning not long after, Paul took a call from Steve Marriott, the increasingly wayward singer and guitarist of the Small Faces, who was putting the band back together. McCartney remembers that Marriott said, "Oh, hi mate. Er, me and Jimmy have been up all night, and he's decided he wants to leave your group and join mine." Feeling miffed, but stuck for an answer, Paul replied, "Hey, good luck to you guys, I hope it works out," knowing in his own mind that it wouldn't. Then McCulloch came to the phone and said, "Look, thanks a lot. See you around."

When the rift went public, both Paul and Jimmy offered anodyne quotes to the press. "It is a pity he's leaving," said McCartney, "but problems have been building up for quite a while now and so the rest of us are happy to carry on without him."

"I enjoyed playing with Wings and I learned a lot from Paul," remarked a butter-wouldn't-melt McCulloch. "But I felt it was time for a change and the ideal change for me was the Small Faces. They're old friends of mine whose music I've always enjoyed."

Only later would either publicly reveal his true feelings about the whole messy affair. "I don't think anyone was too upset about the parting," said Jimmy. "We had some very good times together. Although Linda doesn't know much about music, she's a really nice chick."

For McCartney, the breakup had been a long time coming. In hindsight, there had been two unspoken options: either the group could have struggled through the making of another record, suffering the likely agonies and arguments, or McCulloch would have had to knuckle down and do what McCartney asked of him. "Jimmy decided to leave," Paul said to one reporter. Then he added, sounding a touch self-serving, "Luckily, he'd done all the required stuff on the album that we wanted him to do, so it worked out quite well for us."

Behind this front, Paul was becoming increasingly infuriated by his inability to maintain a lasting lineup of Wings. Having tried to loosen up and allow the musicians more creative freedom, he was now attempting to shield the carefully tended normality of his family life from the rock piggery happening only a short distance away on his farm. As ever, he painted a sunny face on the situation. Asked about the various trials of keeping a group together, he vaguely reasoned, "You get all sorts of weird little problems that you can't do much about."

Along with the ever reliable Denny Laine, McCartney got his head back down into songwriting. The chorus for the soon-to-be-ubiquitous "Mull of Kintyre" had been kicking around since 1975. In the mornings on the farm, Denny would wander over from his cottage to High Park to have breakfast with the McCartneys. One day this unhurried routine slipped into the afternoon, when Paul suggested that they climb up the hill with a bottle of whiskey and a couple of acoustic guitars. There the pair shared ideas for the verses of "Mull of Kintyre" and completed the misty-eyed anthem.

Realizing that it needed a suitably rousing climax, McCartney invited Tony Wilson, the leader of the local Campbeltown Pipe Band, up to the farm to play him the freshly written song and ask him if he could score an arrangement for bagpipes. At first, the two sat in the small kitchen at High Park working through the tune, before Wilson suggested that they perhaps step outside, since the bagpipes were piercingly loud. It quickly became clear that the song naturally suited the sound of the ancient drone. A plan was made to add an accompaniment of massed pipes and drums to the upcoming recording.

When Wilson broke the news to the other pipers at the band's next meeting at the local church hall, it got a mixed response. Some of them were thrilled by the notion; others felt that they were selling out their traditionalism by agreeing to play on a pop single. The youngest member, Jimmy McGeachy, only fifteen, at first suspected it was a practical joke, even though he often spotted the McCartneys in the town. "You'd see Paul walking about in his Welly boots," he remembers. "Mary and Stella, you'd see them with Linda. And Heather was there quite a bit, 'cause she used to hang about with the young farmers' set. She would take the mickey out of us, about the Bay City Rollers and all that. She was an early punk, the first time we'd seen a spiky haircut. It was all happening down in London, so for us boys on the west coast of Scotland, it was the first time we'd seen somebody come up from London who looked pretty cool."

In the early evening of Tuesday, August 9, 1977, the members of the Campbeltown Pipe Band—by day joiners and electricians, farmers and schoolboys—all piled into a minibus, wearing their full kilted regalia, and headed up to the McCartneys' estate. Waiting for them at Low Ranachan were Paul, Linda, Denny Laine, Joe English (whose drumming contribution was in this instance redundant), Geoff Emerick, John Hammel, and, most welcomingly, tour manager Trevor Jones with a wheelbarrow full of cans of McEwan's Export. Clearly well rehearsed, the pipers' stirring contribution was nailed in one take, and the beer flowed. The drums were added next, recorded alfresco beside the barn. Listening to a playback in the studio, the now merry local musicians suggested that the song was a definite single, one that would likely appeal to expat Scots the world over.

Paul wasn't so sure about "Mull of Kintyre." Photographer Robert Ellis remembers McCartney playing an acetate of the single—counterbalanced with the relatively rocking "Girls School"—to him and various members of ELO in London soon after. "He was going, 'Ooh, which is the A side, what do you think?' I was going, 'Well, what are you talking about? It's "Mull of Kintyre," isn't it?' He was saying, 'Oh, I don't know. I think it's a bit too twee and sugary.' Of course, the vote round the room was quite clearly for 'Mull Of Kintyre.' But he still wasn't convinced. He was definitely not that secure about that song." In the end, hedging his bets, McCartney released "Mull of Kintyre/Girls School" as a double A-side on November 11, 1977, the same week the iconoclastic, game-changing *Never Mind the Bollocks, Here's the Sex Pistols* was sitting at No. 1 on the U.K. albums chart.

The cover of the single revealed another truth: Wings was once again reduced to a trio, after the departure of Joe English. The official reason given was that the American drummer had found it hard to acclimate to life in Britain. But, still hiding his addictions, English was suffering from a lot more than homesickness. He later admitted that his life was a wreck and that in his heart he knew he had to leave the situation. In addition, in a now all too familiar complaint, he said he was becoming dispirited with his lack of creative input within the band. English returned to the States and soon became a born-again Christian, enduring more years of drug problems before finally, with the help of his renewed faith, going clean.

Meanwhile, it was a heavily pregnant Linda who added her harmonies to "Mull of Kintyre." Secretly, the McCartneys were hoping that their fourth child would be a boy, and to Paul one strange omen suggested as much. For the past few months he had taken to wearing an old tweed coat he had thriftily picked up at an Oxfam secondhand shop. Reaching into a pocket one day, he pulled out a baby bootie that, spooking him, was blue. "It was like a *Twilight Zone* moment," he marveled. On September 12, 1977, James Louis McCartney was born at the Avenue Clinic in St. John's Wood in London.

A month later, a promo clip for "Mull of Kintyre" was filmed, featuring McCartney perched on a wooden fence gate strumming his acoustic guitar, as in the background Linda emerged carrying baby James in a shawl. McCartney was joined by Denny, and the pair strolled toward Saddell beach, where in the distance the Campbeltown pipers could be seen striking up and stridently marching over the sands. In the final scenes, locals gathered around a towering bonfire on the beach at night, singing along with the closing refrain.

This cozy picture was bound to vex the punk-fed critics. But, once released, "Mull of Kintyre" assumed a life entirely of its own, selling half a million copies within three weeks of its release and hitting No. 1 in December for the start of a nine-week run. It seemed to reach out to the kind of record buyers who never really bought records, while confirming McCartney's fears that the song would cement his image as a comfy, middle-aged balladeer. At the same time, the single's inexorable success far surpassed any expectations he might have had for it, which clearly tickled him. It was the monumental hit record that he'd never anticipated or, deep in his rocker heart, necessarily wanted. "The song touched me," he said, "but I wasn't sure it was everyone's cup of tea."

As demand ramped up, other video performances of "Mull of

Kintyre" were filmed. One featured the three members of the band sitting on a grassy mound in a wobbly-looking pastoral studio set at Elstree; another, for the Christmas TV special of comedian and impressionist Mike Yarwood, had them arranged on high stools, a carpet of dry ice billowing around their feet, as the Campbeltown pipers filed in from behind. In a sketch later in the show, Yarwood, dressed as Chunky Punky—a spiky-haired and safety-pin-wearing incarnation of chancellor of the exchequer Denis Healey—visited the McCartneys in their pretend living room. Paul was seen quickly stuffing a wad of banknotes under the lid of a piano, playing up his stingy image, forever the beloved light entertainer.

Some members of the Campbeltown Pipe Band, meanwhile, were becoming disgruntled about where exactly the humongous profits from the song were going. They aired their grievances in the papers, moaning that they'd only been paid flat session fees for their arguably crucial contribution to the record. This wasn't entirely true. After recording the song, Jimmy McGeachy remembers, the musicians were given "an envelope with some cash in it, ready to get spread around. We thought, Oh, this is all right." They were given £30 each for the recording session itself, plus another £300 each for their appearance in the video, with around £300 each following in royalties. "To me, it wasn't an issue," says McGeachy. "Some of the older guys . . . it was a bit of a hindsight thing that some of them thought about it."

Wings' performance of "Mull of Kintyre" on *Mike Yarwood in Persons* was, staggeringly, watched by more than twenty-one million people, almost 40 percent of the British population. "From there on," says Denny, "*whoosh,* up it went." For those who had perhaps let the Beatles slip to the back of their minds, Paul McCartney was once again a household name.

When the millionth copy of the single, containing a hidden certificate, was bought by a fan named David Ackroyd, EMI gave him a gold disc. But the Campbeltown pipers had been wrong about the support of the expatriates in one key territory: the record flopped in America, where bewildered DJs focused on "Girls School," which struggled to No. 33 on the *Billboard* chart. Back home, however, "Mull of Kintyre" was to top 2.5 million sales, nudging past the Beatles' "She Loves You" and, for a time, becoming the biggest-selling U.K. single ever. Effectively, in terms of his sales power, McCartney had lapped himself.

————

It was to be a commercial blip, however. The singles subsequently pulled from the album recorded in the Virgin Islands, now entitled *London Town,* showed diminishing returns in Britain: the gliding synth pop of "With a Little Luck" made it to No. 5, while the stomping, mock-pissed-off rocker "I've Had Enough" faltered just outside the Top 40.

There were signs that Paul was touchy about the completed album. Playing it for Tony Bramwell, who had worked for the Beatles at both Brian Epstein's NEMS and Apple, McCartney casually asked for his opinion. "Well, it'll be all right when it's finished," said Bramwell. At this, McCartney lost the plot, apparently shouting at his former associate, "What the fuck do you know? I fucking brought you down from Liverpool."

After a run of years characterized by self-assurance and validation, doubt was beginning to creep back into Paul's mind. "We didn't seem to be writing any real hard rockers," he admitted in the wake of the album's release. "Next time around we'll go for a bit more sweat."

This mood of uncertainty was reflected by the press launch of *London Town,* held on a miserable, wet, and windy day in March 1978, on a boat sailing up and down the Thames. The McCartneys and Laine were hustled around by photographers; afterward, they tried to adopt a cheerful demeanor while eating fish and chips from newspapers in the rain. It was another boat, but this time in a very different climate. After the splash of sun, the outlook had returned to cloudy.

12

TAKE THESE BROKEN WINGS

Making McCartney II, *back on your own again. Was this a conscious move away from Wings?*

Y'know, it was really 'cause synthesizers and sequencers came in and I was intrigued. Since leaving the Beatles, I've done that, working on my own thing. Which I always think of as sort of being a nutty professor. You're just holed up in this little laboratory, experimenting with sounds.

THERE WERE SIGNS that McCartney was growing tired—and, more specifically, tired of Wings. "It was getting a bit boring, to tell the truth," he would later admit. "I was getting a bit fed up with *yet another lineup.*" But, of course, given his determined work ethic, at times bordering on the obsessive, he found himself putting together yet another lineup.

Amusingly, he first met the guitarist who was to replace Jimmy McCulloch in Wings in a restroom at CTS Studios in Wembley, during the marathon mixing sessions for *Wings over America*. Laurence Juber, a twenty-four-year-old session musician, was hawking his skills around London. His recent gigs had included various TV shows and the qualifying rounds for the Eurovision Song Contest. It was Herbie Flowers, the bassist responsible for the elastic low-end riff on Lou Reed's "Walk on the Wild Side," who introduced him to Paul over the urinals. The two awkwardly shook hands in the gents' and weren't to see each other again for eighteen months.

Juber subsequently met Denny Laine when he played a version of the Moody Blues' "Go Now" in the house band on the *David Essex* TV show, impressing Laine by perfectly mimicking the guitar solo from the live Wings version of the song. Six months later, Juber got a call from Laine asking him if he'd like to come for a jam in the basement of the MPL offices.

The guitarist, who didn't own a Wings record, borrowed a couple of their albums from his brother in order to bone up. "I can't say that I had been a huge fan of the band," he confesses, "because at that point I was busy trying to be a hot-shot studio guitar player." When Juber arrived at the audition, Paul introduced him to Chris Thomas, the producer who had started his engineering career with the Beatles at Abbey Road on *The White Album,* then gone on to work with Pink Floyd and, most recently and intriguingly, the Sex Pistols. Having laughed at the idea of punking up his sound, Paul was now clearly serious about wanting to toughen up the band. Thomas was someone from McCartney's past who might help guide him into the uncertain post-punk future. Juber picked up on this, even as he was being offered the gig: "There was a sense that there was a desire to take things more in a rock direction."

The calm, polite, softly spoken guitarist, born in the East End of London and a music major at Goldsmiths College, where he'd even studied the lute, was the polar opposite of the tempestuous Jimmy McCulloch. This very likely endeared him to the worn-out Paul and Linda, along with the fact that he was a strict vegetarian, which interested the couple, at the time nearing the end of their long transition into forever forgoing meat.

At the same time, a new drummer arrived on the scene, also via Denny. Steve Holley had recently played with Elton John, so he wasn't unnerved by the idea of working with a famous face. Introduced to Laine by a mutual friend, he turned up at a housewarming party at Denny's place and within minutes was behind a drum kit, jamming with Paul and Linda. "I just sat down and started playing," he says. "I think they saw an easy way to get a replacement drummer, as opposed to going through a long audition process."

The new Wings fell together quickly and painlessly. But it was the first time McCartney had been backed by essentially jobbing musicians, for hire by anyone from jazz singer Cleo Laine to Kiki Dee; the two new members of Wings perhaps lacked the musical character of his former bandmates, however turbulent his relationships with them had been. Later, Paul admitted as much. "Even though they were good players," he said, "my enthusiasm had peaked."

This Mark III version of the group first convened in June 1978 at the Scottish barn studio, now named Spirit of Ranachan. Unlike several of their predecessors, Juber and Holley weren't at all sniffy about being asked to live and work in such a far-flung and relatively unrefined environment. The drummer, who acknowledges that he was still fairly green at the time, says, "I didn't really know how anything worked in the music business at that level, so for me it was a complete surprise." The guitarist, who had a little more experience, notes, "There were some creature comforts there, but nonetheless it was a converted barn."

The pair were clearly just thrilled to be working with McCartney. There were early indications, however, that things weren't quite right. One evening at the barn, Linda confided to Holley that she really didn't want to be in the band anymore. "All I truly want," she told the drummer, "is to be here with my family." Denny, meanwhile, could suddenly pull rank in unpleasant ways. Holley says that he'd written the heavy, loping guitar riff for what became "Old Siam, Sir" in rehearsals one day, before Denny picked up on it, aped it, and claimed it as his own when Paul arrived. An argument, verging on a fistfight, broke out between Laine and Holley and had to be calmed by McCartney, who, perhaps through loyalty, sided with Denny.

Holley was given a strong indication of the level of dedication required from him now that he was a member of Wings when, out of the blue, he got a call from Jimmy McCulloch, asking him to play on his first solo album. Not knowing exactly what the deal was regarding his extracurricular playing, not least with someone who had split from McCartney not so long ago, the drummer asked Alan Crowder at MPL how he thought this information might go down with Paul. "I remember it not being well received," Holley notes. "He said to me, 'You'd be out of your mind to do that.'"

As the making of the album moved south to England, Paul and Linda began looking for a place to work that was an easy commute from their home at Peasmarsh, so that they wouldn't have to schlep up to London every day. Lympne Castle in Kent seemed to provide the answer, and it let them continue their ritual of recording in unusual locations while being within a short drive of their home. A medieval castle with arched Gothic windows and spiraling stone staircases, it brought a sense of otherness to the proceedings. "It had battlements and even a ghost," says Juber. The band set up in the ballroom, snaking their cables up the medieval stairwells to the drawing room turned control room upstairs.

Paul threw everything into the record that was to become the maligned *Back to the Egg*, recording dozens of songs that ranged from rattling new wave–ish rockers like "Spin It On" (which still sounded too smoothed out to be truly edgy) and the power-popping, Squeeze-echoing "Getting Closer" to the old-timey crooner swing of "Baby's Request." There were weird—and not in a good way—collages of spoken word by Lympne Castle owners, Harry and Deirdre Margary, who quoted obscure literary texts over funky grooves ("Reception") and faux-classical arrangements ("The Broadcast"). There was too much material, and yet not enough of it to gel into a cohesive album.

For their part, the two new musicians might have started to sense that Paul was a touch jaded about the whole affair. "*Jaded* is a loaded word," points out Juber. "But you have Paul's work ethic, which is just to keep working. The goal was productivity."

"If he was jaded," Holley argues, "well, how could you not be? He'd achieved so much. There was a disappointment that was evident in a lot of areas."

The 1970s were coming to a close, and just like the low, fuggy mood that had surrounded the end of the previous decade, there was a feeling that, for McCartney and his generation of 1960s musicians who had survived the subsequent years, a familiar kind of hangover was beginning to kick in.

This became all too dramatically evident at the beginning of September 1978, in the wake of what had been established as the annual Buddy Holly week, inaugurated by McCartney two years earlier. For Paul, this yearly occurrence worked on two levels: he was able to pay tribute to one of his formative musical heroes and, since back in 1971, at the urging of Lee Eastman, he'd bought Holly's song catalog as an investment, he was able subtly to promote his business interests.

The first event, in September 1976, after Wings had returned from the U.S. tour, saw producer Norman Petty ceremonially present McCartney with the cuff links Buddy Holly had been wearing on his fatal flight in 1959. In 1977, the late singer's former backing band the Crickets reunited for a performance. This year would be marked by the British premiere of the biopic *The Buddy Holly Story,* starring Gary Busey, at the Odeon cinema in Leicester Square. The guests, including David Frost, Carl Perkins, Eric Clapton, members of Roxy Music, and Keith Moon (wearing a black leather jacket and a Wings T-shirt), were treated to dinner beforehand at the voguish Covent Garden restaurant Peppermint Park.

Moon, who was sober at this point but had been snorting cocaine earlier in the evening, looked both wired and weary, and older than his thirty-two years. He fell ill during the screening and left. Along with his girlfriend, Annette Walter-Lax, he returned to the Curzon Place flat in Mayfair that he was borrowing from Harry Nilsson. Four years earlier, the flat had been the scene of the death from a heart attack of Mama Cass of the Mamas and the Papas.

The Who's drummer, after scarfing down a sedative called Heminevrin to take the edge off his alcohol withdrawal, fell asleep in bed in front of the TV while watching the Vincent Price horror flick *The Abominable Dr. Phibes.* In the morning, Moon woke and ate a breakfast of steak and eggs made by Walter-Lax after an argument during which he had told her to "fuck off." He popped more pills, watched the rest of the film, and nodded out. At three-forty on the afternoon of September 7, his girlfriend woke to find him dead.

Less than four weeks after his death, Keith Moon was the ghost at the scene of McCartney's next grand venture. As if a cocky display by Paul and his contemporaries to celebrate the fact that they'd survived the tumultuous 1970s, a performance by the supergroup Rockestra found McCartney conducting his musician mates as they made a big noise. On October 3, at Abbey Road, he assembled this mock orchestra of premier-league bassists, guitarists, keyboard players, and drummers to create the "Rockestra Theme."

Those who accepted the invitation and made up the numbers included musicians who had come up alongside McCartney (Hank Marvin, Pete Townshend), those who had followed (Gary Brooker of Procol Harum, David Gilmour of Pink Floyd, John Bonham and John Paul Jones of Led Zeppelin), and even a sole representative of the new wave

community (bassist Bruce Thomas of Elvis Costello's band the Attrac-
tions). Among the no-shows were Jimmy Page (although a roadie did
set up his amp so that it would be ready for his arrival), Jeff Beck (who
didn't like the idea that he had no control over the final track), and Eric
Clapton. "He didn't feel like it," Paul commented tersely about Clapton's nonappearance.

The resulting, largely instrumental track, a chugging, bluesy rocker
aspiring to the grand movements of big-band swing, was nailed in five
takes; it was perhaps more fun to play than it is to hear. There was certainly no shortage of high jinks that day, including, according to Jo Jo
Patrie, a line of coked-up rock stars queuing up to use the men's room.
Even with the specter of Keith Moon haunting the proceedings, the
party went on. The comedown, however, was to be a long one. Two
years later, John Bonham, too, would die, by choking on his own vomit
after a heavy drinking binge.

Denny Laine's indulgences were also worsening, though he still
found time to get married, on a yacht in Boston Harbor on November 5,
to Jo Jo. The bride in particular was a bit put out that the McCartneys
didn't show for the ceremony, only weeks later sending the happy couple a silk bedding set, unwrapped, in a shopping bag, with no card.
There was clearly still no love lost between the McCartneys and the
untamable former groupie.

Paul and Linda were, at the same time, being surprisingly profligate
in other respects. For the cover for the forthcoming hits compilation
album *Wings Greatest*, a design team was flown to the Swiss Alps to
shoot a figurine of a burlesque dancer—with her arms outstretched, as
if ready to take to the air—positioned in the snow. It became something
of a ridiculous endeavor: a snowdrift was artificially created, and shots
were taken from a helicopter. Ultimately, the image used might have
been captured in any decent photographic studio back in London for far
less than the $8,000—or $25,000 in today's dollars—it cost to create the
sleeve of *Wings Greatest*. "It really did not need that degree of money
and time and effort spent on it," reckoned photographer Robert Ellis.
"It was a complete and utter obscenity."

The spending didn't stop there. Irked by the fact that he was frequently
unable to book time at Abbey Road, his spiritual recording home, with

entire months at the facility having been blocked out by EMI's new darling, Kate Bush, McCartney, at great expense, turned the basement at
MPL into a facsimile of that studio, pointedly naming it Replica. The
making of *Back to the Egg* continued there, running over into the first
weeks of 1979. It was becoming clear, though, that Denny Laine, never
one for spending days and weeks poring over takes and mixes, was
growing weary of the endless recording. "I'm desperate to be on tour,"
he said. "I get twitchy sitting around in a studio. I'm quite sure we'll be
touring soon, otherwise I honestly feel that I wouldn't be able to stay in
Wings."

McCartney still drove himself relentlessly onward. "It was hard to
get Paul not to work," says Laurence Juber. "I remember being in Replica studios when he had a lousy cold and he was still at it. It took a lot
for Paul to call the session off and say, 'I just don't feel up to it.'" In
many ways, McCartney was striving for the breakthrough that never
came. Even when he'd bagged the Latin-tinged dance-floor groove of
the naggingly catchy "Goodnight Tonight," an obvious single, Paul had
reservations about the track. Still searching for a likely hit, at the close
of one fruitless session at Replica he threw down a challenge to the
other members of Wings: come up with a song over the weekend and
we'll consider it for the next single. Obviously, for the other musicians,
this was a potentially lucrative opportunity. Separately, Juber, Holley,
Laine, and even Linda got their heads into writing mode over the weekend, only for Paul to arrive at the studio on Monday and trump them all
with "Daytime Nighttime Suffering," a song he'd written himself over
the previous two days. It was as if, missing the games of creative one-
upmanship he'd enjoyed playing with Lennon, McCartney was manufacturing a false sense of rivalry.

Indecision set in again, this time over whether "Goodnight Tonight"
or "Daytime Nighttime Suffering"—mixed and remixed nearly fifty
times—should be the A side, with Paul doubting the firm opinion of the
others that the former was the clearly superior song. "We sat around for
years—well, it seemed like years—discussing it," McCartney said. "The
normal soul-searching you go through. And we decided, No, it isn't
right, we won't put it out. And about a week later, I played the record
again. I thought, That's crazy, we've made it . . . why not put it out?"

As the tracks for *Back to the Egg* were being completed, McCartney
turned to David Bowie, himself nearing the end of a peerlessly inspired

1970s, to ask for his opinion of the new songs. Chris Thomas recalled that Bowie sat there saying, "Like this . . . not that. . . . This is good . . . keep this . . . not that one," doubtless relishing the novelty of being required to critique an ex-Beatle. His art-rock-slanted views were perhaps not to be trusted, however. Bowie, mischievously, suggested that the abstract, minute-and-a-half-long track "The Broadcast" should be Paul's next single.

Instead, Wings released "Goodnight Tonight," complete with a video shot at London's Hammersmith Palais, featuring the band sporting 1930s garb—black suits and bow ties, their hair slicked back with gel. Fooling around on the stage during the long day, the group ran through rock'n'roll standards including the enduring "Twenty Flight Rock," McCartney's acid test for any band. But this was a more vanilla and conservative outfit in many ways, lacking the wildness of spirit that Jimmy McCulloch, Henry McCullough, and even Geoff Britton had brought to the party. Holley, unable to find the makeup artist at the end of the shoot, was nervous about being forced to drive home with his hair pinned and greased, wearing thick foundation. "I just thought, I hope to God I don't get stopped," he says.

McCartney had just signed a new U.S. record contract, fueling the procrastination over the first single to be released by the new if not entirely improved Wings. His arrangement with Capitol having lapsed, he'd moved over to Columbia, cutting himself a money-hoovering deal that made him the highest-paid recording artist in the world, with a $2 million advance on his future albums and an unparalleled 22 percent royalty, at least 4 percent more than any of his rivals had secured. The president of the company, Walter Yetnikoff, even threw in a clause that allowed Paul and Linda the use of the company's private jet.

Paul was a prestige signing for the record label. When he first visited Columbia's offices in New York for a grip-and-grin meeting with its employees, some of them trembled with nerves, as if they were being granted an audience with the queen. Still, there were those at the company who felt that the deal was over the top. Later, one anonymous employee would say, "It was too much money for an artist who was obviously past his prime. We knew we would have to really work our asses off to try to earn some of that money back."

At the same time as business was booming for McCartney, Allen Klein was being jailed in New York. Found guilty of tax evasion, he was given a two-year sentence, of which he would have to serve only two months. Commenting at the time, Paul tried not to sound too pleased. "I feel sorry for him now," he said. "But I was caught in his net once, and that panicked me. I really wanted to do everything to get him. I was contemplating going to where he lives and walking outside his house with placards. I was really crazy at that time."

With the villain of the piece in jail, the ex-Beatles seemed to be in a more playful mood. At the May 19, 1979, wedding celebration thrown by Eric Clapton at his home in Surrey to toast his marriage to Pattie Boyd—notably, of course, George Harrison's first wife, the two friends having reached some kind of peace in the aftermath of the difficult affair—the former bandmates were practically on frolicsome form. Paul described Ringo and George as "two old flames" as he called them to the stage in the pavilion pitched on the lawn of the estate, and along with Clapton they drunkenly hammered through some old rock'n'roll standards and even a few Beatles numbers, including "Sgt. Pepper's Lonely Hearts Club Band" and "Get Back." "The music was terrible, absolute rubbish," said Denny Laine, who watched this impromptu and overrefreshed three-quarters Beatles reunion from the audience of par-tygoers. "It's lucky nobody made a tape."

Back to the Egg was launched with a surreal press conference held in the hallowed Studio Two at Abbey Road, its interior decked out as if it were the inside of a giant frying pan. Journalists sat at tables under parasols made to resemble enormous fried eggs. Asked about his future intentions, Paul, unsurprisingly, said he was planning to take this new lineup of the band on the road.

The marketing budget for the album, underwritten by Columbia, was far higher than for any of the previous Wings albums. The band returned to Lympne Castle to shoot a number of expensive promo videos, including one for the ballad "Winter Rose," which the production team decided needed a snowy setting, requiring them to spray gallons of white foam over two areas of the grounds. "They'd promised the Margarys, the owners of the castle, that it wouldn't damage any of the grass or foliage," Steve Holley remembers. "But then it washed away and it had turned everything brown."

A minute-long TV ad, screened during prime time, announced *Back* to the Egg as "a timeless rock'n'roll flight through twelve superbly produced new songs on an album that really is perfection." It was certainly an album made by a perfectionist, even if he was one unable to wholly trust his creative instincts.

Upon its release, in May, "Goodnight Tonight" reached a respectable No. 5 in both the United Kingdom and the States. The album followed, peaking at No. 6 in Britain and, disappointingly, No. 8 in America. *Back to the Egg* sold more than a million copies in the United States, a respectable figure in the middle of the economic recession of 1979, but this didn't quite satisfy McCartney's investors at Columbia. Part of the problem was that—in a practice that harked back to the 1960s, when it was thought that not putting a single on its parent LP offered value for money—Paul had argued against including "Goodnight Tonight" on the album. But times had moved on and, particularly in America, every album release needed a radio hit or two to push sales. By not featuring the hit single on the album, opined one record executive, Paul had shot himself in the foot, particularly when the follow-ups released from *Back to the Egg* in the States—the chiming, upbeat "Getting Closer" and the tailored-for-FM-radio homage to Philly soul "Arrow Through Me"—failed to even puncture the Top 20.

Acknowledging its relatively poor sales, Paul joked that *Back to the Egg* was less a concept album and more a "bomb-cept" album.

Unperturbed, and flush with the proceeds of the Columbia deal, that summer the McCartneys bought the property neighboring their Sussex home, Lower Gate Farm, for £250,000, planning at some point in the future to knock down its semiderelict farmhouse, perched on a hill, and build in its place a house designed by Paul. The plan was purposely modest: a five-bedroom house, which would provide each of the kids with their own room, it was not overly expansive. The couple hated the idea of living in some huge, posh country home where the children might be "rattling around in the east wing, and you never see them."

They reinstated the property's original name, Blossom Wood Farm. Within its 159 acres there were stables, a windmill building that Paul earmarked for a recording studio, and an old cottage that Linda turned into a pottery studio. Linda took a hippieish, Mother Nature's daughter approach to owning so much green space. "I was lent all this for a little while," she told her friend Danny Fields. "And I have to take good care of it, so I can give it back just the way it is."

July found Paul alone, in his studios in Sussex and Scotland, messing around with the tracks for what was to become his second solo album, *McCartney II*. Without Wings, he began experimenting with synthesizers and sequencers, recapturing the freedom he'd enjoyed when making the first record. Once again he found himself at play, balancing a snare drum on the rim of a toilet and whacking it with a stick to see what kind of resonant sound it made.

Almost all of the songs were entirely improvised, beginning with the bubbling synths of "Front Parlor" and the bouncy falsetto dub reggae of "Check My Machine." "Temporary Secretary" was a letter song, in the style of "Paperback Writer," directed at the head of the Alfred Marks Recruitment Agency and requesting the services of the typist of the title, delivered in a cartoon American accent over a clubby beat. It was frivolous and liberating stuff. "Check My Machine" and the hypnotic electronic track "Secret Friend"—which weren't to make the original cut of the album, surfacing only on subsequent reissues—were long and unhurried. Other songs weren't quite so forward-looking and experimental, however, with "On the Way" and "Nobody Knows" essentially being bluesy rock knockoffs.

There was a real maturity evident elsewhere, though, Paul having just turned thirty-seven. "Waterfalls," inspired by the natural feature at the Sussex estate, found McCartney plaintively fretting about the safety of his loved ones. "One of These Days" might have been lifted from *The White Album* and captured Paul peering into the future with a certain serenity, writing in the becalmed hours after a visit from an acquaintance who was devoted to the Hare Krishna movement.

The making of *McCartney II*, in isolation and in secret, was a real indication of the fact that Paul was tiring of the complications of working with other musicians. It had been ten years since he'd last done the same, hiding himself away in Cavendish Avenue during the dark days of the end of the Beatles. It was a closing of the circle.

Then, on September 27, 1979, Jimmy McCulloch died. In the two years since leaving Wings, the guitarist had continued his drinking and drugging around London, moving into a posh Maida Vale flat and ripping through the not insubstantial royalties that had followed his time with the band. The reformed Small Faces had, as McCartney predicted, been a short-lived enterprise. Jimmy had subsequently played in Wild Horses, with similarly hard-edged, hard-living former Thin Lizzy guitarist Brian Robertson, and in an outfit called the Dukes, signed to Warner Brothers.

McCulloch had gone AWOL for a couple of days in September, failing to show up for a rehearsal with the Dukes at Dingwalls nightclub in Camden. Phone calls to him went unanswered. Worried, his brother, Jack, made his way over to the flat in Maida Vale. When there was no reply to his knocks and he noticed a strange, unpleasant smell emanating from inside, he took his shoulder to the door and burst it open.

Jimmy was discovered sitting up in an armchair, with a burned-out spliff between his fingers, clearly dead. He was twenty-six. There was some evidence that someone had been with him and had absconded, likely scared. Cannabis, morphine, and alcohol were found in the guitarist's blood, but other than the joint roach, no drugs were in the flat. The police concluded that the place had been tidied up in a hurry. The door's chain had been broken by someone other than Jack.

Deputy coroner Dr. Paul Knapman concluded, "There are certainly some odd circumstances and, because of this, I think an open verdict is the proper one." Jack McCulloch was quoted as saying, almost threateningly, "I'm sure somebody was in that apartment when my brother died and I'd like to find out who it was." The exact circumstances of Jimmy's death remain a mystery.

"I was shocked . . . it was crazy," says Dave Clarke, McCulloch's former partner in White Line. "But I have to say there was always that thought at the back of your mind. Knowing Jim as I did and his personality . . . it wasn't something that I thought *couldn't* possibly happen. I never saw him near any heroin. I think it probably came later. It was all uppers and drinking and grass."

It was perhaps no surprise that Paul, who, of course, couldn't bear funerals, didn't attend McCulloch's wake. But neither did Denny Laine. "I was pissed off with Jimmy over lots of things and I'd kind of fallen out with him," he admitted. "I know it sounds funny to say, but when somebody dies you can still be angry with them." Paul said of Jimmy's death, "In the end, he was just too dangerous for his own good."

That autumn, the sales of Wings albums topped one hundred million. At the same time, the people behind the *Guinness World Records* book series presented McCartney with an award to mark his landmark achievements, naming him the most successful recording artist of all time. The trophy handed to him was made of rhodium, a substance twice as expensive as platinum. The organizers had originally wanted to cast it in osmium, before discovering that the rarer metal was highly toxic.

Still, this elevated status appeared to do little to firm up McCartney's sagging belief in himself. In once again trying to step away from his fame and downsize his ambitions, Paul had suggested that the new Wings, still untested live, should go out on a low-key tour of small British clubs, to refine their performance and get closer to their audiences. The notion perhaps revealed McCartney's inner doubts about the band. "At the moment, we don't want a great big tour of the world with everything it entails," Paul announced in the pages of the Wings newsletter *Club Sandwich*, "so it looks as though we'll just be turning up with our guitars and plugging them in wherever they want to listen to us."

In the end, promoter Harvey Goldsmith managed to up the scale, talking Paul into nineteen theater dates. As it transpired, throughout the jaunt, Paul and Linda were there with the band, but somehow apart. Whenever possible, they would drive home after the shows, to Sussex or London.

McCartney had promised to launch his next tour back on his hometown turf, in Liverpool. Demand for tickets overwhelmed the box office of the Royal Court Theatre, forcing the line to be closed on more than a thousand fans who had queued outside overnight in the autumn cold. Similar scenes were repeated up and down the country.

Waiting to go on stage at the Royal Court on November 23, the first night of Wings' British tour, saxophonist Howie Casey was amazed to see just how nervous McCartney was. Paul turned to him, minutes before showtime, and said, "Oh God, I hope this goes well." Casey, taken aback, replied, "Paul, this is like the Second Coming. You're gonna go down well just walking on the stage."

The Royal Court, which Paul had frequented as a kid, was at the time struggling financially. McCartney had donated £5,000 to the cause, which was seen by its directors as "a great boost to the theatre," while attracting some criticism from the local government. One of the city's Labour councillors carped, "I don't see why Paul McCartney should be singled out for special praise. The Beatles could have given a million and not missed it. They made their millions and we've not seen them since."

He was a lone voice, and one that failed to be heard in the clamor caused by Paul's arrival back in Liverpool. "I feel I'm not judged with the same harshness by the people here as elsewhere," McCartney said.

On the afternoon of the opening night in the city, Paul played a free matinee show for pupils from his former high school, the Liverpool Institute, organized by his former geography teacher, Bertram Parker, nicknamed Blip. Parker, who was now the school's headmaster, remembered Paul as "a bright and cheerful lad who did a reasonable amount of work." He recalled, with a smile, that the last time he'd seen McCartney, in his pre-fame days, had been when Paul repaid a small debt to Parker's wife. "A sixpence that he'd borrowed to go to the cinema," Parker noted with a grin. That afternoon, upping the headmaster's cool, Paul started the show by saying, "Hello, Blip, nice to see you."

The media trailed after McCartney the whole day: the *Liverpool Echo* joined him for a trip on the Mersey on the *Royal Iris* ferry, the setting of some early Beatles performances, and a camera crew from the BBC teatime magazine show *Nationwide* captured his every move for a twenty-minute documentary. Before the evening show, in a news item on local radio, one reporter frothed up the atmosphere in the city. "Theatre staff are predicting the greatest explosion since the Merseybeat mania of the 1960s, and the police are taking no chances," he babbled. "They're prepared to draft in extra men at the first signs of the hysteria McCartney attracted during the heyday of the Beatles."

In truth, despite the roaring responses, Paul felt the band was underrehearsed, the performances phoned in. *Rolling Stone* reviewer Mick Brown could tell that the singer's heart wasn't in it. "Everything seemed designed to take the spotlight off Paul McCartney and spread it among the rest of Wings," he noted. "The impression given was not that of a deity with a box of thunderbolts, but a band onstage for the hell of it." Howie Casey says he felt that, from his vantage point at the back of the stage, something had changed in the Wings setup beyond the shake-up in personnel. They had turned even less rock'n'roll, effectively becoming a showband in some ways. "They gave us black suits and it became almost formal," he says.

In Steve Holley's view, despite the impression given to its audiences, McCartney hated the 1979 tour. Backstage after one underwhelming show in Brighton, Paul told the drummer that he thought it "stank." Finding themselves once again trying to juggle touring and family life heaped more pressure on the McCartneys' relationship. "It caused a lot of trouble between us," said Paul. "We both work at it and have a laugh or have an argument," said Linda. "But we always end up in the laugh."

In Edinburgh, partway through the gig, the power failed, and, in the semidarkness, the bandmates turned into troupers and rallied the crowd. Denny performed a jokey striptease and unveiled some acrobatic skills; Linda and the horn section roused everyone into a sing-along of "When the Saints Go Marching In." On the last night in Glasgow, the Wings musicians turned up in kilts and brought the Campbeltown Pipe Band on for a roof-lifting "Mull of Kintyre." "We did the encore and everybody went ballistic," says Jimmy McGeachy. Performing the rubbery funk of "Coming Up," a song Paul had recorded solo during the *McCartney II* sessions, he zeroed in on one particularly enthusiastic audience member. "This kid was bopping away," he recalled. "I thought, Oh, this is a hit." Luckily, the show was being recorded by a mobile studio unit that night, and this B-side live version was to be favored by DJs in the United States over Paul's solo A-side version, reaching No. 1.

Rising up the British charts during this time was McCartney's first attempt at a festive 45, "Wonderful Christmastime," a bright, synthy concoction recorded alone in the summer and destined to become a perennial. In the slightly muted aftermath of the British tour, he sat down with promoter Bill Graham to plot a U.S. jaunt, due to follow a trip to Japan early the next year. It may be no coincidence that, knowing how Linda might feel about this, he presented his wife with a marriage-sweetening, grand-gesture gift of a ranch in Arizona, a property she'd visited and adored back in her university days.

Wings closed out the year with a show at the Hammersmith Odeon in London on December 29, set up following a plea from U.N. Secretary-General Kurt Waldheim to reunite the Beatles for a benefit to raise funds for the victims of war in Kampuchea. The fact that this was always going to be highly unlikely did nothing to dampen the raging press speculation that, finally, nearly ten years on, the four were to re-form. In fact, calls were indeed placed to Ringo and George, who agreed to appear, though not as part of the Beatles. John, in New York, wasn't interested. Then, when the papers got wind of Harrison and Starr's agreement to participate, the two pulled out. And so it was left to McCartney to tell Waldheim that Wings would play the show.

It was a long, rambling night, and flat in its execution. Denny

Laine was drunk, but not as spectacularly as Pete Townshend, who turned up for a live gathering of the Rockestra and proceeded to fuzz his way through "Let It Be." The assembled musicians—among them Robert Plant, John Bonham, ex-Faces bassist Ronnie Lane, and James Honeyman-Scott of the Pretenders—all agreed to wear the requisite uniform for the evening, a silver suit and top hat. The Who's guitarist, though, noisily refused to dress up, shouting, "I'm not wearing that fucking shit."

"Pete was breathing Rémy Martin fumes down my neck," Laurence Juber remembers. "I put the top hat on him, at one point and he took it off and threw it into the audience."

The final Wings show of this difficult year proved both an anticlimax and an inauspicious end to the decade. "There was a growing sense from Paul that it was getting to the endgame of the band," says Juber.

No one could know that the group had just played its last gig.

13

STUCK INSIDE THESE FOUR WALLS

Japan, 1980: what was going through your mind?

How the hell did that happen? But it did. Then it became just a film, y'know. A slow-motion film of Japan. The inside view of Tokyo. An insider's view! Jesus! It was just unbelievable.

L ATER, McCARTNEY WAS TO WONDER if it had been some strange act of self-sabotage.

It was almost as if I *wanted* to get busted, he thought to himself.

The first days of January 1980 saw Wings regroup at Hog Hill Mill Studios, McCartney's newly completed facility at his Sussex estate. Maybe it had something to do with rehearsing at home. Maybe the dawning of the new year, and decade, only served to remind him of his waning passion for the band. But for Wings, rehearsing for merely a week in preparation for a major tour, the pall of lethargy was all too obvious.

"We hadn't really rehearsed enough," Paul admitted. "For the previous Wings tour we rehearsed a lot."

Steve Holley didn't think the band was ready for the upcoming Japanese tour, either. "I didn't feel at my best when we set off," says the drummer. "I remember the rehearsals being less than satisfactory. They hadn't yielded enough security for Paul. So when we left, there was a cloud hanging over it."

On Saturday, January 12, Paul and Linda, with the four kids, flew to New York on the Concorde, booking into the Stanhope, on Central Park. Once there, through an East Coast connection, they bought half a pound of grass. Legend would later have it that McCartney then phoned Lennon at the Dakota, the call taken by Ono, to say he could come over with some "dynamite weed." The offer was declined, but, in the aftermath, the rumor spread that Yoko—incensed that the McCartneys planned to stay in the Lennons' favorite suite at the Hotel Okura in Tokyo—tipped off a cousin who worked in Japan Customs that McCartney was coming in carrying a hefty bag of dope. Ono would dismiss the accusation, saying drugs hadn't been mentioned in the conversation and she didn't even have a cousin who worked at the airport.

Puncturing another hole in this conspiracy theory, of course, is the fact that no one could have imagined that Paul would ever have been stupid enough to try to smuggle dope into Japan, the country that just over four years earlier had banned him for his drug conviction.

But, leaving for Japan, he couldn't bring himself to flush the stuff down the toilet. It was to be the dumbest thing he'd ever done in his life. "I was," he says, "an idiot."

Paul hadn't set foot in Japan since 1966 with the Beatles. Having had his visa turned down nine years later, forcing the cancellation of the Asian leg of the 1975 tour, he was now to be allowed back into the country for eleven concert dates over eighteen days, the authorities having taken into consideration McCartney's popularity with Japanese fans.

Straight off the plane, on January 16, 1980, Paul—with Linda and the kids and Laurence Juber, who had joined them on the flight from New York—grinned and capered around for the photographers and reporters. Once the storm of flashbulbs died down, the party moved through to an immigration holding area, where they spent two hours going through paperwork with officials. "It was tedious, to be honest," says the guitarist.

From there, they made their way with their luggage through to customs. Blue-uniformed, white-gloved Japanese officers began opening bags at random, performing standard spot checks, pulling an item or two, though not everything, from each. One unzipped a beige canvas suitcase. Inside, lying on top, was Paul's folded jacket. The official reached inside it and pulled out the clear plastic bag of grass.

Paul, recalls Juber, who was standing next to him, "turned kind of white." The officer, visibly stunned and embarrassed, almost made to cover up the bag of weed again with the coat. Then he quickly realized that he couldn't possibly ignore what he had just seen. He duly alerted his superior, and Paul was hurriedly ushered into a back room.

Juber was dumbstruck. Alan Crowder from MPL had warned the band that, prior to entering Japan, they had to take every precaution to ensure that they weren't carrying a crumb of dope. They were to vacuum their pockets, scrub their fingernails. Now, because of the foolishness of the boss, a stony-faced Japan Customs man was handing Juber a screwdriver and ordering him to remove the panels from his guitars, to search for any other stashed packages.

"All of us had been warned, whatever you do, don't take stuff into Japan," says McCartney. "And there it was. The look on the customs man's face when he pulled a bag of pot out of my suitcase was priceless. I mean, it was just like a sort of mad movie."

But however much Paul felt as if he were outside himself, looking in, this was really happening.

When it was all over and done with, no one could ever work out why such a stupid thing had been allowed to occur. There were those who said it revealed the superstar bubble that McCartney floated around in. Paul, on some level, felt he was above the law, a hangover from the Beatles' sense of diplomatic immunity. "I think of my kind of drug involvement as harmless," he later said, "so I walked straight into Japan after a fourteen-hour flight thinking, It's not that bad. Most people taking that kind of thing into the country would give it to the roadies. That just shows that I wasn't really thinking about it. I was taking *my* opinion of it instead of the legal opinion."

Maybe his rebellious side told him he could get away with it. Even if he was caught, he was likely assuming, his power could effectively snuff any legal difficulties, just as it had done in the past. "I'm still not quite sure how it all happened, to tell you the truth," he offers now.

This time around, though, his fame and wealth couldn't protect him. In order to secure the visa, McCartney had signed an affidavit declaring that he no longer smoked marijuana. The minister of justice had rubber-stamped the application and approved the visit. Now the singer seemed to be making a fool of Japanese law. In losing face, the authorities decided that an example had to be made of McCartney. He was arrested and handcuffed, and was filmed leaving the airport amid a scrum of police officers and reporters. Outside the fans were screaming, as if it was Beatlemania all over again. "But instead of going to a gig," says Paul, "I was going to a cell."

McCartney was taken to the Kojimachi police station, in central Tokyo, and questioned for an hour. "I made a confession," he says, "and apologized for breaking Japanese law." The promoter, Seijiro Udo, issued a statement saying that a decision about the shows would be made imminently. Some phone calls having been made, the announcement followed: the tour was off. One hundred thousand tickets had been sold, making for a possible loss of 100 million yen, or nearly £200,000.

Denny Laine and Steve Holley, who had flown in first-class from London on TWA with the crew and management an hour earlier, were sitting in a bus outside the airport, wondering what was causing the delay. Alan Crowder came to tell them there had been a "slight problem" with the McCartneys' flight. After a period of waiting, the band was driven to the Hotel Okura. Exhausted after the eighteen-hour trip, the drummer went to bed and was woken by a call from Linda, telling him that Paul had been arrested. "I actually thought she was just playing a trick on us," he says. Emerging from the elevator in the lobby, Holley was met with the sight of a mob of journalists. He spotted the crew in the bar, slumped over with their heads down, looking dejected. "I went, Oh no."

Meanwhile, Howie Casey and the rest of the brass section were sitting in a room at the Okura, drinking wine and smoking cigars, in celebration of the fact that they'd had their wages raised to $1,000 a gig for the Japanese tour. "So we're mid-cigar and half a bottle of wine gone," says the saxophonist, "and Alan comes in and says, 'Have you heard the news? Paul's been arrested.' We're going, 'Fuck off, Alan, don't take the piss.' And of course, it was true." Casey and the others were baffled by the risk McCartney had taken, everyone having been quietly advised prior to the trip that marijuana could be freely bought through contacts at the U.S. Army bases in the country. "They could have got it no problem," he points out.

Holley says the musicians were quickly made to feel as if they were personae non gratae in the country. To fox the press, they faked their exit from the hotel, making a big show of leaving via the front door before nipping around the back to a waiting van that would take them to the train station and on to Kyoto, where they could sit out the fuss.

Transferred after questioning to the Metropolitan Jail and stripped of his personal effects, including his wedding ring, Paul was now prisoner No. 22. He was appointed a public defender, Tasuku Matsuo, who soberly informed him that two Japanese men had recently been sentenced to three years after being caught with only half the amount of marijuana found in McCartney's suitcase. The truth was that he could be facing up to seven years in prison.

Linda was at the Okura, with the kids, waiting for news. "It's a strain," she told reporters. "I wouldn't mind if we knew what was happening and knew he was getting out." Sick with worry, she couldn't help letting sinister fantasies about what was now happening to her husband creep into her mind. "I was thinking they might be torturing him."

She was eventually allowed into the prison to see Paul, on the other side of a metal grille, having been informed that she couldn't bring the kids. Her husband didn't tell her that he could be looking at a seven-year sentence. "If I'd known what Paul was really facing," she said, "I'd have fallen apart." At the same time, her father, Lee Eastman, in New York, apparently furious, said his son-in-law was in "a hell of a mess" and dispatched John Eastman to Japan.

Stuck in his cell, McCartney was quietly terrified: "It was scary for the first couple of days, I must say. I felt worse for what I'd landed the family in. If I'd just been some single guy, I'd have sort of thought, You're a total nutter and you deserve to get nicked. But it was more the impact it would have on them that was really doing my head in. And also, unless you're an old lag, you don't know the scene. So it takes you a few days to sort of see what's going on."

The first night, he couldn't sleep, and a blinding headache set in. His biggest fear was being raped. "So," he says, "I slept with my back to the wall."

Each morning, the lights in his eight-by-four-foot cell would come on at dawn. McCartney, as he had been instructed to, would then roll up his tatami mat, designed for the Japanese stature and thus too short for him. He then had to sit cross-legged and wait for cell inspection. Throughout this process, he still felt oddly detached. "I kept thinking I was watching a war film. They shouted out 'Twenty-two' in Japanese, and I had to shout back, '*Hai.*'" Pushed through the door was a breakfast of three bread rolls with miso soup, which, once he was freed, he would never be able to face again. Supper was a bowl of rice. The lights went out at eight.

On the second day, with Matsuo at his side, Paul was interrogated in English for six hours by the police at Kojimachi. He insisted that the marijuana had been for his personal use and added that he continued to take a pro-dope stance, arguing that it was less toxic than alcohol. "I tried to tell them ciggies were worse," he says. "They wouldn't listen, of course, because many of the police there chain-smoke." The line of questioning often seemed bizarre to him. "They wanted to know everything, I had to go through my whole life story—school, father's name, income, even my medal from the queen."

As he attempted to leave the station, around two hundred fans chanting, "Free Paul" blocked the exit. The police pulled McCartney back into the building. Officials were still refusing to say whether he would be deported or face a trial. In the press, one well-known Japanese music journalist, Ichiro Fukuda, was damning of the singer, saying, "For a man like McCartney to violate the law means he has no respect for Japan." A media ban was even imposed, prohibiting the playing of any of his records. But encouragingly, perhaps, the minister of justice noted in a statement that Paul "had not legally landed when he was seized."

On the third day, prosecutors asked the Tokyo District Court to allow them a further ten days to question McCartney. It was clear that they were determined to continue to take a tough line, particularly in light of the fact that the news had made front pages the world over, effectively becoming an international incident. When Paul put in a request to be allowed a guitar in his cell, it was flatly denied.

He was visited by the British consul, Donald Warren-Knott. They talked for fifteen minutes, the U.K. official apparently cheerful, but ultimately powerless. An official statement was put out by the press office at the detention center: "He slept well in jail, but he is concerned about his wife, Linda, and four children."

"Linda wasn't going to go back to England," Paul points out. "I was looking at the kids being brought up in Japan."

On the other side of the world, several days after McCartney had been jailed, a clearly distressed twenty-nine-year-old fan named Kenneth Lambert arrived at Miami International Airport, walked up to one of the desks, and hysterically demanded a ticket to Japan in order to, as he put it, "free Paul." Being unable to produce either any money or ID, he began arguing wildly with the airline clerk, then pulled a genuine-looking toy gun from his pocket. A policeman shot him dead on the spot.

Across the country, Laurence Juber landed in Los Angeles and exited the airport to find bootleggers hawking unofficial T-shirts commemorating Wings' tour of Japan, with the word CANCELED slashed across them. "It was a big deal," he points out. The band had lingered on in the Far East until January 19, three days after Paul's arrest, leaving, slightly dazed, only when it became clear that there was no chance of the tour being rescheduled.

As part of their deal, all of the members of Wings had been given a round-the-world first-class air ticket allowing them unlimited stops en route back to London. Denny Laine flew to the MIDEM music industry conference in Cannes to cut a deal for a solo album. This annoyed McCartney, riled by the thought that his guitarist was sunning himself on the French Riviera while he was locked in his cell, facing a highly uncertain future. A slightly aimless Steve Holley traveled to Australia to visit family. "I thought, Well, I'll go there and I'll hang out and I'll see what happens," he says. "I just didn't really know what to do. It wasn't clear."

Back inside the Metropolitan Jail, as letters and telegrams flooded in, Paul felt his spirits begin to lift. "Well, I'd seen *Bridge on the River Kwai*," he says. "I knew what you had to do when you were a prisoner of war. You had to laugh a lot and keep cheery, 'cause that's all you had. So I did a lot of that." One of his jailers, Yasuji Ariga, was quoted as saying, "He is very polite and has made a good impression on the guards."

On January 22, Linda visited her husband for the second time, taking him some sci-fi novels, a cheese sandwich, and some fruit, and staying for half an hour. "He looks incredibly well," she said upon leaving. "He was managing to smile and crack jokes. In fact, he was laughing so much he even got me laughing, and, believe me, I haven't been able to do much laughing during the last week."

As the days passed, and he realized that the jail wasn't quite as dangerous as he'd imagined it might be, McCartney began banging on the walls and communicating with other prisoners, who shouted back vaguely British references like "Maggie Thatcher!" and "Bell's whiskey!" He responded by making "the worst jokes in the world . . . but they helped to relieve the tension." He began a dialogue with the prisoner next door, who could speak a bit of English and who, similarly, was inside for smuggling dope. "I became quite matey with the chap," he says. "We sang and laughed together as if we had been mates for ages."

He was allowed two cigarettes a day, smoked outside during the daily exercise period. Given the option of a private bath, he decided to show solidarity by agreeing to wash in the communal bath with his fellow inmates. "I wasn't shy," he says. "You're not as proud in jail. It knocks it all out of you." As grinning guards looked on, he sang the prison work song "Take This Hammer" and the perky 1920s hit "When the Red, Red Robin (Comes Bob, Bob, Bobbin' Along)." "Their favorite, though, was 'Yesterday,'" he points out.

Naked among a group of convicts, here he found himself finally performing in Japan, if not in a way he might ever have imagined.

He initiated a game he called See Who Can Touch the Ceiling, knowing that, at five feet ten, "with my great Western height," it was no contest. One of the larger, more imposing prisoners, tattooed with the image of a samurai warrior all over his back and talking through another who could interpret, asked McCartney why he was in the prison. When he replied, "Marijuana," the heavy looked at him with a frown and indicated through the other that he was sure to get seven years. "He was just trying to frighten me," Paul reckons. "I said, 'No, no, no . . . ten.' And they were all over on the floor in a heap, laughing at that."

Elsewhere, the other three former Beatles reacted to Paul's imprisonment in different ways. George and his new wife, Olivia, sent a telegram saying, "Thinking of you all with love. Keep your spirits high. Nice to have you back home again soon." Cornered by reporters in the south of France, Ringo sounded simultaneously judgmental and sympathetic, telling them, "It's the risk you take when you're involved with drugs. He's just been unlucky."

John, meanwhile, told his photographer friend Bob Gruen that Paul couldn't have predicted, as an ex-Beatle, that he would have had his bag properly searched. Like everyone else, though, Lennon was wondering, "Why would he carry pot when he finally was allowed in?" His personal assistant Fred Seaman later claimed that John sent him to fetch every available newspaper so that he could pore over all the reports, and that he sat watching TV for hours, trying to catch every bulletin detailing McCartney's progress.

"You know, it serves Paul right," Lennon told Seaman. "Paul wanted to show the world that he's still a bit of bad boy." Without being aware of it, he agreed with McCartney's assessment that on some level he'd knowingly invited trouble. "I think subconsciously," said Lennon, "he wanted to get busted."

By January 24 the details in the Japanese press were being exaggerated, with one claiming that the marijuana McCartney had been caught with was worth £700,000, or just under £100,000 an ounce. In truth, customs representatives had estimated that the 219 grams they had confiscated from the singer had a street value of 600,000 yen, or just over £1,000. At the hotel, a journalist asked Linda how long she planned to stay in the country. She firmly replied, "I'm prepared to stay in Japan for as long as it takes."

It didn't take long. The next day, the charges were suddenly dropped—the result of the pressure put on the authorities by Eastman and Matsuo, added to the fact that Paul was contrite and obviously not a drug smuggler. Moreover, the whole messy affair was becoming an embarrassment to the Japanese, who clearly couldn't decide how to deal with the problem and wanted it swiftly resolved. Technically, they decided, because McCartney's visa had been taken away from him the minute he was arrested, he was now an illegal alien and should be deported. The statement from the Japanese police read: "Charges were not brought against Mr. McCartney because he had brought in the marijuana solely for his own use and already he has been punished enough." After ten days in a cell, Paul was released. "We were so lucky," said Matsuo.

At the airport, booked on the first available flight out of the country, which happened to be on Japan Airlines, leaving at 12:30 P.M. for Amsterdam, a sheepish if jocular Paul grabbed a guitar and serenaded the press with a brief snatch of "Yesterday," the song carrying a very different resonance in the circumstances. The day before, Paul's troubles had been all too evident. Now, his mood was one of acute relief.

On the plane, Paul was tearfully reunited with Linda and the kids. Booked on the same flight, however, was a pack of opportunistic journalists, and in the air the couple were continually hassled for quotes. "I'll never come back to Japan again," Linda promised. "It's my first trip and my last."

Paul was depressed about the fact that when his belongings were returned to him, his wedding ring was missing. "That made me very, very low," he admitted. In its place he now wore a curled paper clip, saying, "It's the sort of gesture that Linda and I will look back on rather romantically."

Clearly emotional, he told the *Daily Express,* "This is the longest I've ever been away from my family in ten years. I don't want a separation like it again." He confessed to another reporter, "I've been a fool. What I did was incredibly dumb. I was really scared, thinking I might be imprisoned for so long and now I have made my mind up *never* to touch the stuff again. From now on, all I'm going to smoke is straightforward fags and no more pot."

It was a long, exhausting flight, with a stop to refuel in Anchorage, Alaska. After finally touching down in the Netherlands, the McCartneys were flown by private jet to Lydd Airport, in Kent. From there they were driven home, disappearing up the driveway of their Sussex estate.

Even in jail, Paul had still been thinking about work. "In the clink I had time to think," he said. Further marking the distance he felt from Wings, he resolved to finish the tapes he'd recorded alone the previous summer and release them as the solo LP *McCartney II.*

At the same time, in an act of catharsis, he wrote a private memoir he called "Japanese Jailbird," penned in longhand over ten days and stretching to twenty thousand words. "I wrote it all down," he said. "I sort of thought, God, this is like writing an essay for school. I can't do it. I'm frightened of the piece of paper. But I knew I had to write it down to remember the incident. I forced myself to write it." Ultimately he decided against publishing it, reasoning that it would only drag this unfortunate episode in his life back into the public mind. Instead he bought a printer and produced one paperback-sized copy that he could fit into his pocket.

The next time Laurence Juber saw McCartney, he says, the singer was "a little chagrined . . . but also, kind of, 'Well, that was an interesting experience.'" The whole sorry matter had also proved costly. In the final tally, McCartney lost nearly half a million pounds: £200,000 to refund the promoter, who had threatened to sue, with an additional £100,000 in legal bills, plus the living costs of the stranded family, band, and crew, which totaled around £10,000 a day.

In the January 26 edition of *The Sun,* a headline quote from McCartney declared, "I'll Never Smoke Pot Again." From here on in, he would certainly change his tune in terms of his public advocacy of marijuana use.

He met the press at the gates of Blossom Wood Farm. "I'd prefer to forget this incident right now," he told them. Asked whether he was now planning to get back to "the English way of life" and spend time with his family, Paul tetchily responded, "Yeah, if you fellas would leave me alone, that *would* be possible."

The last thing Paul wanted to do, it seemed, was to return to rehearsing with the group. "It sucked the momentum out of Wings," says Juber. This was partly as a result of a sudden rift between McCartney and the long-serving Denny Laine, who in the wake of the debacle had returned to England and spent most of his time at Rock City Studios in Shepperton, recording his own solo album. Indicating his ambivalent feelings about the drama, Laine called it *Japanese Tears,* after the opening song, which found him comforting a Wings fan distraught about the canceled tour. Throughout, it transpired, the musicians had still been paid their weekly wage retainers, but had each lost in the region of £50,000 in tour profits. Laine admitted he was miffed: "I felt I was entitled to an explanation, but I never got one. He felt very sorry for himself when he came out of prison but he didn't seem to understand he'd upset a lot of people."

McCartney next resurfaced on January 30, when he filmed a prere-corded tribute for a forthcoming edition of the TV show *This Is Your Life,* dedicated to George Martin. Later, he talked to Paul Gambaccini for *Rolling Stone,* saying that his Japanese arrest had reminded him of when, as a kid, he would get on a train in Liverpool with a second-class ticket and sneak into a first-class compartment. "And I *always* got caught," he stressed.

It was clear that Paul's freewheeling years were over. "I suppose I was treated this way because I am Paul McCartney," he reflected, not acknowledging the fact that anyone who had tried to smuggle half a pound of dope through Japan Customs would have wound up in the same situation or, moreover, that his fame had saved him from a long prison sentence. "It's not bad for you to be humiliated at times," he reckoned. "It's sort of cleansing." Meanwhile, this newfound notoriety upped his cool, *Rolling Stone* naming him "the world's most famous pot smoker."

Looking back now, he refuses even to entertain thoughts of whether or not he could have endured a seven-year stretch in a Japanese prison.

"I'd prefer to not even let that question go round my brain," he says with a sigh. "I've put it away and it's over with now."

14

THE WAKE-UP CALL

What effect did John dying have on you personally?

It was just a huge loss. As it was to all his mates and, in actual fact, to the rest of the world. It was a combination of the fact that he wasn't coming back, the circumstances in which he'd died, the whole futility of it all. I don't know if you ever get over those things.

LINDA WAS COMING UP THE DRIVEWAY of the Sussex farm, returning from the school run, when Paul emerged from the house. As soon as she saw his face, she knew something was wrong. He was sobbing; he looked desperate. She'd never seen him in this state before.

It was the morning of Tuesday, December 9, 1980. "He told me what had happened," she remembered, "and then we were both crying."

For all their carping and sniping, bitterness and petty disgruntlement, Paul and John had been getting on better. Their relationship had progressed via a series of infrequent telephone calls that had become warmer than their scattered bursts of sharp words in the media might have suggested. During the small talk and trivia of one conversation, early in 1980, McCartney casually asked Lennon whether he was writing songs. "Just out of my curiosity," Paul explained. "He told me he was finished doing that."

In May, *McCartney II* was released, intended as a double but, perhaps sensibly, edited down to a single album. Exploring new possibilities in video technology, Paul shot a promo for "Coming Up" in which he played all the parts of a group named, with a nod to new wave, the Plastic Macs. Lennon would later point out that it was an ideal fantasy scenario for McCartney, since he'd essentially always wanted to be a one-man band.

For the clip, Paul dived into the dressing-up box to play out various rock archetypes: the hairy Neanderthal drummer, the spaced-out hippie guitarist, the four members of a greaser horn section. On keyboards, he mimicked the discomfitingly expressionless Ron Mael of Sparks; on second guitar, the grinning Hank Marvin of the Shadows, in thick horn-rims. On bass, most surprisingly, in a collarless jacket and mop top, pumping away at his old violin-shaped Höfner, he reinhabited the character of Beatle Paul, with all the "woo"s and cutesy hair tosses.

It was a stranger experience than he might have anticipated. "I almost chickened out," he admitted. "But once I put on the old uniform, I thought, Ah well, it's a laugh, what the hell." Taped to the body of the bass he found an old Beatles set list from their final 1966 tour that he'd forgotten was there, instantly zapping him back fourteen years. As he walked onto the set dressed as Beatle Paul, the mood among the studio technicians instantly turned buzzy; some suddenly asked him for his autograph. He found it "a very kind of weird, exciting feeling, really. I felt like I was at a TV show twenty years ago. It felt exactly the same."

Only in the days after did he realize that, for him, it had been an exorcism of sorts. "I'd actually gone and broken the whole voodoo of the Beatles," he said, "'cause I'd been him again and it didn't feel bad."

Lennon was being driven by Fred Seaman through Cold Spring Harbor, Long Island, when he first heard "Coming Up" on the radio. "Fuck a pig, it's Paul," he exclaimed, before turning up the volume and nodding along. "Not bad," he decided at the song's conclusion. He asked Seaman to buy him a copy of *McCartney II* and set up a new stereo system in his bedroom specifically so he could listen to it. The next day, "Coming Up" was still rattling around John's head. "It's driving me crackers," he told Seaman, before venturing the opinion that even if its parent album was patchy, at least Paul was back trying to do something eclectic and experimental.

While Lennon had apparently retired and disappeared, McCartney maintained his public profile and began to pile up the awards: he was named Outstanding Music Personality at the British Rock and Pop Awards, won Best Instrumental for "Rockestra Theme" at the Grammys, and was presented with an Ivor Novello award by Yul Brynner, the star of *The Magnificent Seven* and *The King and I*. Even Linda was picking up some belated recognition, with Argentinian director Oscar Grillo's animation for her single "Seaside Woman," released three years earlier, bagging the Palme d'Or for Best Short Film at Cannes. The McCartneys slipped into the cinema unannounced and watched the screening, quietly touched by the unexpected applause it prompted.

In France, McCartney held a press launch of sorts for *McCartney II*, handing out free LPs to journalists. He was asked by one if there was ever the chance of new Lennon/McCartney material. "Well, I wouldn't say there would be, actually," he replied, explaining that John had told him he had no interest in making music. "Most of us do our jobs to arrive at a point where we no longer have to do our jobs," he reasoned, "and we can put our feet up and enjoy life for a change. I think John's probably reached that point."

Secretly, in fact, John was writing again, his dormant competitive rivalry with Paul awakened after hearing *McCartney II*. In Bermuda, over the summer, the songs began to pour out of him. First came the eerily prophetic reggae of "Borrowed Time," to be followed by the tetchy fame-rejecting "I Don't Wanna Face It" and the serene, absence-explaining "Watching the Wheels." If the passing of time had softened his edges, there was real self-awareness and maturity surfacing in his music, beyond the sloganeering and abstract aphorisms of the past. It was his last creative surge.

Meanwhile, Paul was still on the campaign trail. In June he shot the strange fantasy video for "Waterfalls," in which he appeared oddly straight, his hair trimmed like a banker's, sporting beige cords and a Fair Isle waistcoat, backdropped by multicolored fountains of water and at one point sharing the set with an eight-foot polar bear named Olaf. Revealingly, because of the Cannes success of "Seaside Woman," Linda was on the promotional treadmill, too. She informed *Woman's*

Own that she and Paul had yet to make wills. Elsewhere, she told the *Daily Mirror* that the couple saved money by cutting one another's hair.

In the meantime, Paul talked to Southern Television's weekday local news program *Day by Day*. The interviewer, taking an unsettlingly prescient line of questioning in the light of what was to come, asked the singer about the problems of being an aging rock star. No one could escape growing older, said McCartney.

"Except people like Buddy Holly and Elvis Presley," the presenter pointed out, before hastily adding, "Hopefully, nothing like that will happen to you."

"Sorry, what do you mean by that?" Paul interjected sharply.

"I mean they were stopped in their prime by death, right?" the presenter blundered on. "For that reason they will always be remembered. In a sense, they're immortalized."

"Oh yeah, I know," Paul replied. Then he turned gently facetious: "I mean, I'd rather stick around and get old than, like, be terrific and famous and die young. *Myself,* y'know. Some people like going out in a blaze of glory. I'm not one of them."

From there, the interviewer segued into the obligatory Beatles reunion question. There was currently no chance of it, according to Paul. "No, no, no," he said. "I don't think John would ever be interested in getting the group back together again."

For his part, around the same time, in the press John dismissed the notion of a Beatles reunion as "an illusion." As ever, Lennon's feelings toward McCartney were highly erratic. He confessed that he'd liked "Coming Up" but said he thought Paul "sounded like he was depressed" on "Waterfalls." "I don't follow Wings," he curtly told *Newsweek*. "I don't give a shit what Wings are doing." The journalist then apparently quoted Paul as saying that, in his opinion, Lennon had gone to ground because he had done everything else in his life "apart from be himself." At this, Lennon exploded. "What the hell does that mean?" he roared, accusing Paul of knowing nothing about his life during his househusband years. "He was as curious as everybody else was. It's ten years since I really communicated with him. I know as much about him as he knows about me, which is *zilch*."

That wasn't entirely true, since the pair would still sometimes talk. On October 9, John's fortieth birthday, Lennon and McCartney spoke for the last time on the phone. John had just completed most of his return album, *Double Fantasy*. Paul called in the evening, and the pair—Lennon perhaps regretting his most recent caustic comments—discussed how they were always being baited to put each other down in the press.

"Do they play me against you like they play you against me?" John wondered.

"Yeah, they do," said Paul.

In June, six months after their last rehearsals, Wings got back together for two weeks in the abandoned concert hall at Finston Manor, Tenterton, Kent. This lackluster affair found them jamming a heap of songs for possible inclusion on an album called *Hot Hits, Cold Cuts,* to be part old singles, part new tunes. It would never be released. Instead, most of the new McCartney material was tested out in a rudimentary fashion before being squirreled away by Paul for use on his future solo albums. Denny Laine, bored, announced that he was going out on tour on his own.

Meanwhile, Paul decided to return to cartoonland, entering AIR Studios in central London and reuniting with George Martin, for the first time since "Live and Let Die," to begin work on the soundtrack for a planned animation centered on the plaid-trousered *Daily Express* comic-strip character Rupert Bear. Songs worked on included the *Ram* outtake "Sunshine Sometime" and others with the kid-friendly, slightly stoned-sounding titles "Tippi Tippi Toes" and "Flying Horses." Paul even revived "The Castle of the King of the Birds," an ornate piano piece he'd first tinkered around with in January 1969, during the Beatles' *Let It Be* sessions in Twickenham.

In the gaps, McCartney halfheartedly started work on a Wings album at home in Hog Hill Mill Studios. The sessions were due to relocate in the new year to George Martin's newly completed AIR studio on the Caribbean island of Montserrat. With the old Beatles producer back on the team, rumors perhaps inevitably began to percolate that John was due to join Paul there in the early months of 1981.

Not one ever to stray too far from a TV camera during this period, Paul, sitting next to Linda, made a high-profile appearance on the coast-to-coast U.S. breakfast show *Good Morning America,* relayed live from their Sussex home. During the interview, as the power failed and the lights continually cut in and out, the McCartneys said much to host David Hartman but revealed little beyond trivialities.

Did they celebrate Thanksgiving? Yes, they did, because Linda was American, but as vegetarians, they had a "macaroni turkey." Who had "Yesterday" been written about? "Your wife," quipped Paul, ribbing the host. Had Linda idolized Paul before she met him? No, she'd actually preferred John. "No accounting for taste," McCartney tutted. "These women. I mean, what can you do, Dave?" How, in the face of his status as a top-flight rock star, did the family manage to maintain a reasonably normal lifestyle? "We've got a ridiculously small house with four kids in two bedrooms, would you believe?" Paul volunteered, referring to the circular Waterfall house, where the six were still living as they waited for McCartney's plans for the new building to be approved. "So by doing things like that, just not living with a big style, it seems to naturally keep pretty close and intimate."

It was November 27, only eleven days before the looming tragedy. The interviewer turned to the subject of Lennon's apparently lingering resentment of McCartney. Recognizing the fact that John might be up and watching at home in New York, Paul's response was cautious, and at the same time untypically frank.

"After all of that stuff that has gone down over the years," he said, "I actually kinda keep a bit quiet now. 'Cause, I mean, anything I say, he gets resentful of. So I dunno, really, it's just a weird one. I don't quite know why he thinks like that. I mean, what do you do about that?"

On December 8, his final day, Lennon, doing an interview for RKO Radio, performed a public volte-face as regards McCartney, recognizing him, along with Ono, as being the major creative collaborator of his life. "There's only been two artists I've ever worked with for more than a one-night stand, as it were," he said. "That's Paul McCartney and Yoko. I think that's a pretty damn good choice. As a talent scout, I've done pretty damn well."

Later there would be some comfort found in the fact that his final words on Paul were ones of positivity, approaching some kind of love.

The call came in just before nine on the morning of December 9. Steve Shrimpton from MPL phoned Paul in Sussex to break the horrific news that John had been murdered in New York, just under five hours earlier; he'd been shot by a deranged fan on the street outside the Dakota, before taking his last, stumbling steps into the building's lobby. The details, at this point, remained sketchy.

The news had first flashed up on Reuters at 4:55 A.M. U.K. time. Five minutes later, grave announcements were made during the 5:00 A.M. radio bulletins.

Neither of the McCartneys could ever quite remember the words Paul used when breaking the news to Linda. "I just sort of see the image," Linda said later. "It's like a picture . . . a snapshot. Soul's camera."

McCartney, distraught, phoned his brother, Mike. "Paul was too distressed to talk properly," Mike recalled. "He just said, 'Keep sending the good vibes down from Liverpool,' to help him through the day."

Paul didn't know what to do with himself. Dazed, and due to be recording in AIR Studios with George Martin that day, he made the decision to go ahead with the session. At eleven-thirty A.M. he was driven out of the gates of Blossom Wood Farm, telling the waiting reporters, "I just can't take it in at the moment." Later he would try to explain why he'd thought it was appropriate to travel to the studio: "I was in shock. We all went to work that day . . . to not be sitting at home, is the truth."

Upon arrival at AIR, McCartney and George Martin, as the latter remembered, "fell on each other's shoulders, and we poured ourselves tea and whisky and sat around and drank and talked and talked." Clearly, for Paul, there was some security to be found in being with his and Lennon's onetime father figure. "We grieved for John all day," said Martin, "and it helped."

Denny Laine was there, and naturally had wondered whether McCartney would show up at all. A physically shaken Paul told him, "I just don't know what to think." Always utterly thrown by death, McCartney was in a state of emotional paralysis. "Even at the best of times," said Denny, "he wasn't really too articulate when it came to expressing how he felt about things." As ever, McCartney turned to his music.

Everyone attempted to do some work on a track, the appropriately titled "Rainclouds," the lyrics of which found the singer pleading for the dark formations above his head to be blown away. Of course, little progress was made with the recording. Paddy Moloney, of traditional Irish folk group the Chieftains, had flown in from Dublin that day to add uilleann pipes to the song. Paul said to him that Lennon's death was "tragic and useless and didn't make sense," while looking utterly stunned.

"There was a kind of unspoken sadness," Moloney said. "It was subtle, and there wasn't any crying or moping about. I don't think it had really sunk in yet. I don't think at the end of the session that it had really penetrated either . . . that John was dead, gone forever."

At the end of one attempt at a take, McCartney and Laine were standing beside an enormous floor-to-ceiling window overlooking Oxford Circus when a green lorry painted with the words LENNON'S FURNISHINGS passed by below.

"Oh God, look at that," said Denny, before noticing that McCartney's eyes were filling with tears.

"I'll tell you one thing, man," Paul confided in him. "I'll never fall out with *anyone* again in my life for that amount of time and face the possibility of them dying before I get a chance to square it with them."

Later in the afternoon, he called Yoko in New York. McCartney remembers that Ono "was crying and cut up and had no idea why anyone should want to do this." She told him how warmly John had often talked about him in private. "It was almost as if she sensed that I was wondering whether the relationship had snapped," he says. Later, he would look back on his last conversation with Lennon and realize "we were still the best of mates."

Leaving the studio at the end of the day, McCartney offered short responses to the questions of the journalists who had been standing all day on the pavement in Oxford Street. He said that he'd been in the studio "just listening to stuff. . . . I just didn't want to sit at home." One, inanely, asked why. "I just didn't feel like it," Paul responded, obviously irritated. As he made to leave, his final comment to the reporters was: "It's a drag, isn't it?"

"I probably should've said, 'It's the world's most unholiest . . . worst-ever drag . . . in the universe,'" he says now. "Y'know, that might have explained what I was thinking a bit better. But I just sort of said, 'It's a drag.' And that came out very flippant. It wasn't flippant. And anyone who saw me on that day knows it wasn't."

The words would haunt McCartney for years. More than flippant, in the light of the deep shock and open grief that was spreading around the world, his lasting comment in reaction to the death of Lennon was seen as offhand, uncaring, and even callous. When this brief but provocative statement began to filter out, Paul was instantly damned by the media. "I felt every inch for him," said George Martin. "He was unwise, but he was off his guard."

Paul tried to put out the media fire by issuing his own statement: "I have hidden myself in my work today. But it keeps flashing into my mind. I feel shattered, angry and very sad." He acknowledged that John had often been rude about him in the press but said, "I secretly admired him for it. There was no question that we weren't friends. I really loved the guy." He concluded by saying that his late friend would be remembered in future years as an international statesman, whose "Give Peace a Chance" had helped hasten the end of the Vietnam War. "He often looked a loony to many people. He made enemies, but he was fantastic. He was a warm man who cared a lot."

Later that night, back at home in Sussex, the McCartneys and the kids sat and, like the rest of the world, watched the news reports on TV. As music-industry pundits began to turn up on the screen, offering their in-depth analyses, Paul felt his anger rising. "I thought it was well tasteless," he said. "Jesus Christ, ready with the answers, aren't we? Aren't we just ready with a summary?" Ultimately, of course, he was enraged by the fact that these journalists were being relatively eloquent in their tributes to Lennon, when he had been awkward and inarticulate. "They were the ones who came off good because they said suitably meaningful things," he sadly points out. "I was the idiot who said, 'It's a drag.'"

He raged against the now identified killer, if impotently and still somehow inexpressibly: "I remember screaming that Mark Chapman was the jerk of all jerks. I felt so robbed and emotional. It was crazy. It was anger. It was fear. It was madness. It was the world coming to an end."

Finally, behind closed doors, he allowed himself to break down. "I wept like a baby," he says. "It was a heavy personal blow."

15

END OF THE ROAD

These days you pay tribute to both John and George in your live shows. What goes through your mind when you play those songs? Are you aware of the heightened emotion in the crowd?

You're not as aware of it as the people in the audience are. But you're aware of a feeling. The nice thing is, it's a common feeling, 'cause it's you and them feeling it. Obviously when I do "Here Today" or "Something," I'm thinking of John or George. There's an inherent emotion in those songs. The music just touches a raw nerve.

THE DAY AFTER THE WORLD LEARNED of the death of John Lennon, there was a pheasant shoot in the forest near Blossom Wood Farm. Linda was forced to go outside, locate the hunters, and quietly tell them that, in the circumstances, the sound of gunfire was the last thing the McCartneys wanted to hear.

Paul was in a fogged state of disbelief. The next time he left the farm, it was for the MPL Christmas lunch in London, where, understandably, it was hard to rouse the festive spirit. "There was a lot of sadness there," says Laurence Juber. "It was overshadowed by not only the fact that Paul had lost his musical soul mate, but also there was a certain kind of threat to the fact that, if somebody could assassinate John, they could also do the same to Paul."

The fear of being next was never far away. "Paul," said Linda, "was in so much pain," and he found it hard to shake the dread that he or a member of the family might be targeted. This was an anxiety he shared, naturally, with the other two surviving Beatles. "That was a question that was whipping around the three of us," McCartney admitted. "Like, Are you next?"

Inevitably, perhaps, bizarre threats came in from unhinged individuals. One report said that a stalker carrying a knife had been caught attempting to break into the McCartneys' estate. From here on in, Paul and the family were always accompanied by security guards. Laurence Juber dropped by AIR Studios in January 1981 to find the singer's every move being shadowed by a protection detail. "Somebody had been making death threats in New York," he remembers. "It was scary."

Linda explained to her friend Danny Fields that the family was forced to maintain a low profile, more for the sake of the children than anything else. "There were some nuts," she told him, "but we had to take them seriously. We have so much more security around us now. Our lives have really changed."

As time wore on, however, Paul realized something. Having never allowed his fame to hamper or hinder him in the past, having taken a determinedly ordinary approach to his everyday activities, he decided that living behind a wall of security was not for him.

"There are crazy people everywhere," he reasoned. "I was really worried for a few weeks afterwards. But I couldn't really live like that. My attitude is to try and push it out of my mind."

As planned, on February 1, 1981, the McCartneys flew to Montserrat to continue work on the next album, with Denny Laine, but notably without Laurence Juber and Steve Holley, indicating that Wings was once again reduced to their core trio, at least for studio purposes. Back at the helm was George Martin, the thinking being that the producer's old-fashioned record-making values would ensure tighter quality control over the material. There had been moments of inspiration on *Back to the Egg*, while *McCartney II* had worked as a creatively liberating experience. But still, Paul rightly acknowledged that there had been something lacking in his most recent albums.

While the previous trips to far-flung destinations had allowed him a window of escape, in the light of Lennon's murder there was to be no such relief on Montserrat. The paparazzi constantly shadowed him on the island, tailing him in cars and on scooters. It was the first time he'd experienced this kind of behavior—to be expected perhaps in London,

Paris, or New York—in what was essentially a holiday setting, and it riled him. He tried to ram them with his hired jeep, calling them "monsters."

Over the coming weeks, a parade of invited musicians arrived at the Caribbean studio. A fortnight in, Ringo showed up with his new girlfriend and soon-to-be wife, actress Barbara Bach, adding his rolling drum parts to McCartney's future single, the sunny "Take It Away." Following him five days later was the rockabilly musician Carl Perkins, a hero to the nascent Beatles, who traded lines with Paul in the skiffle swing of "Get It." The American, like others before him, was impressed by the McCartneys' apparent normality and familial closeness. "We tried the jet set, Carl, and it's plastic," Paul told him. The next to fly in was Stevie Wonder, to make a cameo appearance on the synthy funk of "What's That You're Doing" and duet with McCartney on the race-blurring "Ebony and Ivory." As time passed, it was clear that the record was becoming less a Wings album and more of a solo outing, exploring the burgeoning 1980s trend for major-name collaborations.

Not surprisingly, Denny Laine felt increasingly sidelined and undervalued. His dwindling creative influence aside, he was annoyed that once again Jo Jo hadn't been allowed to come on the excursion. At the same time, he was stewing over his perceived lack of financial reward for his contribution to McCartney's output over the previous ten years. He flew home, peeved and disillusioned.

When the sessions returned to AIR in London, one day early in March, Laine simply didn't turn up. Trevor Jones and then John Hammel both placed calls to his house, with the guitarist refusing to come to the phone. Then Paul rang and spoke to Jo Jo. She told him, with no little satisfaction, that Denny had "asked me to give you and everyone else the message" that he wasn't coming back. After a decade of loyal service, Laine was quitting.

"It was obvious we wouldn't tour again," Denny said at the time, by way of explanation. "But touring is the purpose of being in the business as far as I'm concerned." Laine knew, of course, that essentially McCartney was making another solo album and Wings probably wouldn't survive. In truth, he jumped before he was pushed.

"It would've been Wings, plus all these other names," he said of the record that was to become *Tug of War.* "But it became his album because I left and there was no Wings anymore."

In private, though, George Martin had been encouraging McCartney to drop the façade of the band and release the album under his own name. "The idea of working with Wings again . . . in truth, it would have just been limiting, I thought," said Paul. "And George agreed. I slightly blamed it on him a bit. Only a bit, though."

In the last week of April, the Associated Press got wind of the split and issued the following story:

> Ex-Beatle Paul McCartney, who formed the group Wings after the Beatles split up in 1970, is now facing problems with his band. Denny Laine, the band's drummer [sic] since it was formed in 1971, quit suddenly on Tuesday in a disagreement over McCartney's decision to halt the group's public appearances temporarily. The departure left only two members of the group, McCartney and his wife, Linda. "There is no row," said Laine's manager Brian Adams. "But Denny likes to tour and Paul has decided that Wings will not make any tour plans for the future."
>
> A London newspaper reported Laine, 36, decided to quit the group during a recent recording session in the West Indies, where the next Wings album was made. McCartney halted public appearances because he had received several death threats since the murder in New York of fellow ex-Beatle John Lennon on Dec 8. A McCartney spokesman denied the report, adding that Wings would still exist.

This official denial was merely a delaying tactic, of course. Steve Holley, having read of the breakup in the *Evening Standard,* phoned McCartney to ask him if it was true that the band was over.

"Uh, yeah, I've been meaning to call you," Paul said.

"It was just horrible the way it went out," says Holley. "Even though every fiber of my body was telling me that it was going to happen, it was awful."

For Juber, there was a sense of missed opportunity. The guitarist feels that if the bust in Japan had never happened, the group would have gone on to tour America successfully in the summer of 1980, establishing *Back to the Egg* as a major, as opposed to minor, album. "Then," he reasons, "Wings would have gone out with a bang, rather than a whimper."

Denny, rehearsing with his new band at Rock City Studios in Shepperton, talked to the press to confirm that the schism had been created by McCartney's refusal to tour. One prying reporter, exploiting the apparent fallout, asked Laine if, as the gossip suggested, Paul was a difficult man to work with. "Well, I've had my moments," the guitarist offered, as if leaving much unsaid.

The key problem, as Laine saw it, was that McCartney was too famous to tour on a relatively normal level, without the accompanying hoopla his presence attracted. "Because of who he is," he says today, "that was one of the drawbacks, really. I was ready to go out and do my own thing."

In truth, it was only half the story. During this period, Laine was suffering from various problems in his personal life. At a Mayfair nightclub he was involved in a tussle with Jock McDonald, singer with punk band the Bollock Brothers; the matter was resolved without charges being brought. Following that, he crashed his Ferrari into a fence. "I don't seem to be having much luck lately," he noted at the time. Then, far more seriously, Jo Jo Laine suffered a drug overdose at the couple's home in Laleham, Surrey, after her father—shot and paralyzed two years before by her schizophrenic brother—died in America. She was rushed to hospital, where she made a full recovery.

The couple's marriage had already been in trouble, exacerbated by Jo Jo being left behind in England while her husband was in the Caribbean. At the time, Laine blamed the McCartneys: "Paul and Linda's refusal to allow Jo Jo on Montserrat went a long way to destroying my marriage." Upon Denny's return from the *Tug of War* sessions, Jo Jo confessed that she had been unfaithful to him with John Townley, a singer signed to EMI. "I'd always denied any affairs I'd had," she said, "but this one I was open about."

The feud between McCartney and Laine was to go public, the former pointing out that the latter had quit the group, saying that he missed playing live, and yet hadn't been on the road since leaving. "But that was my problem," says Denny. "It was hard for me to go out and play live after Wings, like it was hard for him to play live after the Beatles. It's very difficult when you've been in a big band. I couldn't go out doing Moody Blues material. You want to move forward."

Only much later, in the face of ongoing accusations of his financial tightness, did McCartney address Laine's money grumbles about his time in Wings, saying that there were receipts in the MPL office for over

£1 million paid to the guitarist over the years. "Now, you tell me a guy in any group who got that for the period we were together," Paul argued. "If you think I sound mean after that, I've got to disagree with you. I mean, these people like Denny Laine, 'He didn't pay us enough.' Well, what I think is, Yeah, well, I did. I know exactly what I paid him. It's a million."

From the perspective of one unnamed former Wings employee, Denny was paid more than the other group members to act as Paul's second-in-command, keeping the band on an even keel, particularly when sailing through stormier waters: "He was the go-between. But he didn't really share the McCartney family circle. Denny was his own man, and unfortunately Jo Jo didn't see eye to eye with Linda."

Later, living in Spain, Denny fell in with a couple of journalists who offered to write a biography of him. He says the pair absconded to London and filleted their interview transcripts for the juiciest details before selling them to *The Sun*, without his knowledge or approval. The revelations were of the lurid and druggy variety—Paul and Linda spent over £1,000 a week on weed, smoking joints "the way ordinary people smoke cigarettes"; they smuggled dope through an airport in the hood of toddler James's coat; Paul's head was so clouded by the stuff that, because of chronic indecision, his albums took forever to make.

Worse, perhaps, Laine claimed that in all of his time with McCartney, he got no closer to knowing the real and "complex" Paul. "Even though I've written countless songs with him and we've been stoned together hundreds of times," he was quoted as saying, "I still don't feel I am very close to him. He is the best person I've met in all my life at hiding his feelings."

In the wake of the apparent exposé, the McCartneys largely kept quiet, although Linda was to venture the opinion that "so much of it is rubbish. I thought Denny came off badly. I could see some girlfriend or an ex-chauffeur writing such rubbish, but a musician?"

Looking back today, Denny insists, "We never fell out. Nothing like that. But it certainly looked like we did."

In the final reckoning, Wings had proved to be a long and difficult endeavor. "To me," Paul said, "there was always a feeling of letdown, because the Beatles had been so big that anything I did had to compare directly with them." Linda, controversially, given her own musical struggles, declared that none of the members of the group, across all of the lineups, had ever been accomplished enough to work with an increasingly frustrated McCartney, who was forced to carry their weight. "They were good," she said, "but not great."

The death of Lennon, meanwhile, had caused the remaining ex-Beatles to turn reflective about their relationships with one another. In a reunion of sorts, McCartney and Starr were to come together to play on Harrison's playful Lennon reminiscence "All Those Years Ago," the first time all three had appeared together on a record in more than ten years. Parts of *Tug of War* revealed more of Paul's own feelings about John. The title track concerned itself with the push and pull of competitive relationships, while the highly emotional, "Yesterday"-echoing "Here Today" was clearly directed at his lost friend.

One verse recalled an event in September 1964, during the Beatles' first U.S. tour, when their flight to Jacksonville, Florida, was diverted to Key West in order to avoid the destructive path of Hurricane Dora. Grounded, and with a rare evening off, Paul and John sat up all night and got drunk and bared their souls to each other, ending up in tears. McCartney said that while writing the ballad he imagined a cloud parting in the sky above his head and Lennon blowing a raspberry at him. "This is what the song is, y'know," he said. "I'm sort of saying, 'Even though you blow that raspberry, I really did know you.'

"Songwriting is like psychiatry," he went on, possibly disclosing more about his creative urge than he had ever done before. "You sit down and dredge up something that's deep inside and bring it out front. And I just had to really say, 'I love you, John.' I think being able to say things like that in songs can keep you sane."

After the shock of Lennon's passing, and the sobering lesson of Japan, the McCartneys' hunger for traveling the world as a merry band was gone. Ten years in, particularly for Paul, the desire for constant forward motion had finally subsided. "We just thought," he said, "we've done it now." In reality, of course, post-Tokyo, there was every likelihood that securing visas for many territories would be a long, involved, and painful process, and possibly one it was best to avoid.

Mission accomplished, more or less, the couple returned to their now semipermanent base in Sussex. There Paul could record, free from pressure or worry, at his studio, while Linda wandered around on the farm, tending the horses, taking pictures. If the McCartneys were hankering for a quieter, more self-sufficient life, here was their chance. After all, he was still only thirty-eight, his wife thirty-nine.

"Really, I try to lead a pretty normal life," he said, repeating a familiar refrain, before revealing a certain truth. "The only abnormality is being Paul McCartney."

In just over ten years, he had come full circle. Here he was, doing it all over again: splitting with his band, making a record by himself, disappearing with his family.

In the summer of 1981, the ramshackle cottage on the hill at Blossom Wood Farm was torn down to make way for the building of the new house, plotted, as everything was, to McCartney's design.

It would be another eight years before he would tour again. For Paul, for now, it was the end of the road.

EPILOGUE

Almost thirty years later, in his office at MPL in London, Paul was talking about Linda. Following her death from breast cancer, aged fifty-six, on April 17, 1998, at the ranch in Arizona, McCartney was obviously devastated. He lay low for close to a year, but when he emerged, he was creatively reenergized and seemingly ever more determined to make some of his best music since the 1970s.

In 2007, with *Memory Almost Full*, it appeared as though he had paid coded tribute to Linda, a perhaps overstudious fan having worked out that the album's name could be reshuffled into an anagram that read, "For my soul mate LLM," the initials standing for Linda Louise McCartney. In truth, the title came from a message that flashed up on McCartney's phone, which he felt held a certain poetic quality, particularly in his advancing years.

"It's such a clever anagram," he said. "At first, I thought, Maybe I won't tell anyone I didn't know it was there, just let 'em guess, y'know. It was very weird. I found out about it on the anniversary of Linda's passing when my eldest daughter told me about it. She said, 'Thanks for that dedication, Dad, that's great.' I said, 'What d'you mean, babe?' She said, 'The anagram.' I thought, What's she talking about? She told me, and I said, 'God, that's pretty spooky.' She said, 'I'll tell you what's spooky, is you didn't know about it. It would be pretty spooky anyway that you could get that anagram out of it. But the fact that you didn't even know about it . . .'"

He paused in mid-sentence as suddenly, outside, there was a loud bang that sounded like a gunshot.

When a second explosive crack quickly followed, McCartney was up on his feet and over to the window. "Murder in Soho!" he exclaimed. "Shock horror!"

"It's probably just a car backfiring," I said as I joined him to look down over Soho Square, seeing nothing.

"Probably is," he said, distracted, if not visibly nervous.

"I'll protect you, Paul," I joked, pretending to fling myself in front of him. "I'll take the bullet."

He laughed and turned to his publicist Stuart Bell, sitting in a corner of the room. "Oh all right." McCartney grinned. "Okay, then. You heard that, Stu."

"Actually, I won't," I added. "I'm just being nice."

" 'Yeah, you can take it, Paul,' " he said, putting imaginary words in my mouth. " 'Go on then . . .' "

We sat back down, and McCartney picked up his conversational thread.

When he talked about Linda, he was in turns protective of her memory and wistful about what might have appeared to be minor recollections.

In the early 1990s, a bootlegged tape had done the rounds, featuring her vocal cruelly isolated from the mixing desk at a live show as she sang along to "Hey Jude" and failed to hit the notes. "It was dreadful," he admitted. "She'd sort of go, 'Oh, Jesus Christ' when she heard it. And it was mean, whoever did it. You couldn't get it back. It was one of these things, where she'd be"—he began clapping above his head—"the crowd leader in the band. But, y'know, you just had to take all that stuff."

At the same time he remembered their frequent drives in their Mercedes up to AIR Studios from Sussex, where they would phone ahead to a Chinese restaurant en route and order veggie spring rolls to collect. "Great memories of that," he said, nodding. As trivial as this perhaps seemed, it held a certain poignancy: for all his wealth and fame and power, Paul, of course, couldn't bring Linda back and relive the simpler pleasures the couple had enjoyed.

The mock-gunfire incident had maybe served to illustrate a point that I was now a bit nervous about bringing up. When he didn't tour for most of the 1980s, some people assumed it was because he was scared to appear in public after Lennon's murder. Was there any truth in that?

"No, y'know," he said, dismissively. "We've said already, people speculate about anything. They always credit me with motives that I haven't even dreamed of. It's kind of interesting really, the way they sort of *perceive* my life and analyze it for me. I just find it very strange. 'Cause they're hardly ever right. In that case, I never thought about touring much. People used to say to me, 'Oh, it's ten years since you've toured.' I'd go, '*Is it?*' What was I doing? I dunno. Bringing up kids, writing some songs, going on holiday. I just know that I haven't done it for a little while. That's all that was, really. I don't know why. Maybe I didn't fancy it."

"But, understandably," I added, "after the circumstances of John's death—"

"That's the least likely explanation," he said, cutting in before I could finish the sentence. "I didn't give up touring 'cause I was scared to. It wasn't that. It was just 'cause I didn't fancy it. I can't remember, to tell you the truth. I didn't have a band, probably. I think that was the reason, if you think about it. I mean, it's pretty straightforward, really. Why didn't he tour? 'Cause he hasn't got a band."

"You can always find a band, though, can't you, Paul?" I pointed out.

"You can," he replied, a touch abruptly. "If you can be bothered. But I don't suppose I could be bothered."

He accepted that, over time, he had been forced to recognize that he could never find a replacement for Lennon as a songwriting partner, having tried to form subsequent creative partnerships with both Eric Stewart of 10cc and Elvis Costello.

"I think the inevitable thing that I realized," he said, "and that I sort of knew all along, was that John was an impossible act to follow. He and I were just so sort of natural and read each other and did such good work . . . he said modestly."

"I think you can cut yourself some slack there," I offered.

"But to pick up that ball and run with it is very difficult for anyone," he continued. "So I did a little bit of collaboration, but obviously none of it could match up to working with John, which was just the magic mix. We just fell into it. We were kids, we learned how to do it together. We read each other, y'know. I knew where he was going, he knew where I was going. We corrected each other and directed each other. So that was the thing. What John brought to the collaboration was unique. And I think what I brought to the collaboration was unique. We just happened to hit it."

———

It was clear McCartney had no regrets about some of the weirder choices and stranger records he made in the 1970s. Ultimately, he just shrugged them off.

"I think the more sophisticated people or the more hardcore rock'n'roll fans were going, '*What* is he *on*? I'll have some of those drugs,'" he laughed. "I mean, people still do think of it like that. 'What was it, man? There must have been some special . . . substance he had to make him do that.' But really, y'know, I don't embarrass myself by stepping out of the box. I almost don't notice myself doing it."

We returned to the idea that he really has no grasp of how people perceive him, which in many ways, is a blessing. "I get some feedback," he said. "And some people'll talk about my composing history and might be very flattering. Then some people will just sort of say, 'I think a lot of what he's done's rubbish.' So . . . I don't know. I hear these opinions and I just carry on regardless. I'm not gonna let any of that stuff affect me, 'cause I just do what I think is right at a given time. And it may or may not be right. But I don't care if it's wrong. 'Cause it's what I have to do. It's what I *fancy* doing."

He has always been, he stressed, a man without a career plan. "I don't think of myself as someone with a *career*," he said, as if the word brought a nasty taste to his mouth. "I just think of myself as someone who likes to have a go at various things. I'm certainly not one of these people who's really clever and goes, 'Well, I can't do that because that will ruin my image.' I don't even know what my image is. I'm making it up as I go along."

If McCartney spent the 1970s trying to outrun the ghost of his Beatles past, it proved to be an impossible task. Over the years he was slowly to come to terms with his legacy, introducing more and more Beatles songs into his live repertoire, while gently kicking against the virtual canonization of John Lennon.

Sometimes the latter seemed petty and pointless, such as when, on his 2002 live album *Back in the U.S.*, he controversially reversed the Lennon/McCartney credits on many Beatles songs to reflect the fact that he had made a greater contribution to the composition, consequently provoking the ire of Yoko Ono. Nevertheless, in settling scores and tidying up the truth, he was, in effect, keeping his and John's rivalry alive, much as Lennon would surely have done had he lived.

I asked him if he believed, post-Beatles, that he'd had the respect he deserved.

"I dunno, man," he said. "I think on and off, yeah. Sometimes I think, Yes I have, sometimes, I haven't. But I don't necessarily think I deserve anything. I'm not one of those people, 'How dare you? Do you know who I am?' It's like, Hey man, if you don't dig it, fine by me. You don't have to like me. But if you do, I'd probably prefer it. Like anyone.

"But I would never say I've not had the respect I deserve. It's too pompous to say that. If I do something right and someone likes it, cool. And I'm always trying to get it right. It doesn't always come off. But it won't have a large bearing on my next attempt.

"My *career* is certainly not carefully considered," he stated breezily. "And I think that's probably quite obvious."

Looking back, he said, for him his time in the 1970s represented achievement.

"Achieving the impossible, really," he emphasized, before remembering the words of those critics who rejected the idea that he would ever create anything that could be held up against the golden light of the Beatles. "It had always been, 'You can't do that, that's not gonna be possible.' I *slightly* believed that and thought, Yeah, but I want to be in music, so I'm gonna have to do *something,* and this is my best shot.

"But, y'know, it was doubtful. So the idea of actually achieving that impossible target, by *Band on the Run* and by the tour of 1976, was great. It was very gratifying, and the other thing was, I'd taken along my missus, who had no stage experience whatsoever, but who had agreed to accompany me on this adventure. And it was a wacky thing. But, come on, man, we were hippies.

"So it was nice that even against all odds and all of the trials we went through—and there were a few—that suddenly we found that we'd done it . . . we'd cracked it."

I wondered how he felt the period had changed him.

"I suppose it taught me to be a bit independent," he said. "Calmed me down a bit. 'Cause it was kind of frightening leaving the Beatles, I think, for all of us, to some degree. So to just come out of that period was a good thing. I survived."

We were done and began to say our goodbyes.

"Escort this man from the building," McCartney instructed one of his assistants with a smile, shaking my hand firmly. Five minutes later, we bumped into each other again two floors down in the MPL reception area, Paul struggling to open the front door while wrestling with an unwieldy pile of papers.

As we stepped onto the sidewalk together, McCartney heading for a black minivan with smoked windows, he paused to reconsider everything we'd talked about.

"Hope I don't end up coming off like the world's greatest nutter," he said with a grin. "And if I do, then that'll be good for my image." A mischievous glint could suddenly be detected in those world-famous eyes. "Give them something to think about."

And with those parting words left hanging in the air, Paul McCartney, former hippie renegade turned knight of the realm, walked away, leaving the past behind him.

ACKNOWLEDGMENTS

For their generous interview time and for quotes that made their way into this book, thanks to Paul McCartney, Ringo Starr, Yoko Ono, Michael Parkinson, May Pang, Denny Laine, Denny Seiwell, Henry McCullough, Clive Arrowsmith, Laurence Juber, Steve Holley, Robert Ellis, Dave Clarke, Bob Gruen, Robin Black, Alan Parsons, Howie Casey, Jimmy McGeachy, and Jimmy Iovine. For allowing me to use additional transcripts of interviews with Denny Laine and Denny Seiwell, thanks to Tom O'Dell and Elio Espana of Prism Films.

Thanks also to Phil Alexander and Paul Rees, under whose editorships the original McCartney interviews were conducted for *Mojo* and *Q*. For continuing to employ me and putting up with me in general, not to mention indulging my frequent disappearing acts while writing this book, I'd like to thank: Danny Eccleston (with special thanks for his idea for the interstitial quotes), Ian Harrison, Andrew Male, Jenny Bulley, Ross Bennett, Mark Wagstaff, Andrew Harrison, Ted Kessler, Chris Catchpole, Niall Doherty, Matt Mason, James Mannion, Gordon Thomson, and Sam Inglis. To my writerly comrades—keep the faith, people: Sylvia Patterson (the big sister I never wanted), John Aizlewood, Craig McLean, Mark Blake, Andy Fyfe, Dave Everley, Mark Ellen, John Harris, Gareth Grundy, Helena Drakakis, Louise Millar, Allan Brown, and Daryl Easlea.

Very special thanks to Simon Goddard for his Staropramen-induced, lightbulb-above-the-head notion that gave this book its title, and to Dorian Lynskey, who also came up with the same title, only just a bit later.

I'm grateful to all at Polygon: Neville Moir, Sarah Morrison, Vikki

Reilly, Jan Rutherford, Maria White, and especially my utterly ace editor, Alison Rae, who calmly extended my deadline more than once with a reassuring "Oh, don't *worry*." To my unflappable agent, Kevin Pocklington, at Jenny Brown Associates, for "getting" this book and getting it off the ground. For the U.S. edition, thanks to Susanna Porter, Priyanka Krishnan, Paolo Pepe, Caroline Teagle, Richard Callison, Karen Hoffman, and Stacey Witcraft.

Additional thanks to Stuart Bell at DawBell and to Claudia Schmid at MPL.

For allowing me to bore them senseless in the pub about Paul McCartney for an entire year: Anth Brown, Mike Brown, Steve Aungle, Derek Hood, Steve Wilkins, Dave Black, Dave Scott, Nick Roberts, Paul Esposito, Sophie Mayerhoeffer, Robbie and Parm Gunn-Hamilton, Alan Shaw (who's still wrong about "Smile Away"), Allan Shanks, Aidan Rose, Kieran Leonard, Martin Low, Steve Hands, Dave Tomlinson, Jon Bennett, Steve Donoghue, Kris O'Mahoney, Nick Holywell-Walker, Jon Mills, and Gary Clark. For simply just encouraging me or sorting stuff or helping with research: the McCombies, Paul Salley, Lorraine Wilson, Roddy Isles, Linda Barclay Isles, Rosha Kasravi, Richard and Ben at Audio Gold, and Nick de Grunwald at Isis Productions.

To my family up in Scotland, for understanding why I didn't phone so often: Dad and Heather, Brian, Caroline and Ryan. And to the all-knowing, all-suffering, saintly patient love of my life, Karen, and to Milly, who manages to get bigger and cheekier and funnier and cleverer and more beautiful with every day.

SELECTED DISCOGRAPHY

ALBUMS

Paul McCartney

McCartney

> U.K.: Apple PCS 7102, April 17, 1970
> U.S.: Apple STAO 3363, April 20, 1970
> Reissued: Commercial Marketing B004WJRF6C, June 13, 2011
> The Lovely Linda / That Would Be Something / Valentine Day /
>   Every Night / Hot as Sun/Glasses / Junk / Man We Was Lonely /
>   Oo You / Momma Miss America / Teddy Boy / Singalong Junk /
>   Maybe I'm Amazed / Kreen-Akore

McCartney II

> U.K.: Parlophone PCTC258, May 16, 1980
> U.S.: Columbia FC-36511, May 22, 1980
> Reissued: Commercial Marketing B004WJREMW, June 13, 2011
> Coming Up / Temporary Secretary / On the Way / Waterfalls / No-
>   body Knows / Front Parlor / Summer's Day Song / Frozen Jap /
>   Bogey Music / Darkroom / One of These Days

Tug of War

> U.K.: Parlophone PCTC259, April 26, 1982
> U.S.: Columbia TC37462, April 26, 1982
> Reissued: Parlophone B000005RT9 August 9, 1993
> Tug of War / Take It Away / Somebody Who Cares / What's That
>   You're Doing / Here Today / Ballroom Dancing / The Pound Is

Sinking / Wanderlust / Get It / Be What You See (Link) / Dress Me Up as a Robber / Ebony and Ivory

Paul and Linda McCartney

Ram

U.K.: Apple PAS 10003, May 21, 1971

U.S.: Apple SMAS 3375, May 17, 1971

Reissued: Commercial Marketing B007L96VCY, May 21, 2012

Too Many People / 3 Legs / Ram On / Dear Boy / Uncle Albert/Admiral Halsey / Smile Away / Heart of the Country / Monkberry Moon Delight / Eat at Home / Long Haired Lady / Ram On / The Back Seat of My Car

Paul McCartney and Wings

Red Rose Speedway

U.K.: Apple PCTC251, May 4, 1973

U.S.: Apple SMAL3409, April 30, 1973

Reissued: Parlophone B0000721M, June 7, 1993

Big Barn Bed / My Love / Get on the Right Thing / One More Kiss / Little Lamb Dragonfly / Single Pigeon / When the Night / Loup (1st Indian on the Moon) / Medley: Hold Me Tight, Lazy Dynamite, Hands of Love, Power Cut

Band on the Run

U.K.: Apple PAS10007, December 7, 1973

U.S.: Apple SO3415, December 5, 1973

Reissued: Commercial Marketing B003XX2O8C, November 1, 2010

Band on the Run / Jet / Bluebird / Mrs. Vandebilt / Let Me Roll It / Mamunia / No Words / Picasso's Last Words (Drink to Me) / Nineteen Hundred and Eighty Five

Wings

Wild Life

U.K.: Apple PCS 7142, December 3, 1971

U.S.: Apple SW 3386, December 7, 1971

Reissued: Parlophone B00005RPU, June 7, 1993

Mumbo / Bip Bop / Love Is Strange / Wild Life / Some People Never Know / I Am Your Singer / Bip Bop Link* / Tomorrow / Dear Friend / Mumbo Link*

Venus and Mars

U.K.: Capitol PCTC 254, May 30, 1975
U.S.: Capitol SMAS 11419, May 27, 1975
Reissued: Parlophone B000007210, June 7, 1993
Venus and Mars / Rock Show / Love in Song / You Gave Me the Answer / Magneto and Titanium Man / Letting Go / Venus and Mars Reprise / Spirits of Ancient Egypt / Medicine Jar / Call Me Back Again / Listen to What the Man Said / Treat Her Gently / Lonely Old People / Crossroads Theme

Wings at the Speed of Sound

U.K.: Parlophone PAS10010, March 26, 1976
U.S.: Capitol SW11525, March 25, 1976
Reissued: Parlophone B000007221C, June 7, 1993
Let 'Em In / The Note You Never Wrote / She's My Baby / Beware My Love / Wino Junko / Silly Love Songs / Cook of the House / Time to Hide / Must Do Something About It / San Ferry Anne / Warm and Beautiful

Wings over America

U.K.: Parlophone PCSP 720, December 10, 1976
U.S.: Capitol SWCO 11593, December 11, 1976
Reissued: Capitol B000007638, February 19, 1990; HRM-34338-02 May 27, 2013
Venus and Mars / Rock Show / Jet / Let Me Roll It / Spirits of Ancient Egypt / Medicine Jar / Maybe I'm Amazed / Call Me Back Again / Lady Madonna / The Long and Winding Road / Live and Let Die / Picasso's Last Words (Drink to Me) / Richard Cory / Bluebird / I've Just Seen a Face / Blackbird / Yesterday / You Gave Me the Answer / Magneto and Titanium Man / Go Now / My Love / Listen to What the Man Said / Let 'Em In / Time to Hide / Silly Love Songs / Beware My Love / Letting Go / Band on the Run / Hi Hi Hi / Soily

*Reissues only

London Town

> U.K.: Parlophone PAS 10012, March 31, 1978
> U.S.: Capitol SW11777, March 31, 1978
> Reissued: Parlophone B0000072lI, June 7, 1993
> London Town / Café on the Left Bank / I'm Carrying / Backwards
>   Traveller / Cuff Link / Children Children / Girlfriend / I've Had
>   Enough / With a Little Luck / Famous Groupies / Deliver Your
>   Children / Name and Address / Don't Let It Bring You Down /
>   Morse Moose and the Grey Goose

Wings Greatest

> U.K.: Parlophone PCTC256, November 2, 1978
> U.S.: Capitol SOO11905, November 13, 1978
> Reissued: Parlophone B00002U8M, June 7, 1993
> Another Day / Silly Love Songs / Live and Let Die / Junior's Farm /
>   With a Little Luck / Band on the Run / Uncle Albert/Admiral
>   Halsey / Hi Hi Hi / Let 'Em In / My Love / Jet / Mull of Kintyre

Back to the Egg

> U.K.: Parlophone PCTC257, June 11, 1979
> U.S.: Columbia 3-11020, June 8, 1979
> Reissued: Parlophone B0000072lD August 9, 1993
> Reception / Getting Closer / We're Open Tonight / Spin It On /
>   Again and Again and Again / Old Siam, Sir / Arrow Through Me
>   / Rockestra Theme / To You / After the Ball / Million Miles / Win-
>   ter Rose / Love Awake / The Broadcast / So Glad to See You Here
>   / Baby's Request

SINGLES

Paul McCartney

Another Day / Oh Woman Oh Why

> U.K.: Apple R 5889, February 19, 1971
> U.S.: Apple 1829, February 22, 1971

Wonderful Christmastime / Rudolph the Red-Nosed Reggae

> U.K.: Parlophone R6029, November 16, 1979
> U.S.: Columbia 1-111162, November 20, 1979

Coming Up / Coming Up (Paul McCartney and Wings Live)

> U.K.: Parlophone R6035, April 11, 1980
> U.S.: Columbia 1-11263, April 15, 1980

Waterfalls / Check My Machine

> U.K.: Parlophone R6037, June 14, 1980
> U.S.: Columbia 1-11335, July 22, 1980

Temporary Secretary / Secret Friend (Limited Edition Twelve-Inch)

> U.K.: Parlophone 12R6039, September 15, 1980

Paul McCartney with Stevie Wonder

Ebony and Ivory / Rainclouds

> U.K.: Parlophone R6054, March 29, 1982
> U.S.: Columbia 18-02860, April 2, 1982

Take It Away / I'll Give You a Ring

> U.K.: Parlophone R6056, June 21, 1982
> U.S.: Columbia 18-03018, June 29, 1982

Paul McCartney with Carl Perkins

Tug of War / Get It

> U.K.: Parlophone R6057, September 20, 1982
> U.S.: Columbia 38-03235, September 14, 1982

Paul and Linda McCartney

The Back Seat of My Car / Heart of the Country

> U.K.: Apple R 5914, August 13, 1971

Uncle Albert/Admiral Halsey / Too Many People

> U.S.: Apple 1837, August 2, 1971

Paul McCartney and Wings

My Love / The Mess

   U.K.: Apple R 5985, March 23, 1973
   U.S.: Apple 1861, April 9, 1973

Live and Let Die / I Lie Around

   U.K.: Apple R 5987, June 1, 1973
   U.S.: Apple 1863, June 18, 1973

Helen Wheels / Country Dreamer

   U.K.: Apple R 5993, October 26, 1973
   U.S.: Apple 1869, November 12, 1973

Jet / Let Me Roll It

   U.K.: Apple R 5996, February 18, 1974
   U.S.: Apple 1871, January 28, 1974

Band on the Run / Zoo Gang

   U.K.: Apple R 5997, June 28, 1974

Band on the Run / Nineteen Hundred and Eighty Five

   U.S.: Apple 1873, April 8, 1974

Junior's Farm / Sally G

   U.K.: Apple R 5999, October 25, 1974

Wings

Give Ireland Back to the Irish / Give Ireland Back to the Irish (Instrumental)

   U.K.: Apple R 5936, February 25, 1972
   U.S.: Apple 1847, February 28, 1972

Mary Had a Little Lamb / Little Woman Love

   U.K.: Apple R 5949, May 5, 1972
   U.S.: Apple 1851, May 29, 1972

Hi Hi Hi / C Moon

   U.K.: Apple R 5973, December 1, 1972
   U.S.: Apple 1857, December 4, 1972

Listen to What the Man Said / Love in Song

> U.K.: Capitol R6006, May 16, 1975
> U.S.: Capitol 4091, May 23, 1975

Letting Go / You Gave Me the Answer

> U.K.: Capitol R6008, October 18, 1975
> U.S.: Capitol 4145, October 4, 1975

Venus and Mars/Rock Show / Magneto and Titanium Man

> U.K.: Capitol R6010, November 28, 1975
> U.S.: Capitol 4175, October 27, 1975

Silly Love Songs / Cook of the House

> U.K.: Parlophone R6014, April 30, 1976
> U.S.: Capitol 4293, April 1, 1976

Maybe I'm Amazed / Soily

> U.K.: Parlophone R6017, February 4, 1977
> U.S.: Capitol 4385, February 7, 1977

Mull of Kintyre / Girls School

> U.K.: Capitol R6018, November 11, 1977
> U.S.: Capitol 4505, November 14, 1977

With a Little Luck / Backwards Traveller/Cuff Link

> U.K.: Parlophone R6019, March 23, 1978
> U.S.: Capitol 4559, March 20, 1978

I've Had Enough / Deliver Your Children

> U.K.: Parlophone R6020, September 15, 1978
> U.S.: Capitol 4594, June 12, 1978

London Town / I'm Carrying

> U.K.: Parlophone R6021, September 15, 1978
> U.S.: Capitol 4625, August 21, 1978

Goodnight Tonight / Daytime Nighttime Suffering

> U.K.: Parlophone 12YR6023, March 23, 1979
> U.S.: Columbia 3-10939, March 15, 1979

Old Siam, Sir / Spin It On
> U.K.: Parlophone R6026, June 1, 1979

Arrow Through Me / Old Siam, Sir
> U.S.: Columbia 1-11070, August 14, 1979

Getting Closer / Baby's Request
> U.K.: Parlophone R6027, August 10, 1979

Getting Closer / Spin It On
> U.S.: Columbia 3-11020, June 5, 1979

MISCELLANEOUS RELEASES

The Country Hams

Walking in the Park with Eloise / Bridge over the River Suite
> U.K.: EMI 2220, October 18, 1974
> U.S.: EMI 3977, December 2, 1974

Percy "Thrills" Thrillington

Uncle Albert/Admiral Halsey / Eat at Home
> U.K.: Regal Zonophone EMI 2594, April 22, 1977

Thrillington
> U.K.: Regal Zonophone EMC3175, April 29, 1977
> Too Many People / 3 Legs / Ram On / Dear Boy / Uncle Albert/Admiral Halsey / Smile Away / Heart of the Country / Monkberry Moon Delight / Eat at Home / Long Haired Lady / The Back Seat of My Car

Suzy and the Red Stripes

Seaside Woman / B-Side to Seaside
> U.K.: A&M AASP7461, August 10, 1979; A&M AMS 7458, July 18, 1980
> U.S.: EPIC 8-504403, May 31, 1977

SELECTED GIGOGRAPHY

1972

February 9—Nottingham University, Nottingham, U.K.

February 10—Goodricke College Dining Room, University of York, York, U.K.

February 11—Hull University, Hull, U.K.

February 13—Newcastle University, Newcastle, U.K.

February 14—Lancaster University, Lancaster, U.K.

February 16—Leeds Town Hall, Leeds, U.K.

February 17—Sheffield University, Sheffield, U.K.

February 21—Birmingham University, Birmingham, U.K.

February 22—Swansea University, Swansea, U.K.

February 23—Oxford University, Oxford, U.K.

July 9—Center Culturel, Châteauvallon, France

July 12—Juan-les-Pins, Juan-les-Pins, France

July 13—Théâtre Antique, Arles, France

July 16—Olympia, Paris, France

July 18—Zirkus Krone-Bau, Munich, Germany

July 19—Offenbach-Halle, Frankfurt, Germany

July 21—Kongresshaus, Zurich, Switzerland

July 22—Pavilion, Montreux, Switzerland

August 1—K.B. Hallen, Copenhagen, Denmark

August 4—Messuhalli, Helsinki, Finland

August 5—Kupittaan Urheiluhalli, Turku, Finland

August 7—Kungliga Tennishallen, Stockholm, Sweden

August 8—Idretshalle, Örebro, Sweden

August 9—Njaardhallen, Oslo, Norway

August 10—Scandinavium Halle, Gothenburg, Sweden

August 11—Olympen, Lund, Sweden

August 12—Fyns Forum, Odense, Denmark

August 14—Vejlby-Risskov Hallen, Aarhus, Denmark

August 16—Rheinhalle, Düsseldorf, West Germany

August 17—De Doelen, Rotterdam, the Netherlands

August 19—Evenementenhal, Groningen, the Netherlands

August 20—Concertgebouw, Amsterdam, the Netherlands

August 21—Concertgebouw, Amsterdam, the Netherlands

August 22—Ciné Roma, Antwerp, Belgium

August 24—Deutschlandhalle, West Berlin, West Germany

1973

March 18—Hard Rock Cafe, London, U.K. (benefit concert for the charity Release)

May 11—Hippodrome, Bristol, U.K.

May 12—New Theatre Oxford, Oxford, U.K.

May 13—Capitol Cinema, Cardiff, U.K.

May 15—Winter Gardens, Bournemouth, U.K.

May 16—Hard Rock Cafe, Manchester, U.K.

May 17—Hard Rock Cafe, Manchester, U.K.

May 18—Empire Theatre, Liverpool, U.K. (two performances)

May 19—Leeds University, Leeds, U.K.

May 21—Guildhall, Preston, U.K.

May 22—Odeon Cinema, Newcastle, U.K.

May 23—Odeon Cinema, Edinburgh, U.K. (two performances)

May 24—Green's Playhouse, Glasgow, U.K.

May 25—Odeon Cinema, Hammersmith, London, U.K.

May 26—Odeon Cinema, Hammersmith, London, U.K.

May 27—Odeon Cinema, Hammersmith, London, U.K.

July 4—City Hall, Sheffield, U.K.

July 6—Odeon Cinema, Birmingham, U.K.

July 9—Odeon Cinema, Leicester, U.K.

July 10—City Hall, Newcastle, U.K.

1975

September 6—Elstree Film Studios, U.K. (warm-up)
September 9—Gaumont Cinema, Southampton, U.K.
September 10—Hippodrome, Bristol, U.K.
September 11—Capitol Cinema, Cardiff, U.K.
September 12—Free Trade Hall, Manchester, U.K.
September 13—Hippodrome, Birmingham, U.K.
September 15—Empire Theatre, Liverpool, U.K.
September 16—City Hall, Newcastle, U.K.
September 17—Odeon Cinema, Hammersmith, London, U.K.
September 18—Odeon Cinema, Hammersmith, London, U.K.
September 20—Usher Hall, Edinburgh, U.K.
September 21—Apollo Theatre, Glasgow, U.K.
September 22—Capitol Cinema, Aberdeen, U.K.
September 23—Caird Hall, Dundee, U.K.
November 1—Entertainment Center, Perth, Australia
November 4—Apollo Stadium, Adelaide, Australia
November 5—Apollo Stadium, Adelaide, Australia
November 7—Hordern Pavilion, Sydney, Australia
November 8—Hordern Pavilion, Sydney, Australia
November 10—Festival Hall, Brisbane, Australia
November 11—Festival Hall, Brisbane, Australia
November 13—Sidney Myer Music Bowl, Melbourne, Australia
November 14—Sidney Myer Music Bowl, Melbourne, Australia

1976

March 20—Falkoner Theatre, Copenhagen, Denmark
March 21—Falkoner Theatre, Copenhagen, Denmark
March 23—Deutschlandhalle, West Berlin, West Germany
March 25—Ahoy Sportpaleis, Rotterdam, the Netherlands
March 26—Pavillon de Paris, Paris, France
May 3—Tarrant County Convention Center, Fort Worth, Texas
May 4—Summit, Houston, Texas
May 7—Olympia Stadium, Detroit, Michigan
May 8—Olympia Stadium, Detroit, Michigan
May 9—Maple Leaf Gardens, Toronto, Canada
May 10—Richfield Coliseum, Richfield, Ohio

May 12—Spectrum, Philadelphia, Pennsylvania
May 14—Spectrum, Philadelphia, Pennsylvania
May 15—Capital Center, Landover, Maryland
May 16—Capital Center, Landover, Maryland
May 18—Omni Coliseum, Atlanta, Georgia
May 19—Omni Coliseum, Atlanta, Georgia
May 21—Nassau Coliseum, Uniondale, New York
May 22—Boston Garden, Boston, Massachusetts
May 24—Madison Square Garden, New York City
May 25—Madison Square Garden, New York City
May 27—Riverfront Coliseum, Cincinnati, Ohio
May 29—Kemper Arena, Kansas City, Missouri
May 31—Chicago Stadium, Chicago, Illinois
June 1—Chicago Stadium, Chicago, Illinois
June 2—Chicago Stadium, Chicago, Illinois
June 4—St. Paul Civic Center, St. Paul, Minnesota
June 7—McNichols Sports Arena, Denver, Colorado
June 10—Kingdome, Seattle, Washington
June 13—Cow Palace, San Francisco, California
June 14—Cow Palace, San Francisco, California
June 16—Sports Arena, San Diego, California
June 18—Community Center Music Hall, Tucson, Arizona
June 21—Forum, Los Angeles, California
June 22—Forum, Los Angeles, California
June 23—Forum, Los Angeles, California
September 19—Wiener Stadthalle, Vienna, Austria
September 21—Dom Sportova, Zagreb, Yugoslavia
September 25—St. Mark's Square, Venice, Italy (benefit concert for UNESCO/Venice in Peril)
September 27—Olympiahalle, Munich, West Germany
October 19—Empire Pool, Wembley, London, U.K.
October 20—Empire Pool, Wembley, London, U.K.
October 21—Empire Pool, Wembley, London, U.K.

1979

November 23—Royal Court Theatre, Liverpool, U.K.
November 24—Royal Court Theatre, Liverpool, U.K.

November 25—Royal Court Theatre, Liverpool, U.K.

November 26—Royal Court Theatre, Liverpool, U.K.

November 28—Apollo Theatre, Manchester, U.K.

November 29—Apollo Theatre, Manchester, U.K.

December 1—Gaumont Cinema, Southampton, U.K.

December 2—Brighton Center, Brighton, U.K.

December 3—Odeon Cinema, Lewisham, London, U.K.

December 5—Rainbow Theatre, Finsbury Park, London, U.K.

December 7—Empire Pool, Wembley, London, U.K.

December 8—Empire Pool, Wembley, London, U.K.

December 9—Empire Pool, Wembley, London, U.K.

December 10—Empire Pool, Wembley, London, U.K.

December 12—Odeon Cinema, Birmingham, U.K.

December 14—City Hall, Newcastle, U.K.

December 15—Odeon Cinema, Edinburgh, U.K.

December 16—Apollo Theatre, Glasgow, U.K.

December 17—Apollo Theatre, Glasgow, U.K.

December 29—Odeon Cinema, Hammersmith, London, U.K. (benefit
performance for Concerts for the People of Kampuchea)

BIBLIOGRAPHY

Badman, Keith. *The Beatles After the Break-Up, 1970–2000: A Day-by-Day Diary*. London: Omnibus, 1999.

Baker, Ginger, with Ginette Baker. *Ginger Baker: Hellraiser*. London: John Blake, 2009.

Beatles. *The Beatles Anthology*. London: Weidenfeld & Nicolson, 2000.

Blaney, John. *Lennon and McCartney, Together Alone: A Critical Discography of the Solo Work*. New York: Jawbone Press, 2007.

———. *Paul McCartney: The Songs He Was Singing, Vol.1, The Seventies*. Paper Jukebox, 2010.

Carlin, Peter Ames. *Paul McCartney: A Life*. New York: JR Books, 2009.

Clayson, Alan. *Paul McCartney*. London: Sanctuary, 2003.

Coleman, Ray. *McCartney—Yesterday . . . and Today*. London: Boxtree, 1995.

Connolly, Ray. *The Ray Connolly Beatles Archive*. London: Plumray, 2011.

Davies, Hunter. *The Beatles: The Authorised Biography*. London: Ebury Press, 2009.

Doggett, Peter. *You Never Give Me Your Money: The Battle for the Soul of the Beatles*. London: Vintage, 2010.

Emerick, Geoff, and Howard Massey. *Here, There and Everywhere: My Life Recording the Music of the Beatles*. New York: Gotham Books, 2006.

Fields, Danny. *Linda McCartney: The Biography*. London: Little, Brown, 2000.

Fletcher, Tony. *Dear Boy: The Life of Keith Moon.* London: Omnibus Press, 1998.

Flippo, Chet. *McCartney: The Biography.* London: Sidgwick & Jackson, 1988.

Gambaccini, Paul. *The McCartney Interviews: After the Break-up.* London: Omnibus Press, 1996.

———. *Paul McCartney: In His Own Words.* New York: Omnibus Press, 1976.

Gelly, David. *The Facts About a Pop Group.* London: André Deutsch, 1976.

Giuliano, Geoffrey. *Blackbird: The Life and Times of Paul McCartney.* London: Penguin Books, 1991.

Harry, Bill. *The Encyclopaedia of Beatles People.* London: Cassell Illustrated, 1997.

Jackson, Michael. *Moonwalk.* New York: Doubleday, 1988.

MacDonald, Ian. *Revolution in the Head: The Beatles' Records and the Sixties.* London: Henry Holt, 1994.

Martin, George. *All You Need Is Ears.* New York: St. Martin's Press, 1995.

McCartney, Paul. *Wingspan: Paul McCartney's Band on the Run.* London: Little, Brown, 2002.

McGee, Garry. *Band on the Run: A History of Paul McCartney and Wings.* New York: Taylor Trade Publishing, 2003.

McNab, Ken. *The Beatles in Scotland.* Edinburgh: Polygon, 2008.

Miles, Barry. *Paul McCartney: Many Years from Now.* London: Secker & Warburg, 1997.

Moore, Carlos. *Fela: This Bitch of a Life.* London: Allison and Busby, 1982.

Norman, Philip. *John Lennon: The Life.* London: HarperCollins, 2008.

———. *Shout! The True Story of the Beatles.* New York: Simon & Schuster, 1981.

Pascall, Jeremy. *Paul McCartney and Wings.* London: Littlehampton Book Services, 1977.

Sandford, Christopher. *McCartney.* London: Century, 2006.

Seaman, Frederic. *John Lennon: Living on Borrowed Time.* London: Xanadu, 1993.

Sounes, Howard. *Fab: An Intimate Life of Paul McCartney*. London: HarperCollins, 2010.

Tremlett, George. *The Paul McCartney Story*. London: White Lion Publishers, 1976.

Welch, Chris. *Paul McCartney: The Definitive Biography*. New York: Proteus Books, 1984.

INDEX

ABOUT THE AUTHOR

TOM DOYLE is an acclaimed music journalist, author, and long-standing contributing editor to *Q* whose work has also appeared in *Mojo,* the *Guardian, Marie Claire, Elle, The Times,* and *Sound on Sound.* Over the years he has been responsible for key magazine-cover profiles of Paul McCartney, Keith Richards, Kate Bush, Elton John, R.E.M., and U2, among many other artists. He is the author of *The Glamour Chase: The Maverick Life of Billy MacKenzie,* which, since its original publication, has attained the status of a classic rock biography.

ABOUT THE TYPE

This book was set in Sabon, a typeface designed by the well-known German typographer Jan Tschichold (1902–74). Sabon's design is based upon the original letter forms of sixteenth-century French type designer Claude Garamond and was created specifically to be used for three sources: foundry type for hand composition, Linotype, and Monotype. Tschichold named his typeface for the famous Frankfurt typefounder Jacques Sabon (c. 1520–80).